The Accountant Bes

presents

QuickBooks® for Churches and Other Religious Organizations

Lisa London

Look for more titles in

The Accountant Beside You

series:

Church Accounting: The How-To Guide for Small & Growing Churches

Using QuickBooks® for Nonprofit Organizations, Associations & Clubs

QuickBooks® para Iglesias y Otras Organizaciones Religiosas

The Accountant Beside You

presents

QuickBooks® for Churches and Other Religious Organizations

Lisa London

Deep River Press

Sanford, North Carolina

The Accountant Beside You presents

QuickBooks® for Churches and Other Religious Organizations

ISBN 978-0-9911635-4-0

Library of Congress Control Number 2014956830

Published by Deep River Press, Inc. December 2014

EDITED BY Susan Sipal

COVER DESIGN BY Greg Schultz and Lydell Jackson

Dedication

For Lorene Smith VanLeeuwen, more affectionately known as Granny Great, who always made sure I paid attention in church.

Table of Contents

Introduction

When I originally wrote the first edition of *QuickBooks for Churches & Other Religious Organizations*, it was to answer a specific need I'd encountered with my own church. Many churches were using QuickBooks as their accounting system, an excellent program designed for businesses, but there was no resource to guide them through how to adapt it for the specialized accounting needs of churches. I must not have been the only one at a loss, as thousands of religious organizations and nonprofits are now using my books.

Feedback from readers has been tremendous. The wonderful emails and calls I have received have truly made the project very rewarding. As The Accountant Beside You, I have learned from readers about areas I needed to elaborate further or clarify better. Additionally, there were some topics I did not include in the first book which readers told me they would like to see. Thus, for this second edition, I've not only included reader requests for tracking mission trips, recording a mortgage, entering payroll through the system, and tracking payments to a parent organization, but have updated the guide with changes in the 2015 QuickBooks version as well.

From my experience, I have learned that the best way to set up an accounting system and the related controls is to keep it simple. I'm going to walk you through the church and non-profit specific terminology you need to know, what QuickBooks limitations are for churches, and help you design internal accounting controls. Then, we'll set up your church's accounting system, learn how to pay bills, record payroll, and receive money through the system. Month and year-end reporting and review will be covered, and finally, we'll go over some unusual and non-frequent items that you need to consider.

My approach is designed to quickly and easily get you up and running on the processes churches use frequently and find the most important. This book is not meant to be read once and forgotten. Keep it close to the computer, use what you need, and check my website, www.accountantbesideyou.com, for additional tips and information. Remember, I'm with you all the way. Let's get started.

I. Fundamentals, including Versions, Fund Accounting, & Internal Controls?

A. Will QuickBooks Work for My Church?

Before we start with fund accounting, I think it is important to discuss which QuickBooks version will work for you. QuickBooks is not specifically designed for churches or nonprofits but can function with a few workarounds. There are three different levels of QuickBooks for PC desktops and two levels for online versions. I will not speak to the Mac version as I have no experience with it.

The desktop versions are Pro, Premier (which includes a Nonprofit edition), and Enterprise. Pro is a basic program which will be sufficient if your organization is small. The average Pro user has a business with less than 20 employees and less than $1 million in sales. As of the printing of this book, QuickBooks Pro retails for $250. Premier has increased reporting and budgeting capabilities. The Nonprofit edition changes some of the terminology to donors and adds more nonprofit specific reporting. The Premier and Nonprofit versions retail for around $395.

As a religious organization, your church has access to discounts on software that for-profit businesses do not have. A wonderful online resource, www.techsoup.org, is a perfect example. If your organization meets the requirements, you can buy QuickBooks Premier Edition on their website for as little as $49 (as of the printing of this book). The increased functionality QuickBooks will give you versus using spreadsheets or a personal program like Quicken is substantial.

The average user of the Enterprise version has more than $1 million in sales, 20-250 employees, and multiple locations. It can handle up to 30 multiple users at once. The price starts at $1000 and moves up based on number of users. If you think your organization needs the Enterprise level, I strongly recommend you find an accountant to set it up for you. Search "Find a ProAdvisor" in your web browser to find a QuickBooks expert near you. At this price level, you may also wish to investigate other nonprofit-specific software programs as well.

Intuit, the makers of QuickBooks, is pushing their online options very strongly. These Internet-based programs give the users lots of flexibility, such as allowing multiple users at different locations the ability to review reports, but the online option costs $39 per month. Intuit offers a lower cost option, but it does not allow for class tracking (which will be discussed in chapter 5), so it is not as useful for nonprofits. If you need the flexibility of the online option, this book can be a resource for the basics of setting up an accounting system, but the screens and some of the commands will be different.

B.   Fund Accounting

Note: For simplicity sake, all religious organizations will be referred to as churches; the congregation, parishioners, etc. will be called members; QuickBooks® will be QuickBooks, and religious services will be services.

A church will receive donations for many different areas: general support of the church, an outreach program, a capital campaign, or maybe an endowment. Some of the money given, like the Sunday offering, is considered unrestricted. It is assumed the church will use this money as needed and the donor has not requested any particular use of the funds.

Other times, money will be received for a very specific purpose—an outreach program or a capital campaign—or for a specific time—say next year's pledge. Then the money is considered temporarily restricted. This means it can only be used for the purpose or time period the donor has specified. When the restriction is met, i.e. the building is built or a new year has begun, then it becomes an unrestricted asset. If land is donated for the construction of a new church or an endowment is started in which only the investment earnings may be spent, a permanently restricted fund must be set up.

In accounting jargon, as a nonprofit organization, churches are required to keep their accounting records using a modified form of fund accounting. A fund is defined as a discrete accounting entity with its own set of accounts that must balance the cash and other assets against the liabilities and reserves of the organization. That is a wordy way of saying each significant donation (funds given for particular purposes) should be tracked separately. But as most churches don't keep separate bank accounts for each fund, you will be using a bit easier system called **Net Assets** to keep track of the funds.

For reporting purposes, these funds can be combined by the restrictions placed on them and tracked by net assets. Net assets are the components of equity in the church. It is what is left over after the liabilities (what is owed) are subtracted from the assets (what the church owns). In the business world, this would be the accumulated profit or loss of the company and is called retained earnings.

Net assets are divided into three categories:

1. Total Unrestricted Net Assets
2. Total Temporarily Restricted Net Assets
3. Total Permanently Restricted Net Assets.

One of the limitations of QuickBooks is that because it was designed for businesses, which only have one retained earning account, QuickBooks cannot automatically record net earnings (donations less expenses) in each of the three types of net asset accounts. Therefore, you will have to create the net asset equity accounts and use journal entries to move the balances from retained earnings. I'll walk you through how to do this in Chapter 15.

C.   **Reporting Differences**

Financial reports for churches also have different names than those for a business. The *Income Statement* or *Profit & Loss Statement* that tracks income and expenses for businesses is called **Statement of Activities** for churches. Assets, liabilities, and equity are tracked by companies in a *Balance Sheet*. A church uses a **Statement of Financial Position.** This is important as most versions of QuickBooks will list the reports using business terminology. For purposes of this book, I'll refer to these reports as the Profit & Loss Statement and Balance Sheet, to make it easier to find in the report menus. QuickBooks has a Nonprofit Edition which includes standard reports with the nonprofit titles and a few additional templates for donations, but it is basically the same program as the Premier Edition. Although there are numerous limitations to the standard reporting that QuickBooks offers as it relates to churches, Chapter 13 will go into detail on how to work around these limitations as you set up your reports.

QuickBooks also refers to the people you receive money from as "Customers," so you must remember that Customers = Donors, Parishioners, or Granting Agencies. Grants received will be tracked as "Jobs," and designated monies and programs will be referred to as "Classes." Jobs and classes are ways the system tags information so reports can be run, pulling all the related data together. This terminology may sound strange, but I'll explain it in more detail as needed.

There are a couple of other shortcomings that are involved in using QuickBooks. More expensive accounting packages allow you to set up automatic allocations so you can charge expenses across all of your programs with one step. QuickBooks does not offer that, but I'll show you how to most efficiently record the information. Other packages also offer a 13th accounting period so you can record year-end adjustments and entries separate from the normal transactions of the church. This allows you to have one time period that is only end-of-year transactions. A way to get around this in QuickBooks is to enter all of your December transactions dated on or before 12/30. Then use 12/31 as the date for your end-of-year adjustments. (If your accounting year ends in a different month, use the last day of that month.)

D.   Differences in Terminology

Here is a table showing the different terminology. While learning to use QuickBooks, you may want to make a copy to have by your desk or bookmark it for easy reference.

Description	Church Terminology	QuickBooks Terminology
Your religious organization	Church, Parish, Synagogue, Temple	Company
People or organizations you receive money from	Parishioners, members, donors, etc.	Customers
People you pay money to	Vendors, suppliers, or people you reimburse	Vendors
People who are employed to work at the church	Employees (payroll)	Employees (payroll)
Report to show money in versus money out (track income and expenses)	Statement of Activities	Income Statement or Profit & Loss Statement
Report to show assets (cash, property, etc.) against liabilities (amount owed) to track the accumulated net wealth	Statement of Financial Position	Balance Sheet
Accumulated net wealth/profit	Net Assets	Net Worth
Grants received that need to have the expenses tracked	Grants	Jobs
Monies received for programs and tracked	Funds or Programs	Classes

E. The Case for Internal Accounting Controls

Internal accounting controls are the procedures put in place to assure the integrity of the financial records and the safeguarding of the organization's funds. I know it is easy to think, "Why worry about accounting controls? Only good people work at our church." And as much as we would all like that to be the case, it is not unusual for a church member or employee to steal from a church. Do an Internet search on

"Stealing money from a church," and you will get 12,800,000 hits. Some of these were perpetrated by outsiders, but many of the news accounts mention secretaries, youth ministers, and even pastors guilty of stealing.

Internal controls are not only in place to protect against fraud, but to keep errors from occurring or to make it easier to catch when they do. A good bookkeeper will require strong internal controls to keep himself above suspicion. Additionally, you know that you wouldn't steal from the church, but having controls in place gives you reassurance that the person who takes over after you are gone will also not steal. The smaller the organization, the harder it is to have separate people in the required positions to have strong controls. But don't worry, this book will highlight options and ideas to put in place in the various areas.

The most basic start for establishing internal controls begins at the governing body level (whether a vestry, council, or board). A strong governing body with transparency, stewardship, and accountability sets the tone and is the first defense against fraud.

F.   **Advice for the Governing Body of the Church**

Here are a few basic starting points for the governing council to consider:

1. Financial statements should be reviewed by council on a regular basis (monthly or quarterly).
2. Annual budgets should be prepared and variances reported on a regular basis.
3. There should be a designated treasurer who is NOT the bookkeeper.
4. A conflict of interest policy needs to be established. (This does not mean church or council members can't do business with the church. It simply limits the level of related party transactions and determines steps to make certain the most appropriate price is paid.)
5. An annual audit must be performed. If the church cannot afford an outside auditor, designate an audit committee composed of members not associated with the accounting part of the church.

Within the chapters of this book, there will be recommendations for setting up the internal controls for each process of dealing with the finances. On my website, www.accountantbesideyou.com, I offer a companion handbook to assist you in organizing your data with areas for you to detail your accounting controls procedures. If you have a CPA in your membership, you may wish to ask for additional advice from him.

G. Tips, Hints, and When to Let Someone Else Do It

Throughout this book, you will notice symbols with additional information.

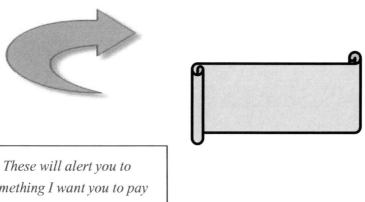

These will alert you to something I want you to pay special attention to or are tips and hints to help make the work go easier.

If you'd like to save time, you can go to my website, www.accountantbesideyou.com, and download a QuickBooks file with the preferences and chart of accounts I recommend in the book. You can then simply edit them for your particular church and not have to start from scratch. There is a charge, but this could save you hours of data entry. Please read over the book first, evaluate the amount of time you have to set up the system, and then you can decide if it makes more sense to spend a few dollars on the file or to input the information yourself.

For the record, I hate sales pitches, but in areas that I have already done the tedious part (like inputting the chart of accounts), I'd like to save you that time. So, periodically check my website to see what downloads or files I offer that can save you time and effort. The book will explain how to do any of these processes, so the download is simply an option.

II. Acquainting Yourself with QuickBooks

A. Layout of the Program

Before starting to enter data for your church, I recommend you spend some time seeing how QuickBooks is laid out and how to move around the program efficiently. Fortunately, QuickBooks includes sample organizations and companies for you to do just that.

When you first install QuickBooks, it will ask if you would like to open a sample company. You can then select which type. The sample nonprofit organization will be the one most like your church.

If the system has already been set up or others have already used it, you will see a screen similar to this one:

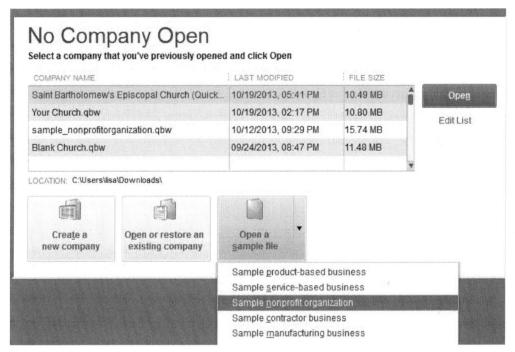

Click on the *Open a sample file* button and you will be offered a list of different business types. Choose *Sample nonprofit organization* and hit *Enter*.

Below is a screen shot of their sample nonprofit company. Depending on your QuickBooks version, you will probably have fewer items listed on the menus.

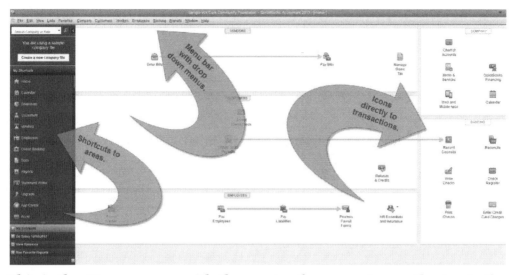

This is the **Home** screen with three sets of menus. Across the top is the **Menu Bar**. To the left of the screen are **Shortcuts,** and the main part is a menu of icons.

In 2015, QuickBooks has added a tab next to the **Home Page** called **Insights**.

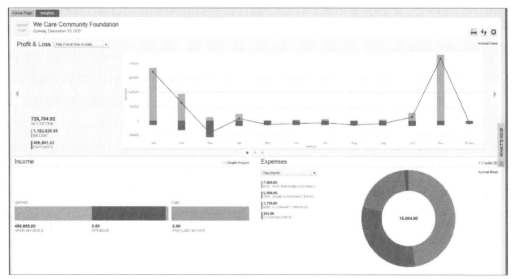

It is designed to give you a quick view of your profit and loss by month, amount of outstanding invoices from donors, and expense breakdowns. If you are using a previous version, look for the **Snapshot** option in the shortcuts area.

The Menu Bar has drop-down menus. We will go over these in detail as we set up each area. *My Shortcuts* take you to a screen for each of the areas. Let's look at the options on the shortcuts list.

There is an option for *Income Tracker* starting in the 2014 edition.

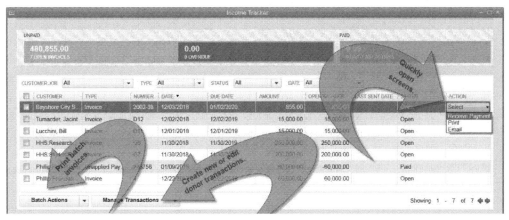

The report displays all open invoices and lets you select a row to quickly open the **Receive Payment** or an email screen. It will also let you batch print or email your outstanding invoices. Starting in 2015, it also includes unbilled **Time & Expense** entries.

The **Calendar** can be set up so you see which bills are due or when payroll payments need to be made. You may want to see donations by month this year, recent payments made, or any variances to budget. If you click on the **Customers** icon, it takes you to the **Customer Center**, where a list of members/donors and their outstanding pledges are listed as well as a history of transactions. The **Vendors** icon does the same for vendors. The **Employees** option allows you to enter and edit employee information, and the **Online Banking** (called **Bank Feeds** in 2014 & 2015) is used to manage any bank accounts that you wish to download transactions from.

Continuing down the list, there is an option **Docs** which allows you to drag or scan documents you would like stored with your accounting system. The remaining are quick links to various areas of the system.

If you ever get lost in the system, you can always go home by clicking on the
Home *tab in the left column.*

The main area of the home screen allows you to click on the task you need and go straight to the correct area. If you want to enter bills, you can simply click on the **Enter Bills** icon and start entering. You could also enter bills by selecting **Vendors** on the top menu or the side menu. QuickBooks makes it very intuitive to navigate their system, depending on how you prefer to see things. Before we go on, take a few minutes just to click on some icons and explore some drop-down menus to see where they go. I'll cover most of these in detail later, but I'd like you to feel comfortable with the system layout. And by using the sample company, you can't hurt anything!

B.   Backing Up. The Most Crucial Part of this Process!!!

Throughout this book, especially through the setup, I will have you stop working and back up your church file. Do not ignore these requests. By backing up the data after each significant input and labeling the backup appropriately, you can change how you set something up without having to redo everything prior to that. Simply reinstall the appropriate backup, and then you won't need to restart from scratch. For example, you have entered your company data, the chart of accounts, and some of your members' information. You then realize you'd rather have the members' "customer number" be a variation of the last name instead of the envelope number. Rather than having to change all the ones you've done so far, it may be easier to reinstall a backup with the company data and the chart of accounts before you started entering in the customer data.

Before we back up your file, let's set up a new folder on the desktop of your computer. I like to have a separate folder on my computer just for backups. In a blank area of your computer's main screen, right click.

Select *New, Folder.* You will see a small icon of a manila folder. If the label below it is highlighted, type *Backup* in the space. If not, right click on the folder to see the following menu:

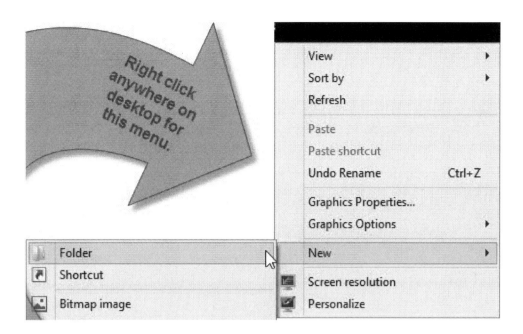

Select *Rename* and type in *Backup*. You now have a file to store your QuickBooks backup.

To back up your data file, first keep in mind that QuickBooks refers to your church as a Company, so we will need to back up the Company File. Select *File, Backup Company, Create Local Backup*.

Next, we'll designate a local backup.

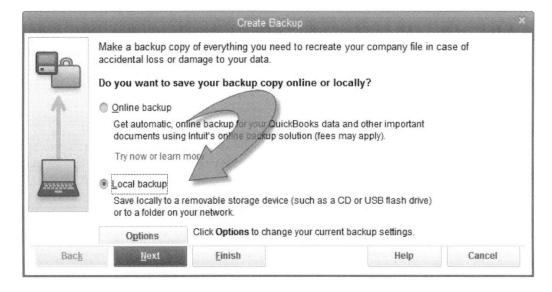

The term local backup means that it is on your computer or a flash drive, not in Internet storage. Don't worry about the online option; it takes you to an Intuit website to sign up for online backups, which are available for a fee.

Select *Options* and it will ask you where you would like the backup to go.

This screen also defaults to adding the date and time to the backup and starts writing over old files after three backups. I strongly recommend leaving the date and time checked, but while we are setting up the church, let's increases the number of copies to 10.

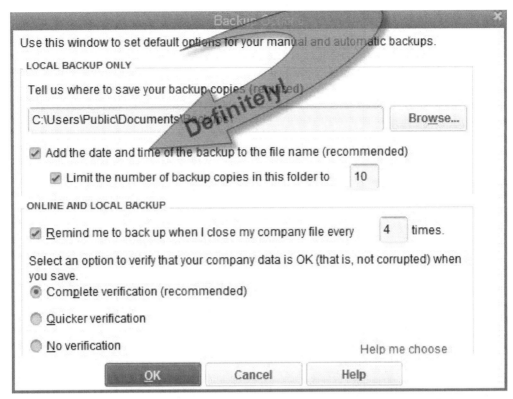

Select *OK* and you may see the following warning.

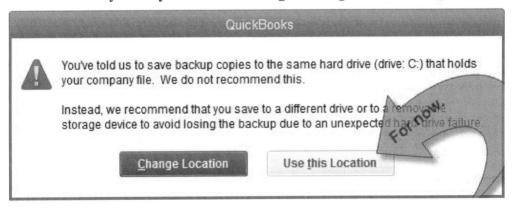

For now, use this location. In the future, you will want to save backups to a flash drive or external file you can store offsite in case the computer hard drive fails or the office catches fire.

The next screen allows you to schedule your future backups, so there is one less thing on your to-do list.

Select *Save it now and schedule future backups,* then hit *Next.*

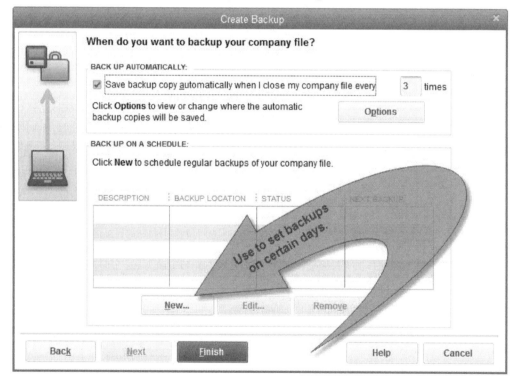

The system will backup automatically every three times you close your system. You can make it save more or less frequently by simply changing the number of times. If you would rather have the system backup on certain days and to different locations, selecting *New* will open up other dialog boxes asking for the dates and your Windows password. To keep it simple for setting up your church, let's leave it to automatic backups.

Once you select *Finish,* you will see the system working and possibly a pop-up box saying *No backups are currently scheduled.* Click *OK,* and once the backup is complete, you will see:

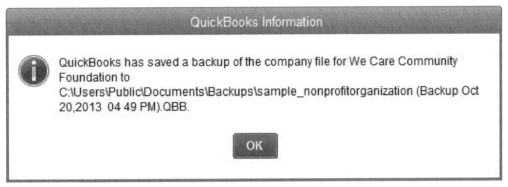

Your backup file name will vary depending on where you saved it. After this first time, you will find backing up the data only takes a few minutes and has the potential to save a lot of headaches.

Where do I store my backups?

If you regularly store your backups on the same drive as the program, you run the risk of losing the data if the machine dies or there is a fire. By storing it in a designated Backup File, you can then copy the folder to a cloud-based storage system. (Dropbox is a manual example; Carbonite is an example of an automatic service.) Another inexpensive option is to save the backup folder to a flash drive weekly and put the drive in a fireproof safe or an offsite location.

C.   Restoring the Data

If you need to restore your data, QuickBooks makes it very easy. There are two options on the **File** menu to help you restore. Near the top is **Open or Restore Company**. This is the one to use if you have moved the program to a new machine and need to reinstall the file. The second option is **Back Up Company** and is the easiest. Choose *File, Back Up*

Company, Restore Previous Local Backup, and then choose your most recent backup file.

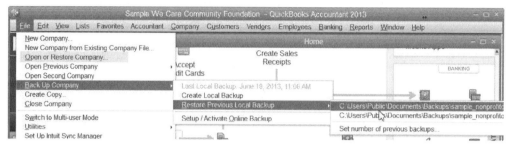

Once you have double clicked on the desired backup, you will see a box with warnings.

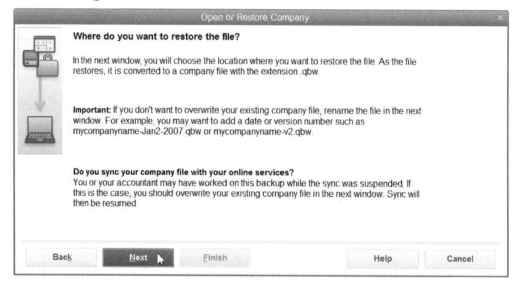

Select *Next* and you will be given a list of company names in the QuickBooks file. Select your church and click *Save.*

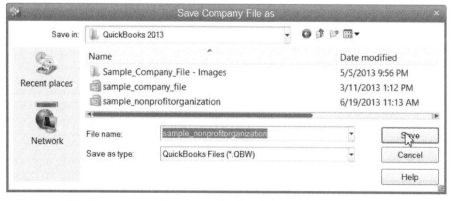

The system will then reward you with the following message.

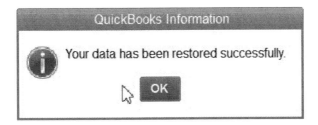

Considering how easy the backup and restore functions are with QuickBooks, there is no excuse to not backup frequently. By backing up your system between each chapter, you have the comfort of knowing that if anything were to happen to your file, you can easily restore it and not lose much work.

*In Chapter 3, we will be setting up your church files and setting preferences to make QuickBooks work most efficiently for you. Now let's close the sample company (from the menu bar, select **File, Close Company**) and start setting up your real one!*

III. Setting up Your Church File

A. Required Information

It is time to set up your church with QuickBooks. (Note: If the church is already set up, you can skip to Chapter 5 to learn to work with transactions, but you may want to review this section to see if you can improve your current system.) To get started, you'll need to pull together some data. Below is what we need to design the data file. A complete list of information needed to set up the system is in the appendix.

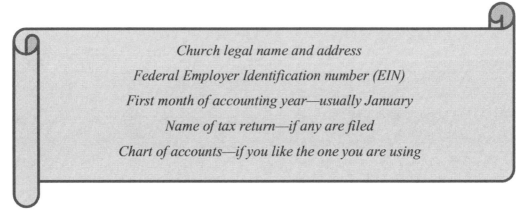

Church legal name and address

Federal Employer Identification number (EIN)

First month of accounting year—usually January

Name of tax return—if any are filed

Chart of accounts—if you like the one you are using

B. Express Start

To set up your church's data file, simply bring up QuickBooks and select *File, New Company* from the top menu bar. This will bring up the following screen:

Let's get your business set up quickly!

Answer some basic questions and we'll do the rest. You can always make changes later. (Recommended for new users)

Express Start

Control the setup and fine-tune the company file.

Create a new company file based on an existing one.

Convert data from Quicken or other accounting software.

Detailed Start   Create   Other Options ▼

Need help? Give us a call

I'm going to have you select *Express Start*. This will allow you to input some information about your church.

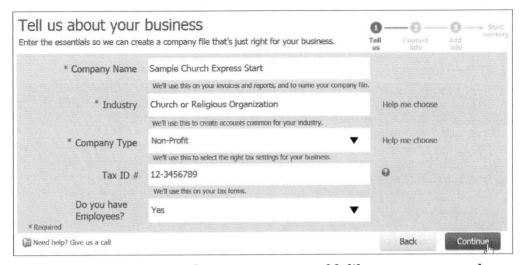

The Company Name is the name you would like on correspondence generated from the system (giving statements, financials, etc.). It may be different from the legal name, but that is okay. We'll update the legal name later if necessary. By selecting the Church as your Industry and Non-Profit as your Type, QuickBooks develops a standard chart of accounts for you. These are names of accounts, not account numbers, which we will discuss in great detail in the next chapter. The Tax ID number is your Federal Identification Number. You should be able to find this on your payroll reports.

Once you click *Continue*, you will see:

After entering your data, select the *Preview Your Settings* button at the bottom. This will display the assumptions QuickBooks has made on your behalf.

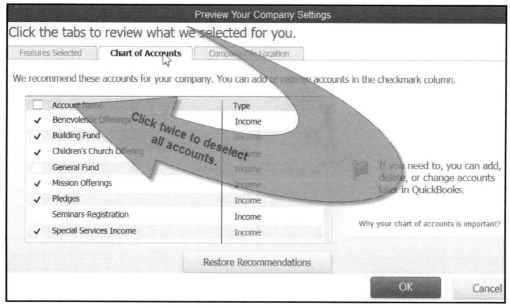

You don't need to do anything about the **Features Selected** or the **Company File Location**. For now, you want to focus on the accounts in the *Chart of Accounts* tab. If you check the *Account Name* box twice, all of the names will be deselected. You can go down the list and select whichever accounts you prefer. But I am going to recommend leaving all the accounts unselected and using the basic chart of accounts that will be detailed in Chapter 4. This will require a bit more data entry, but you will have more flexibility in the names of the accounts, and you will be assigning account numbers to facilitate more detailed reporting. On the other hand, if you are currently using a chart of accounts you like and is similar to this list, by all means use it. We'll add the numbers manually in Chapter 4.

Once you have selected your individual accounts, click *OK* and then *Create Company File*. The first option above allows you to import your contacts from an email contact list or an Excel® spreadsheet.

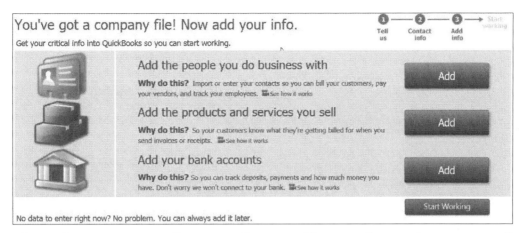

If you have your members, vendors, and/or employees in your email system or in a program that can be exported to Excel, this can be a great timesaver. If not, that's okay, because we can also enter them manually. But you need to first understand the name function in QuickBooks.

Important!

*Read Chapter 6 regarding how the name functions for members and vendors are used in QuickBooks before assigning names above. Names have to be unique and can be numeric. Consideration should be made for data entry ease when setting these up. For now, simply select **Start Working** to get to the **Home** menu. Instead of assigning names in this screen, we'll set them up later after I've explained the naming protocol.*

C. Preferences

Let's set up our preferences next. Preferences determine how the system looks when we bring it up, what information will default on certain screens, and offer lots of flexibility in how to use the system. But because of that flexibility, it is important to understand the options. In order to access the **Preference** option, go to the *Edit* item on the top bar menu.

Preferences will take you to a long list of categories down the left side of the screen. Each of these categories have two tabs; **My Preferences** and **Company Preferences**. Because QuickBooks can be used by several people, the **Company Preferences** tab determines things that have to be consistant across all users and the **My Preferences** tab lets each user set his own defaults. I will walk you through the options on many of these categories, and we'll skip the ones you are less likely to use.

There is a backup file available for purchase at www.accountantbesideyou.com populated with the preferences discussed in this chapter. After restoring the file, you would change the company name and address to your church's name and address. See the appendix for detailed instructions on restoring files.

1. Accounting Preferences

Let's start with *Accounting* under the *Company Preference* tab.

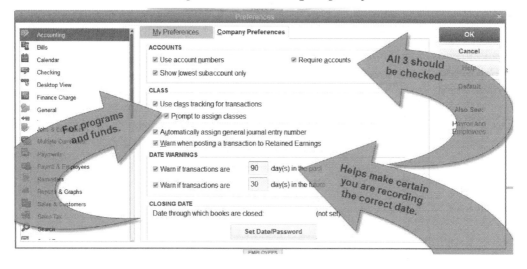

As QuickBooks is an accounting program, it is very important to select *Use account numbers, Require accounts,* and *Show lowest subaccount only.* I'll explain why in Chapter 4 on Chart of Accounts. *Use Class tracking for transactions,* and *Prompt to assign classes* is also crucial to prepare the financial reports on a Net Asset Basis. The other options are there to keep errors from occurring, so we definitely want to leave them selected. We can set a **Closing Date** to keep users from recording data in the previous year or month. I'll show you how to use this in Chapter 15.

Back at the accounting preferences page, click on the *My Preferences* tab. There is only one option, which is to **Autofill** the memo line in a general journal entry. You will want that checked so you do not have to type the same memo on a multiple-line journal entry.

Instead of selecting *OK* when you are finished, select *Bills* from the side menu. This will cause a dialog box to appear asking if you would like to save your changes, select *Yes* and you'll be taken to the next screen. If you select *OK* from the above screen, it takes you back to home and you'll have to bring the Preferences back up.

2. Bills Preferences

The next item down the left menu is **Bills**. There are no personal preferences and only a few company ones.

The warning about duplicate bills helps to keep overpayments down. I like the **Automatically use credits**. This applies any refunds due or overpayments against the invoice currently being paid. If it is not appropriate for a particular bill, it can be overridden, but they are less likely to be forgotten this way. If your vendors offer discounts for early payments, you may want to select that one also, but this is more typical in manufacturing.

3.   Calendar Preferences

The next option relates to the calendar. *My Preferences* control how it is displayed.

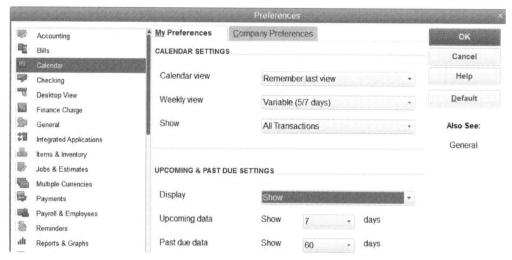

Calendar Settings allow you to set the view to daily, weekly, monthly, or have it remember how you left it last time you were in the system. The weekly view lets you see the calendar as five days per week or seven.

A useful feature is the ability to show accounting transactions on the calendar. The menu under **Show** allows you to show the money received and deposited or bills owed or paid on each day. This is a personal preference area, so play around with them and see which you prefer.

4.   Checking Preferences

The **Checking** item has some interesting options for churches. If you deposit the donations in an interest-bearing account, but pay bills out of a separate account, it allows you to set up the defaults accordingly in the **My Preferences** tab. As you haven't finished setting up your chart of accounts yet, your screens will probably be empty. Either way, leave the defaults or blanks on this page and you'll come back to this screen after Chapter 4.

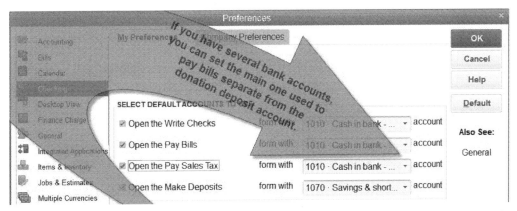

My recommendations for **Company Preferences** are below. (Don't worry if there are no account numbers on your screen).

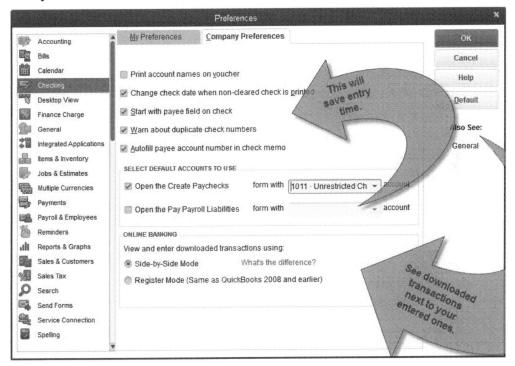

The account name is your accounting code for the vendor, so it really isn't necessary to have on the check stub. You do want to **Change the check date** if a lost check is reissued. If you select **Start with Payee** field on the check, the first thing you will enter is the vendor's name. This can save a few key strokes from having to navigate through the screen. The next two options are fairly self-explanatory.

You can designate the default accounts to use for paychecks and payroll liabilities. If you use an outside service, you won't need to worry about this. If you use online banking, the **Side by Side Mode** will show the downloaded transactions next to the transactions you have already entered in the system. Keep this one checked—it's easier than using the register.

5.   Desktop View Preferences

Now we are at the **Desktop View**. Here you can set the color scheme and unanchor the Help window so it can be moved around as needed. But more importantly, there are two things I want you to note on the *My Preferences* screen. First is the **View** option.   Chose **Multiple Windows** and it is much easier to navigate between windows. The second and most important thing is the **Desktop options**. Select the **Don't Save the Desktop** option.

> *Do not select **Save the current desktop**. If this option is selected and you exit the system with open reports, the next time you start QuickBooks, it will try to repopulate those reports. This not only slows down the startup, but can also cause the system to crash. Once corrupted, it can keep QuickBooks from opening. If this happens, close QuickBooks and then reopen with your finger on the **Alt** key until you have logged in. This forces the software to open without anything saved to the desktop.*

6.   Miscellaneous Preferences

Looking down the column on the left of the screen, you don't need to worry about the preferences for Finance Charges, Integration with other systems, Items & Inventories, Jobs, Multiple Currencies, Payroll, Reports, Sales, Sales Tax, Send Forms, 1099s, and Time and Expense. Depending on your version of QuickBooks, you may not have all of these or you may have a few more. Many of these preferences are not common with churches. Those that are will be discussed in greater detail in later chapters. The next item on the list we will be exploring is the **General** item.

7. General Preferences

My Preferences below has several handy options to allow you to streamline your work.

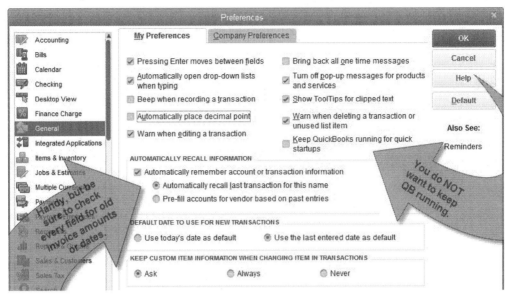

If you do not select the **Pressing Enter** option, the system defaults to requiring you to tab to the next field. If you accidentally hit *Enter* instead of *Tab*, the system saves what you were working on and goes to a new screen instead of a new field. I personally never remember to hit tab and get very frustrated when hitting enter stops what I have been doing, so I find that enabling **Pressing Enter** is a huge time saver. If you are used to tabbing, you will not want to choose this one.

If you have the **Automatically open drop-down lists when typing** enabled, QuickBooks will try to find the donor or vendor automatically once you start typing in a field. It will take you to the first account that matches what you have typed. If you typed a name incorrectly, it does not show in the list. Simply click on the drop-down arrow and you can look for the name manually.

I always deselect the **Beep when recording a transaction** as my life is noisy enough. And I almost always select the warnings so that I don't accidentally make a mistake. But this is simply a personal preference issue.

Another personal preference issue is the decimal place. You can select the **Automatically place decimal point** so that you don't have to touch the period each time. For example, if you need to enter $123.45, you would type *12345*. If you needed to enter $55.00, you would type *5500*. If you are already in the habit of hitting the decimal, you'll want to deselect this.

When you start using QuickBooks, you'll find the system offering you all kinds of messages with the option to click **Never show me this again**. Sometimes after you select that option, you may think it handy to remember a couple of them. If you select **Bring back all one time messages**, it will restore them for you. I'd leave it deselected until you think you need it.

I would, however, select the next one, **Turn off pop-up messages for products and services**, unless you like ads for QuickBooks-related products popping up on a regular basis. This gets rid of most of them, but not all.

Show ToolTips is a very handy feature. If a field has more data in it than you can read in the box, simply move your mouse over that field to see the entire line.

I strongly recommend you do NOT select the **Keep QuickBooks running for quick startups.** If selected, QuickBooks starts up when you power on your computer and stays open in the background. If you are working on an older computer (churches frequently have the hand-me downs) or have other programs running, the extra RAM used can slow your computer dramatically.

The **Automatically Recall Information** options can be another great time saver. The system gives you two options to determine how it will automatically fill in the fields. The first one applies to any name (customer or vendor). When you type in the name, it populates the fields with whatever was saved the last time you used that name. This would include amounts, invoice numbers, account numbers, etc. This is very handy if every time John Smith gives $50, you know it will be posted to the same account. Or if you are paying the electric bill, it will always be posted to Utilities. If you use this option, be certain to review each field to see what needs to be changed, i.e. the invoice number, the amount, etc.

The second option limits this option only to vendors. The system keeps track of the past entries on the vendors and then fills in the information based on the history.

If you only enter transactions every so often, you may want to select the **Use the last entered date as default** instead of today's date. This is especially handy the first week of the month when you are entering bills that were incurred in the previous month. When you bring up a transaction screen, the date area will default to the last date you used. You can then change that date and it will continue to stay the same until you change it again. And don't worry about **Custom item** information.

8. Payments Preferences

The next preference you will want to note is under **Payments**.

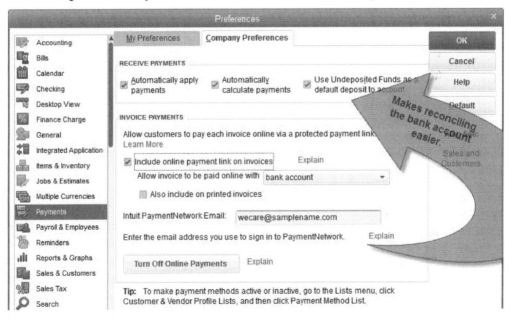

Your only options are under *Company Preferences*. Here, I recommend you select all three of the **Receive Payment** options. This allows the system to automatically apply the dollar amount you designate against the oldest invoices first. You can always manually change it on the payment screen if you do not agree with the system.

Undeposited Funds is an account QuickBooks sets up to allow you to post individual deposits and then group them by deposit slip. This way, when you are reconciling your bank statement, you don't have to guess which donations made up which day's deposit. I'll explain this in more detail when we get to the cash management area, but for now, just trust me.

I've now gone over the general preferences with you, letting you know how I like to work with the system. But you need to make it work for you. If you don't like something, just come back to the preferences and change it.

Before we completely get away from this area, I would like you to take a few minutes and go over the preferences for **Reminders, Search**, and **Spelling**. These are areas that won't affect how the accounting is done, but simply what you would like to see in these areas. Look at the screens and select what you think will work best for you. Then take a well-deserved break and be ready to set up a Chart of Accounts that will be useful to you, your pastor, donors, and any governing boards.

Take a few moments now and backup your system. Refer back to Chapter 2 for instructions.

IV. What is the Chart of Accounts & Why is it Important?

A. Designing the Chart of Accounts

Now it is time to determine your chart of accounts. This is the listing of all the accounts into which you will be recording transactions. For now we are not going to worry about programs or grants; we only want to concentrate on the individual accounts where we will be posting transactions.

If you are currently using a chart of accounts that works for your church, you may wish to design something very similar, but first, read through this chapter so you understand how QuickBooks uses the information for both transactions and reporting. I'd also recommend that you have an accountant or church member who knows accounting requirements review any chart of accounts you are planning to use to make sure it will work for your organization.

I strongly recommend you use account numbers. QuickBooks does not require account numbers, but you will severely limit your reporting options if you do not use them. The numbers can be anything up to seven digits, but unless you have a very complex system, I recommend starting with just four. You will want similar accounts grouped together, so I propose the basic structure shown in the scroll on the next page.

B. Numbering Structure

Within aforementioned structure, I recommend using the following for the balance sheet asset accounts:

1101-1199	Cash and investments
1201-1299	Undeposited monies (I'll explain this in Chapter 9)
1301-1399	Receivables—amounts owed to you
1401-1499	Prepaid assets—this can be insurance, postage, etc.
1501-1699	Available for current assets categories in the future
1701-1799	Church, real estate, and equipment and the related depreciation.
1801-1899	Available for long-term assets categories in the future
1901-1999	Other long-term assets.

1000s—Assets: bank accounts, receivables, computers, etc.

2000s—Liabilities: accounts payable, due to other organizations, payroll, loans, etc.

3000s—Net Assets: unrestricted, temporarily, and permanently restricted.

4000s—Operating Revenues: pledges, donations, pamphlet sales, etc.

5000s—Non-operating Revenues: revenues that are not in the ordinary course of your church's services: bequests, capital campaigns, endowments, sale of buildings or equipment, etc.

6000s—Operating Expenses: facilities, salaries, program costs, etc.

7000s—Non-operating Expenses: extraordinary repairs, depreciations, etc.

8000—Ask My Accountant: a place to record transactions you don't know what to do with. This is then reviewed by your accountant on a regular basis and cleared out.

As you can see, the numbering structure gives you 99 accounts under each of the categories. The chart of accounts in the appendix does the same with the liability, equity, revenue, and expense accounts.

Within these ranges, you may also have sub-ranges, especially in the expense categories. For example, the facility costs may be in 6000-6399, personnel expenses in 6400-6599, and program expenses from 6600-6999. As you need to add accounts within a range, consider adding them by 10s so you will have space between accounts. With Worship Program Expenses at 6610 and Youth Program Expenses at 6620, you have 10 accounts to add between those two.

> *A **current asset** or **liability** is due or used within a year. A **long-term asset** or **liability** is available or due in more than a year. For example, a pledge made for the next year is a current asset, but a capital campaign contribution due in five years is a long-term asset.*

You may be wondering why I am so adamant about designing a specific numbering system with QuickBooks. QuickBooks automatically sorts the chart of accounts by account type and runs reports using this sorting.

Assets are sorted by:

- o Bank
- o Accounts Receivable
- o Other Current Assets
- o Fixed Assets
- o Other Assets

Liabilities are sorted by:

- o Accounts Payable
- o Credit Card
- o Other Current Liability
- o Long-Term Liability

All the other accounts are sorted by number. Therefore, if you have numbers out of sequence with the type, you cannot view your chart of accounts in numerical order. This will become much clearer in Chapter 13 on reports.

C. Naming the Accounts

Now that you have figured out your numbering system, you need to determine how you are going to name the accounts. This sounds very basic, but if you aren't careful, you may have accounts called "Postage and Mailing," "Postage," "Post," etc., which should all be combined. In order to keep things simple, have a policy that significant words are written out with no punctuation marks, and ampersands (&) are used instead of the word "and." If you already have a naming protocol, by all means use it.

> *For now don't worry about the individual programs or grants.*
> *I'll explain how to set those up in Chapter 5.*

D. Chart of Accounts Menus

It's time now to input your chart of accounts. I'll show you how to set up the accounts from scratch, but if you like the list in the appendix and want to save time typing, go to www.accountantbesideyou.com and purchase a download of the chart of accounts file or a backup file that also includes preferences. Instructions on uploading the file into QuickBooks are in the appendix. If you start manually inputting your chart of accounts and decide you'd rather purchase the download, that's okay. You'll simply restore the backup you did after the last chapter and then upload the file. See the appendix for details.

E. Adding New Accounts

From your home page, press the *Chart of Accounts* icon or select from the *Lists* option on the menu bar.

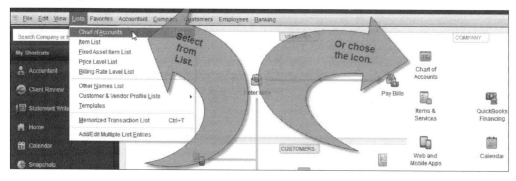

This will bring up a list of accounts the system has input if you chose that option, or, if you deselected the proposed chart of accounts, the system will automatically set up six accounts. Because you selected **Use Account Numbers** under accounting preferences, the system automatically assigns them a five-digit code. Don't worry about this as we will be changing them to fit our chart of accounts.

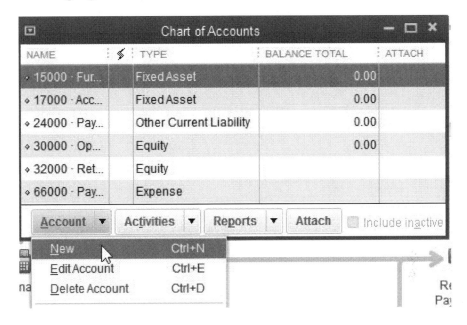

If you select the drop-down arrow next to *Account,* you will see a box that gives us the option of adding, editing, or deleting the chart of accounts. Select *New,* and we will be taken to the area where new accounts are added. Alternatively, if you pressed *Ctrl N,* you would be taken directly to the new account screen.

The first thing you need to do is determine the *Account Type.* As we discussed earlier in the chapter, QuickBooks needs to know what the account's purpose is in order to use it properly. If you select the circle next to a category, QuickBooks will give you a short description in the box to the right. The **More** option will take you to a help screen with detailed descriptions.

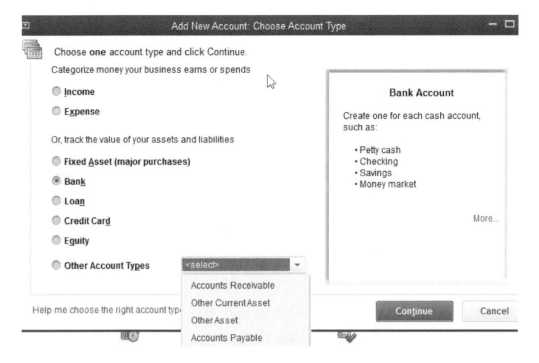

The drop-down menu by *Other Account Types* lets you see all of your other options. If you are not certain of the type, use the proposed chart of accounts in the appendix. It has the related account types listed and is a good reference. Additionally, you can select the *Help me choose the right account type* in blue at the bottom of the screen or call your accountant.

Once you select *Continue*, an entry screen will appear. It will show the account type you selected in the previous screen. The next box is the *Number*. This is where you assign your chosen account number.

The *Account Name* can be typed in, or you can choose *Select from Examples*. This can be a time saver, as QuickBooks will bring up a list of non-profit type accounts for you to select from.

The *Subaccount of* checkbox allows you to assign subaccounts to any of the accounts. For example, if you are going to use the chart of accounts in the appendix, you will notice that most categories have a "Parent" account with one or more subaccounts. Some even have subaccounts of subaccounts. Subaccounts allow you to track your accounts with more detail and give you more reporting flexibility.

For example, if you would like to easily pull up your electricity costs separate from your gas costs, you may have a parent account called **Utilities** and subaccounts named **Electricity** and **Gas**. You could then run reports summing up all utilities or a more detailed report on each of the subaccounts. In order to use QuickBooks correctly for fund accounting, we need to use subaccounts, as you will see later in this chapter.

Let's set up the account for your checking. First you will need the parent for all of your cash accounts. The type will be Bank and, if you are using my proposed chart of accounts, the parent number will be 1100. I've titled it *Cash and Marketable Securities*. Under *Description* or *Note*, you may wish to notate that this account is used to summarize the cash accounts. Select *Save & New* to continue adding accounts.

*When you are inputting the account numbers, you can select **Save and New** to bring up a new **Add New Account** screen with the **Account Type** filled in based on your previous entry. Be VERY careful to change the type when you are inputting other accounts. For example, if you were inputting three different bank accounts and then pledges receivable, the first three times you would not have to change **Type** as it would stay on **Bank**. But when you enter pledges receivable, you would need to change the type to **Accounts Receivable**. Believe me, not remembering is a mistake I've made many times.*

Next in the chart of accounts is the checking account. I'd recommend calling it by the bank name and checking, i.e. First Bank Checking. It will have a number between 1100 and 1199 so that it stays sequentially with its parent account. You will need to select *Subaccount of.* The drop-down menu will give you options of all accounts that have already been set up in this account type.

If you have separate bank accounts for restricted and unrestricted cash, and you will be utilizing the electronic download option from the bank, you will want to enter your bank account and routing number here.

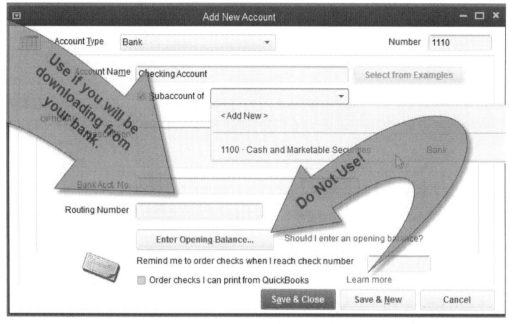

There is an option to *Enter Opening Balance.* **Do not use this!** We will be putting the opening balances in as a journal entry. In accounting, every journal entry must balance. Using a journal entry to record your beginning balances is an important way to make certain that your system balances correctly from the start.

Once you have checks that will work with the system, having a reminder to order more is very handy. You can always add the check number in later. If you select *Order checks I can print from QuickBooks,* you will be taken to a screen to buy checks online or by phone. Intuit (the company that makes QuickBooks) does a good job on the checks, but because QuickBooks is so popular, almost any check printing company will sell compatible checks. Now select *Save & New* to continue entering bank accounts, or *Save & Close*.

You may see a dialog box asking you to set up online accounts. Select *No*. You can come back to the account and set them up later if you'd like.

F.   **Tracking Restricted Cash**

As was discussed in the first chapter, one of QuickBooks' limitations for churches and nonprofits is that it does not handle fund accounting by fund. If your church uses separate bank accounts for restricted versus non-restricted cash, then the cash will be tracked by bank accounts. But most churches have one checking account that all transactions go through.

1.   **Using Custom Reports to Track Restricted Cash**

There are two different ways for you to track the restricted versus unrestricted cash in a single checking account. The preferred and easier approach is to set up your checking and investment accounts by bank account and then design a report to verify the restricted balances versus unrestricted balances. This approach works as long as you use classes for your programs and funds. Chapter 5 will explain the use of classes, and in Chapter 15, I will walk you through the process of setting up the restricted cash report. The chart of accounts list in the appendix assumes you will take this approach.

2.   **Multiple Subaccounts for Cash**

In the second method, you will need to set up subaccounts for any bank account that has both restricted and unrestricted cash. For this approach, set up three subaccounts for each of your checking and investment accounts: Unrestricted, Temporarily Restricted, and Permanently Restricted. When you record payments or receipts, you will always use one of these three, not the parent account. The reconciliation will be done in the parent account, which will have all the transactions.

Once you have set up the cash and money market accounts, your chart of accounts list may look something like this (but you may have to scroll through the screen):

NAME	$	TYPE	BALANCE TOTAL	
◇ 1100 · Cash and Marketable Securities		Bank	0.00	
◇ 1110 · First Bank Checking Account		Bank	0.00	
◇ 1111 · Unrestricted Funds		Bank	0.00	
◇ 1112 · Temporarily Restriced Funds		Bank	0.00	
◇ 1113 · Permanently Restricted Funds		Bank	0.00	
◇ 1120 · First Bank Money Market		Bank	0.00	
◇ 1121 · Unrestricted		Bank	0.00	
◇ 1122 · Temporarily Restricted		Bank	0.00	
◇ 1123 · Permanently Restricted		Bank	0.00	

Because you have already set your accounting preferences to *Show lowest subaccount only,* you do not have to worry about accidentally posting items to the parent accounts. This is important as any cash posted directly to the parent will not be reflected in either the restricted or the unrestricted cash.

This approach allows you to see unrestricted versus restricted cash balances anytime you open the account list, but requires more attention as you enter transactions. Each time you enter a bill, deposit money, or transfer cash, you will need to assure you have selected the correct subaccount.

G.   Enter Chart of Accounts

Now, take your Chart of Account list and start entering each account. It is easiest if you go down the list so the parent accounts are input before the subaccounts. You may also notice a field for mapping to a tax line. Leave it blank. If you file tax returns, print out your chart of account list and take it to your accountant to receive the information you need for the tax field.

Don't worry about messing something up with your chart of accounts. After you've input all the accounts, I am going to show you how to edit, delete, and even hide the accounts.

Plan on an entire afternoon for this process. This is the most tedious step. Don't forget to backup when you finish. I'd hate for you to lose all that work if the computer crashed.

H. Editing, Deleting, and Hiding Accounts

1. Edit Accounts

You have very carefully input your chart of accounts or have uploaded the file from my website, and now you need to check your work. The easiest way to edit your account list is to print it out.

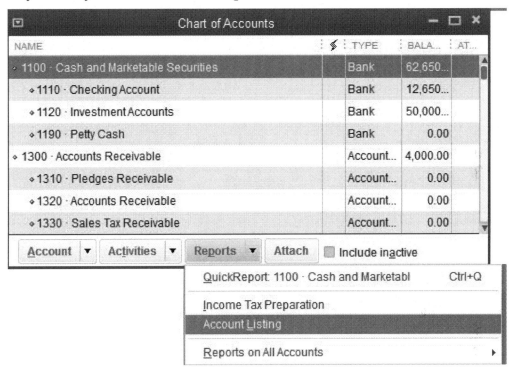

Pull up your *Chart of Accounts* screen and look for an arrow next to **Reports**. Select *Account Listing* and your entire chart of accounts. Now you will see a listing of all accounts and their types.

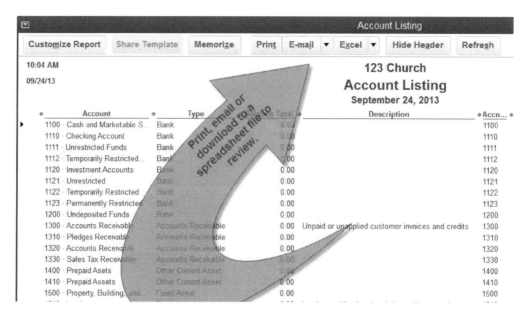

If you find anything you would like to change, **editing** is very easy with QuickBooks.

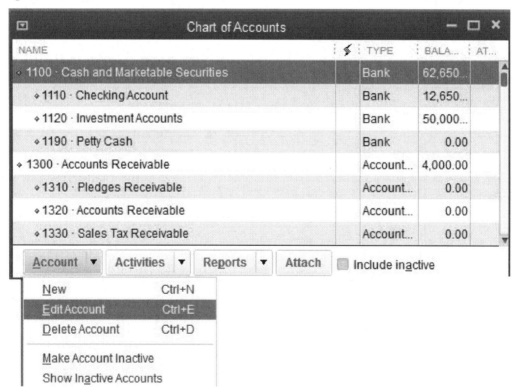

Go to the chart of accounts list, highlight the account you are editing, and select *Edit* under the *Account* drop-down menu. Or right click on the account you'd like to change and select *Edit Account*. This will bring up a screen that looks just like the one you used to set up the account.

You can then choose the field you need to edit and then *Save & Close*. The only exception relates to the account type.

2. Change Account Type

If QuickBooks creates an account automatically, like Payroll Liabilities, the system will not allow the type to be changed. Nor will it allow Accounts Receivable or Accounts Payable accounts to change their types. If you accidentally coded an account as an Accounts Receivable or Payable, the system will not let you change it. You will have to delete the account and reenter it with the correct type. Don't feel bad, however. I do it far more frequently than I care to admit.

If you need to change the type for a parent account with a subaccount, you will first need to unselect the *Subaccount of* option. The account is then no longer a subaccount and you can change the type, first in the parent, then the subaccount. After you've changed all the types, you will then want to go back and replace the subaccount option in each of the appropriate accounts.

Let's say you accidentally set up a prepaid insurance as an *Other Current Liability* instead of an *Other Current Asset*. There are two sub-accounts under prepaid insurance—one for property insurance and one for general liability. You will need to go to both the property insurance sub-account and the general liability sub-account and unselect the **Subaccount of** box. Then go to the prepaid insurance account and change the type to *Other Current Asset*. This corrects the parent account. Bring back up the property insurance, change the type to *Other Current Asset,* and then select **Subaccount of**. Choose *Prepaid Insurance* and save. Now do that for the other subaccount.

This would be a good time to go back to the six accounts that QuickBooks set up automatically and change the account numbers to match your numbering system. Your chart of accounts will then be consistent and reports will be easier to design.

3.   Delete an Account

Deleting an account is even easier. Right click on the account you wish to delete and click *Delete Account* or use the menus as shown below.

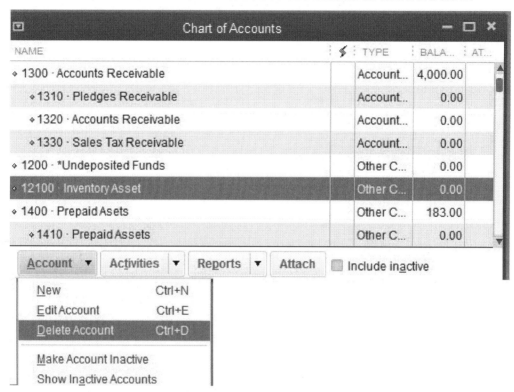

You will then be asked to verify that you really want to do that.

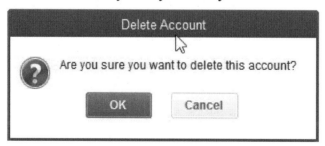

If you press **OK**, the account will be deleted unless it has already had transactions posted to it or subaccounts. You will need to delete any subaccounts first and then the parent account. A warning will pop up if you try to delete an account that the system automatically generates. It informs you that the system will add that account if it needs it in the future.

4.   Hiding Inactive Accounts

If there have been transactions posted, you cannot delete the account. You may instead mark it as **Inactive.** The account can then be hidden to keep anyone else from posting to it. By right clicking on the account, you will get the same menu we have seen before. This time, select *Make Account Inactive.*

If you change your mind and would like to have the account active again, you can do that by checking *Include inactive* at the bottom right corner of the screen.

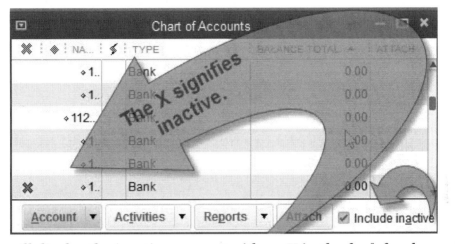

This will display the inactive account with an X in the far left column. To make it active again, just click on the X. If there are subaccounts related to this account, QuickBooks will ask if you want all of them active.

Using the inactive options, you can hide accounts to keep others from posting into them but bring the accounts back later if you need them. These accounts will not appear in the drop-down list, but you can post to them by typing in the name manually.

I.   Beginning Balances

Look how much you have accomplished. You've set up the program, defined your preferences, and even have a working chart of accounts. Now you need to take the beginning balances for each of the balance sheet accounts and put them in the system. If you have an accountant, ask him for this list. If not, you'll need to get them from your previous system or calculate them from bank statements and the like.

The beginning balances will be input as a journal entry. Journal entries are used to enter financial data that does not go through the bank, accounts receivable, or accounts payable. **Journal entries must balance.** This means all of the amounts being coded to assets have to equal the amounts coded to liabilities and equity. Accountants refer to debits and credits in the journal entries.

Here is an example of a beginning balance journal entry.

	Debit	Credit
Checking	$1,000	
Money Market	3,000	
Building	100,000	
Payroll Taxes Payable		1,000
Mortgage Payable		70,000
Equity—Permanently Restricted Net Asset		30,000
Equity—Temporarily Restricted Net Assets-Smith		1,000
Equity—Unrestricted Net Assets		2,000

As you can see, the debits and the credits both equal $104,000. This is a balanced entry.

I recommend using the last day of your previous accounting year as the date of this entry. You can start using QuickBooks anytime throughout the year, but will need to input this year's data to catch up. I'll explain how to do that in Chapters 9 and 10.

 Let me step you through the entry. The **Checking** and **Money Market** amounts should be the reconciled balance as of the start date. The **Building** is based on purchase price or value (ask your accountant), and **Mortgage Payable** is the amount you owe the bank. The **Payroll Taxes Payable** is any money not yet paid for taxes or benefits on payroll.

You may have **Accounts Payables** (bills you owe people) or **Accounts Receivables** (money owed to you) as part of your beginning balances. If so, you will need to input them separately by individual member or vendor and invoice, which we will discuss in Chapters 9 and 10. If you try to input these in the beginning balance entry, QuickBooks will require the amount to go to only one vendor or one customer. Additionally, QuickBooks will not let you post a journal entry with both A/P and A/R data in it.

To record the beginning balances journal entry, you will need another piece of information. Your church probably has several funds, grants, and programs with designated money in the beginning balances. So, in the next chapter, I'll show you how to organize those and how to record the beginning balances entry.

Great job getting all the chart of accounts input. Be sure to back up to a flash drive and put it in a safe place.

V. How do I Track My Grants & Programs?

A.   Classes vs. Jobs

Throughout the years, your church may have received money from members with specific instructions. These are referred to as restricted funds, and it is important to track how these dollars are used. As discussed earlier, QuickBooks is not designed to handle the tracking of funds or individual programs within the church, so you will utilize classes. By using classes, you are able to limit the number of accounts in your chart of accounts and expand your reporting capabilities. For example, most of your church's programs use supplies. Classes allow you to charge the supplies (an account) used to several different programs instead of having to set up subaccounts under supplies for each program.

As you work in the system, every time you see the classes, think programs or funds. Before you set up your classes, I'd like you to look at any reporting requirements you have. If you have an audit, study last year's. If you have a governing body that requires an annual or quarterly report, use it as a good source for the kind of information you may need to track. Review the documents to see what information is required. Nonprofits that file a tax return must designate what money was spent on programs versus administration versus fundraising. You may need to report on money spent on outreach programs versus worship services. Or, if you have a day care associated with your church, you'll want to track its revenue and costs in a separate fund.

Additionally, any funds for special purposes or events will need to be set up as classes. Every program you want to report the related expenses (i.e. supplies, postage, donations) for will need to be set up as a class. Finally, all money restricted either temporarily or permanently should have a class designated.

If you have been given money for a grant with a specific purpose and need to track the related expenditures, you will want to use the jobs option instead. Jobs are set up in the Customer (think Donor) area and are linked to only one donor. This is different than programs, which frequently have numerous donors and related expenses.

The jobs will also be linked to a fund class. In this chapter, you will be setting up program classes and fund classes. The fund classes are necessary to track restricted versus unrestricted funds. The program classes are geared towards understanding program costs.

Here are some guidelines on how to determine if you should set up a Class or a Job.

Description	Program Class	Fund Class	Job
Is it a program within the church?	X		
Are there numerous donors?	X		
Do you need to track the expenses with the fund balance?	X	X	X
Is there a single donor?		X	X
Did the donor specify how the money is to be spent?	X	X	X
Will I be required to give the donor an accounting of the funds?			X

If you answer yes to the last three questions, set up a job under the donor's name in accounts receivable. (More about this is Chapter 6.) If the answer is no, you can simply include those monies with other funds in a fund or program class.

1.   Naming of Classes

QuickBooks allows for subclasses, but does not require you to post to the lowest subclass like you have to do in the chart of accounts. Therefore, you will want to title your subclasses so you know which account the subclass is associated with. For example, if your primary class is 100 Worship, you may have subclasses for different services or locations, i.e. 110Worship-Sunday and 120Worship-Wednesday.

QuickBooks shows the classes using a drop-down menu, listing the names in alphanumeric order. I recommend using numbers in front of your class names to keep program classes together and fund classes together. This also allows you to name the program you will be using the most to show up at the top.

For example, you have classes titled Admin, Education, Social, and Worship, but most of your expenses are Worship related. If you were to title the classes 100 Worship, 200 Admin, etc., then Worship would always be your first option.

Before you start entering the class information, make a list of all the programs you would like to track. I strongly recommend not making this list too long. For example, you may have a social program with a men's group and a women's group. If you are only concerned about the cost of the adult programs in total, use only one class, but if different people are responsible for the expenses of the men's group versus the women's group, use separate classes or subclasses under a Social Programs class. The more detailed you make the classes, the more information you will enter when recording the bills.

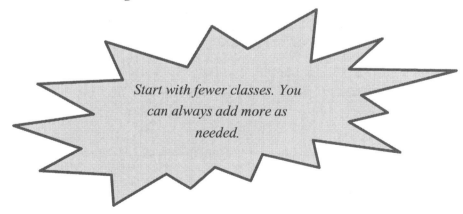

Start with fewer classes. You can always add more as needed.

2. **Example Class List**

Here is an example of a class list

> 100 Administration
>
> 200 Worship
>
> 300 Education
>
> 310 Sunday School
>
> 320 Adult Education
>
> 330 Pastor Education
>
> 400 Social
>
> 410 Men's Group
>
> 420 Women's Group
>
> 430 Teens
>
> 500 Community
>
> 510 Daycare
>
> 520 Bookstore
>
> 530 Soup Kitchen
>
> 600 Fundraising
>
> 899 Ask My Accountant
>
> 910 Unrestricted Funds
>
> 920 Temporarily Restricted Funds

3. **Entering Class Lists**

Now that you have compiled your list, let's input your classes in the system. You will find the *Class List* under the *Lists* option on the menu bar.

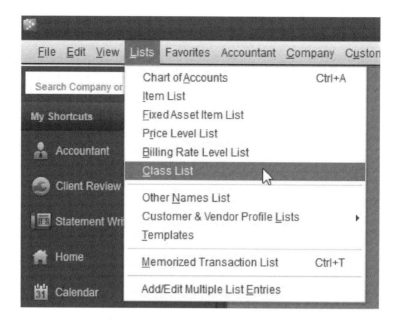

Once you have selected *Class List*, select *Class* and *New*.

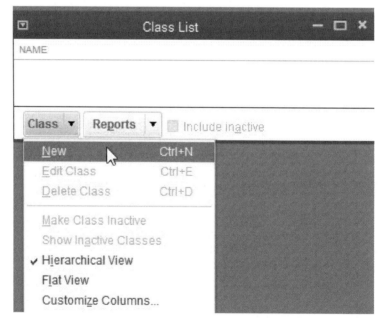

As you can see, this is similar to the screen to add a new account. Type in the name of the class you wish to add.

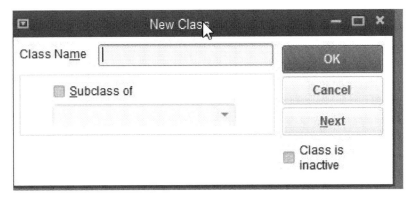

If you wish to set up subclasses, check the *Subclass of* box. The *Class is inactive* option is a way to keep people from recording entries to a particular class but still have it available when you need it.

4. Editing or Deleting Classes

Editing or deleting classes is very simple. Pull up the same menu from Class List that you used to add a new class and right click to select *Edit* or *Delete* instead. The edit option lets you change the name or subclass, make it a parent class, or mark it as inactive. The delete option will ask you to verify that you really want to delete the class.

*Once you have transactions entered in the classes, the **Reports** button at the bottom of **Class List** will bring up a **QuickReport** for the highlighted class which includes of all the entries to review or print.*

By the way, it doesn't hurt to back up your file before you go on.

B. Recording the Beginning Balance Entry

Now that all of your classes have been set up, let's prepare your beginning balance entry. If you will recall at the end of the last chapter, I showed an example beginning balance entry. To record the journal entry, you will need to go to the menu bar and select *Company* then *Make General Journal Entries.*

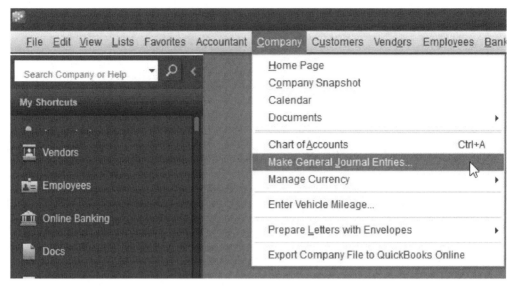

This will bring you to an entry screen with a pop-up warning that QuickBooks automatically numbers journal entries. Just select *OK* to continue. You will then see this screen.

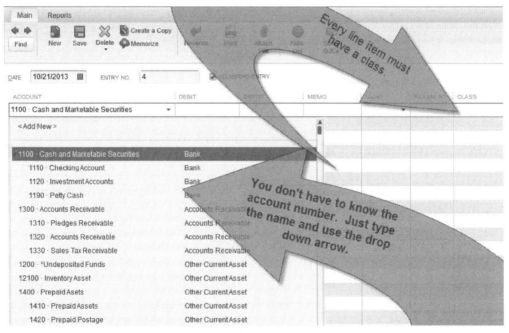

Please note the date will default to today, but you will want to change it to the last day of your previous accounting year. Check the box next to *Adjusting Entry* for the beginning balance entry. Leave it unchecked for normal monthly entries. That is just to let you and your accountant know the entry was something out of the ordinary.

Begin entering the account name for the first line item. The system will "guess" what you want and offer a suggestion. If it is correct, hit enter or tab over to the next field. If not, use the drop-down menu to find the correct account. Once you select the correct account name, you will need to enter the amount in either the *Debit* or *Credit* side. For your beginning balance entry, the assets should be *debits* (except accumulated depreciation), and the liabilities and net assets should be *credits.*

After you have input the dollar amount, press enter or tab across to the *Memo* field. This is where you explain why you are making the entry. I've put "Beginning Balances" in the example above. This memo will be replicated on each line of this entry automatically, but can be changed as needed on the other lines. Next, skip over the *Name* and *Billable* fields. I'll explain how to use them in future chapters. The final column is *Classes*. In order to compile a correct restricted funds report, every line must have a class. Unless the line item is specifically for a restricted fund, use the **Unrestricted Fund** class for the balance sheet accounts.

When the cursor gets to the next line, it will automatically fill in the amount of the opposite side of the entry. This is because the system requires the entry to be balanced with equal amounts of debits and credits. For multi-line entries like this one, just put the next amount in the correct side, and the following system generated amount will be replaced with the correct, balanced amount.

*For the bank balance, put the balance from the bank statement on one line using the checking chart of account number and enter any **outstanding deposits** on separate lines (still using the checking account number) with the amounts on the debit side of the entry. Any **outstanding checks** should be listed separately with the amounts on the credit side of the entry. This will allow you to reconcile your bank account when the previous year's outstanding deposits and checks clear.*

If your church has specific funds, perhaps named after donors or for specific purposes, you will need to enter each one on a separate line with a class specifically dedicated to it. The next illustration shows you a journal entry I recorded as an example based on the information at the end of Chapter 4.

ACCOUNT	DEBIT	CREDIT	MEMO	NAME	CLASS
1110 · Checking Account	3,000.00		Beginning Balance		910 Unrestricted Funds
1120 · Investment Accounts	1,000.00		Beginning Balance		920 Temporarily Restricted Fund
1520 · Building	100,000.00		Beginning Balance		930 Permanently Restricted Fund
1581 · Accum. Depr. Buildings...		20,000.00	Beginning Balance		930 Permanently Restricted Fund
2420 · Payroll Taxes Withheld		1,000.00	Beginning Balance		910 Unrestricted Funds
2900 · Mortgage Payable		70,000.00	Beginning Balance		930 Permanently Restricted Fund
3300 · Perm. Restricted Net A...		10,000.00	Beginning Balance		930 Permanently Restricted Fund
3200 · Temp. Restricted Net A...		1,000.00	Beginning Balance		920 Temporarily Restricted Fund:922 Smith Fund
3100 · Unrestricted Net Assets		2,000.00	Beginning Balance		910 Unrestricted Funds

For each of these net asset accounts, I have chosen a class or subclass to charge them to. If there were several funds under **Temporarily Restricted Net Assets**, each would need its own line. Your previous year's audit or accountant should be able to furnish you with these amounts.

Unrestricted Net Assets is your general fund balance, but it may not yet equal to your audit number. The only difference should be the balance of any accounts receivable or accounts payable at the beginning balance date. Remember that we could not enter Accounts Receivables or Accounts Payables into this entry. In Chapters 9 and 10, we will input the members and vendors open invoices so that this data can be recorded.

After your entry balances and you have coded all the net assets to the correct classes, you will press *Save and Close*. When you do, several messages may pop up with warnings. I'm giving you a heads up here so you'll know what to do.

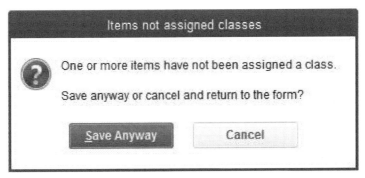

This message is warning you that you haven't assigned classes to each of the balance sheet items. When you see this message, select *Cancel* to go back to your transaction and make certain that classes are assigned to every line.

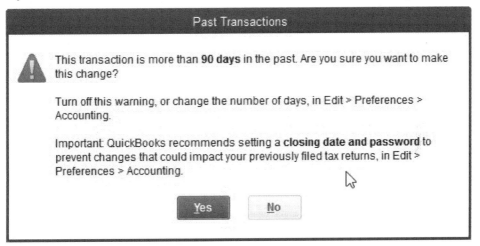

This is a warning that was set up in preferences. Because I had you date this entry at the beginning of the year, it may be past the 90-day window. This time, select *Yes*, but in the future, double check your transaction to make certain you have the correct date.

You may also see a popup box regarding fixed assets. Some versions of QuickBooks do not track fixed assets, so you may need to record them as a journal entry. In Chapter 8, I'll explain fixed asset items, and you can decide if you would like to use them. Just select *OK* to get out of this screen.

You have now posted most, if not all, of your beginning balances. Are you ready to set up your members and your vendors? QuickBooks groups these together under **Lists** which can also be used for sales items, fixed assets, and a few other things. In the next chapter, I'll go through all of the remaining list options QuickBooks offers and help you determine which your church should use and which you can ignore.

> *You have finished another chapter. But before you move on, what should you do?*
>
> *Hint: See page 12.*

VI. How About Members & People I Owe Money To?

A. Setting up Members and Other Donors

Probably the most important accounting function for churches is the ability to receive donations and track them to the correct donor. QuickBooks does this by setting up a *Customer List*. Remember, QuickBooks is designed for businesses with customers, so every time you see the word *customer*, think *church member* or *donor*. I'll continue to call them members for simplicity.

The process of setting up your members is easy in QuickBooks, and if you have a recent version, there is even the option to import your member list from an email or Excel file. I am going to walk you through how to set them up manually in this chapter. This allows those without the upload feature the chance to see what to do and also trains you in how to add new members one at a time.

But first there is always some planning to do. QuickBooks requires a **Customer Name**. This is not the same as the member's full name. It is actually a code used to identify each member. It will not appear on any correspondence; instead the data in the *Company Name* will appear.

To determine the *Customer Name*, think about your members and how you will be entering contributions. The system will try to guess what you are trying to type while entering donations, so let's use that to our advantage. Unless you have already memorized a number code for each of your members, I would recommend using a variation off the last name. That way when you type in *Smith*, the system automatically brings up the names starting with *S*. If you have several *Smiths* in your congregation, you will need to develop a way to differentiate them. The easiest approach is *LastNameFirstInitial* or *LastNameFirstandMiddleInitial*. Note that I intentionally did not put spaces or punctuation. This makes the naming protocol easier to remember.

So now you have *SmithH, JonesA, JonesAB,* etc. Next, you need to decide if you will input all of the members individually or as families. QuickBooks limits you to 14,500 names to be distributed between customers, vendors, employees, and any other name list, with a 10,000 limit on any one of these. For example, if you have 10,000 members in the system, you still have 4500 other names available for vendors and employees. So unless you have an exceedingly large congregation, you should have plenty of room.

The advantage of inputting by family is that you will have fewer name options to choose from when inputting donations. Special fields can be designated to detail spouses' names if you would like to have the data together. If you already have a contact database with your members, there is no reason to have every person included.

1.   Customer Types

Before we look at the donor input form, you need to decide if you would like to use another option that is offered, **Customer Type**. In the business world, this may be wholesale customers or retail customers. If you need data on members' donations versus foundations or other grant agencies, **Customer Type** is where you would set this up. The system allows you to save the customer file without designating a type, but it is easier to choose one now than to have to go back to all of your member files later. I'd recommend setting up at least one type—**Members**. You can always include more as you enter new donors.

To set up customer types, go to *Lists* on the menu bar and select *Customer & Vendor Profile Lists, Customer Type List.*

This is probably starting to look familiar as this screen is very similar to how you set up a new account number.

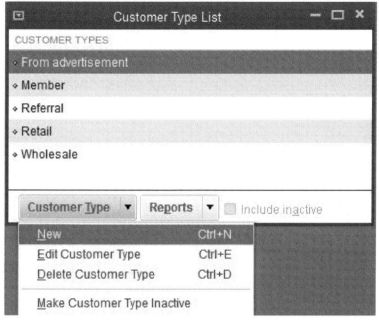

Select *New* from the *Customer Type* button at the bottom of the screen.

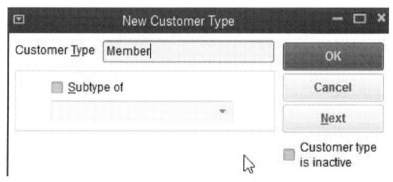

As in the chart of accounts, you can set up subtypes of any *Customer Type* you designate. Think about the type of information you will need. If you will want to know donations by members separate from donations by non-members, you could set up two types: Members and Others.

> *If you would like to run reports by the size and restrictions of the donations, the types may include Big Donor, Regular Donor, and Restricted Donor. These could also be sub-types under your Members and Others types. This can also simplify mailings.*

2. Adding a New Member

Are you itching to get those members' names in the system? Start by opening the *Customer Center* using the side menu.

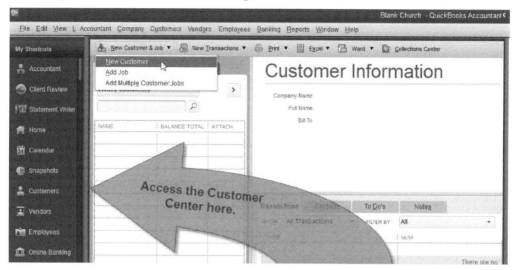

Once you have members and donations recorded, this screen will be populated with the last member you worked on. The middle section will list all members and any outstanding balances which you can easily link to.

For now, however, select *Add New Customers & Jobs, New Customer*. This will bring up an entry screen.

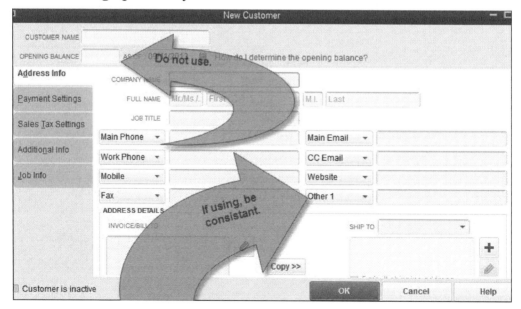

We'll start with the **CUSTOMER NAME**. As we discussed before, this is not your member's full name, but the name you determined using a naming protocol. Type in *SmithH* or whatever your first member's code will be. The **OPENING BALANCE** needs to be ignored. It is too easy to mess up the system by adding an opening balance. If the member owes the church money, I'll show you how to record the receivable in Chapter 9.

The **COMPANY NAME** will be your member's name as you want him or her to be referred to in reports and correspondence. Use the **FULL NAME** to input his legal name. On the bottom of this screen, you will type in the address. If the address is incomplete, a pop-up box will appear asking for more information. Additionally, you can add several addresses for each member.

The next entry fields are self-explanatory. The drop-down arrows by each one allows you to change the order in which these appear or to change the labels.

If you select the arrow next to **FAX**, a list of other labels for that box appears.

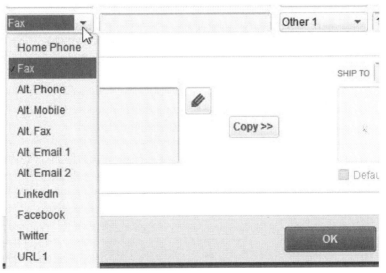

This could be changed to Alt. *Email 1* or *CC Email* (the entire list is not shown above) could be used as the spouses' email. *Other 1, 2 or 3* can be used for whatever you would like, but you'll need to keep it consistent across all members. Some churches use this option to label envelope numbers designated by members. You could put the spouse's name on this screen or in the custom fields you'll be setting up later. Play around and see what fits your needs the best. Select *OK* to be returned to the **New Customer** screen.

The next tab down on the left of the screen is titled *Payment Settings*.

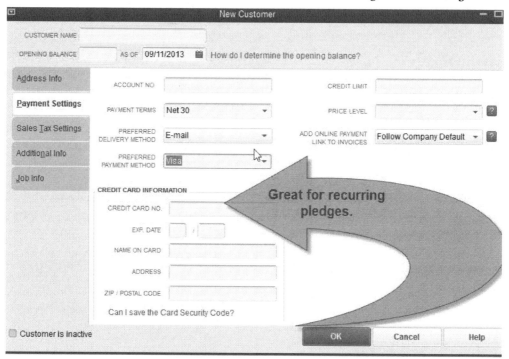

If you send out pledge reminders or have some type of membership dues, you may wish to use the **PAYMENT TERMS**. The drop-down arrow offers several options, or you can add your own. **PREFERRED DELIVERY METHOD** allows you to send out statements via email or print. I'm skipping over **CREDIT LIMIT** and **PRICE LEVEL** as those are rarely used by churches. We'll discuss online payments in the next chapter, so you can leave it empty for now.

A very handy feature of the system is the ability to hold credit card information. Churches have a substantial increase in pledge receipts when their members sign up for a recurring charge on a credit card. Be certain to ask your credit card processor about any laws or regulations regarding the retention of customer credit card numbers.

Most of you will probably not need the *Sales Tax Settings*, so I haven't included any shots. If you invoice items from a bookstore, you may need to use this. Check with your accountant to be sure.

The *Additional Info* tab has several useful features.

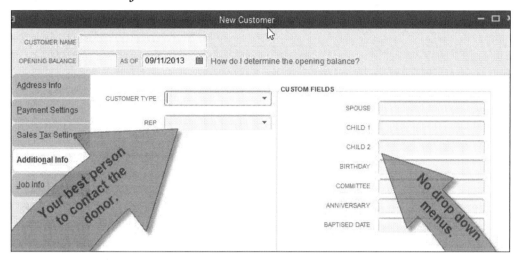

The first item is the **CUSTOMER TYPE** that we set up before we started entering members. The next box labeled **REP** (see below) allows you to designate someone in your organization as the contact person with this member or donor. This can be handy for phone trees or following up on annual pledges.

B.   Custom Fields

Next is the *CUSTOM FIELDS*. You can designate up to seven custom fields. When you select *Define Fields,* you may receive a message to remind you that you can use these fields in correspondence or reports. Select *OK* and the system will bring up the following screen (only blank).

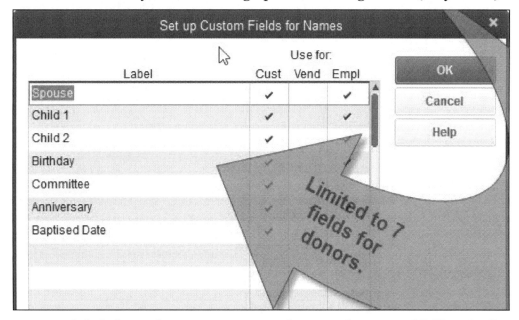

You can label these slots any way you choose. If you would like similar information for your employees or vendors, check those columns. Keep in mind that there will be no drop-down boxes for these, so you need to be consistent on how the data is input. For example, if one of the labels asks for a date, choose a date format and always use it the same way. Custom fields are a good place to keep a record of committee assignments.

If you didn't want to use one of the contact items for the spouse's name, you could designate a line here. Putting them on the contact screen makes their information more accessible, so you may prefer it there. Larger churches probably already have a detailed member database with children, dates of weddings and baptisms, etc., but if you don't, you could use these custom fields for those things. Remember, this is an accounting system, and you will want to give priority to items that relate most to the finances of the church.

*Later in the chapter we'll cover the **Customer Contact** screen. This is the perfect area to list spouses, children, and relations.*

The Custom Fields can be changed. Select *Define Fields* to see the **Set up Custom Fields for Names** screen. Remove the arrows next to the label you'd like to remove and change the name if desired. If you change the name of a current field, realize that the historical data will not change; you're just changing the name. None of these fields are required by the system.

C. Job Entry-Specific Grants or Contracts

Let's move on to the *Job Info* tab. This is where you will track specific grants or contracts.

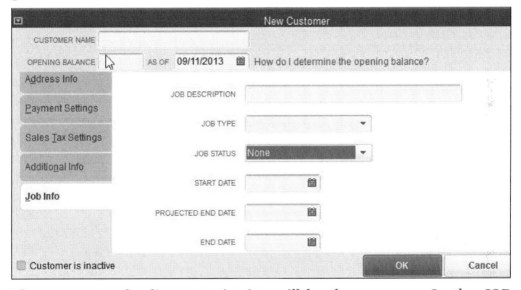

The grantor or funding organization will be the customer. In the *JOB DESCRIPTION* box, explain what the project is. *JOB TYPE* is not required, but you can set them up just like the *CUSTOMER TYPE*.

Options for *Job Types* include Grant, Contract, or perhaps Pass Through (monies received on behalf of other charitable organizations). If you do not need to run reports on different types of funding, you do not need to bother with this.

Finish the *Job Info* tab by entering the appropriate dates and select *OK* to finish up this customer.

D. Other Member Information

That seemed like a lot to do, didn't it? Don't worry, most of your members will not need the payments, sales tax, or job settings tabs. But it is still rather tedious to input each member one at a time. More recent versions of QuickBooks have tried to streamline this. If you are comfortable with computer terminology and working with spreadsheets, I'll show how to import your members from an Excel spreadsheet or from your email contacts in Chapter 7. If not, don't worry about it. You can enter all of your members' data manually.

Go back to your **Customer Center** screen.

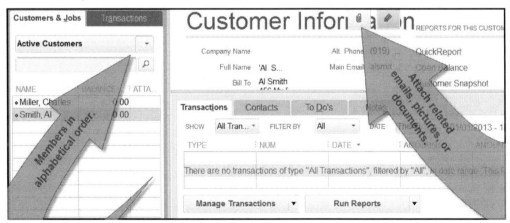

All of the members you have added will appear in the left column under **Customers & Jobs**. To the right will be an information screen with four tabs: Transactions, Contacts, To Do's, and Notes. The 2014 version of QuickBooks added an email management tab. We will be going through the **Transactions** tab in Chapter 9. The other three tabs are there to keep your member information organized and easily accessible. The **Contacts** tab allows you to enter numerous contact and related information. You might use this for children's names and birthdates or which families the member is related to.

The **To Do's** tab is a very handy feature which allows you to record meetings, calls, or tasks under a specific member and records the tasks in the QuickBooks calendar, which then can be set to remind you to complete it on the appropriate date. Tasks can be sorted by type, active status, or date.

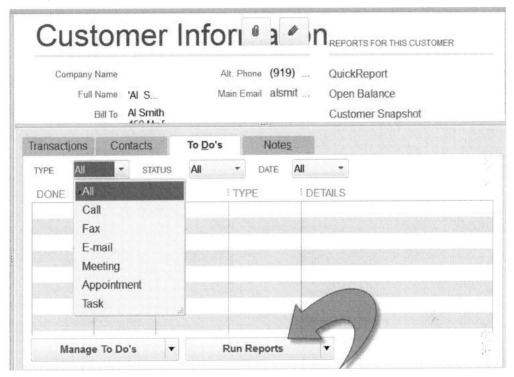

You can run a report listing all of the To Do's for this member by clicking the appropriate tab at the bottom of the screen.

To input a To Do, select *Manage To Do's* at the bottom left corner. Select *Create New* and you will see a screen similar to this one.

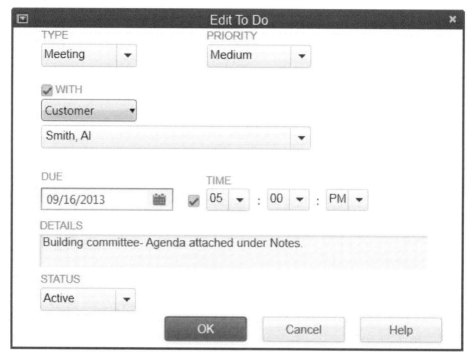

Select the type, priority, who it is with (notice you can chose Customer, Vendor, or Employee), and the date and time. Input the level of detail you would like and the status (Active, Done, or Inactive). Then select OK.

Your QuickBooks calendar will now reflect the to-do item.

E. Attaching Files to Your Member's Account

If you would like to attach a file, there is a paperclip icon in the Customer Information area. The pencil icon is used to edit member files.

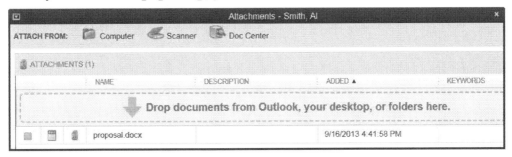

Once you select the paperclip, you will see:

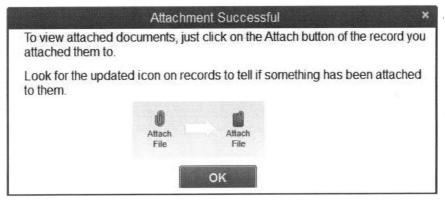

If you had previously attached any documents for this member, it will show up here. The icons across the top allow you to bring in a file from a computer, a scanner, or the Doc Center. The Doc Center is an area to store files that can then be attached to members, vendors, or employees. Select *Computer,* and the system will take you to your computer's document files for you to select which file you'd like to attach. Once it is attached, you will receive the following message:

Attachment Successful

To view attached documents, just click on the Attach button of the record you attached them to.

Look for the updated icon on records to tell if something has been attached to them.

Attach File → Attach File

OK

The **Notes** tab is another area where you can document information about the member and sort it by date.

Wow. Finally we have all of our members input with all the important information we would like to see. Let's now do the same for the vendors.

F.   Setting Up Vendors (The People You Pay)

If you select *Vendors* from the side menu, you will see a screen like this.

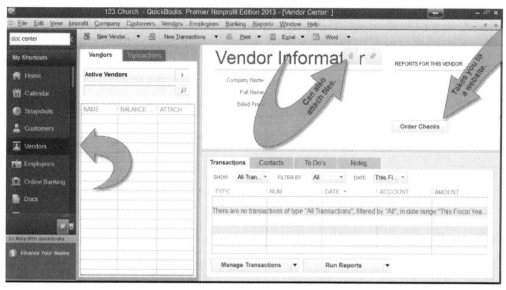

Notice the similarities between the Vendors' screen and the one under Customer. Once you have input vendors, it will list them down the side. Each vendor will have a Vendor Information area where you can attach files, edit, add transactions, contacts, to-dos, and notes in a similar manner as you did with your members. There is also a button labeled **Order Checks**. This takes you to Intuit's check printing website.

1.   Adding Vendors

To see information, we will need to input our vendors. Select *New Vendor* from the top of the list. This screen is very similar to the new member screen. And just like new members, you will need to develop a system to code your vendors.

> *Do Not Use the Opening Balance!! You will take care of that in Chapter 10.*

The **Vendor Name** is not the name on checks; it is the way you will search for vendors in QuickBooks. If you will need to cut separate checks to the same company (perhaps different insurance plans), you will want to have different **Vendor Names**. 123 Insurance-Building and 123

Insurance-Liability are possible examples. Like the new member screen, you can change the titles of any of the boxes with drop-down arrows.

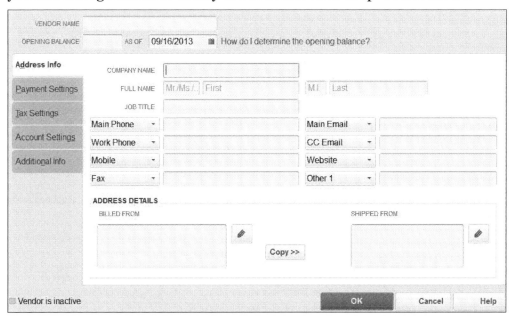

Let's look at the next tab on this screen, **Payment Settings**. This is where you will put any **account number** the vendor may have for you. Later, you can set up your checks so this account number is listed.

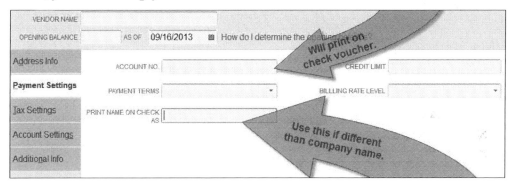

Payment terms aren't used by churches often, but there are choices in the drop-down menu if you need them. The **Print Name on Check As** is handy when the company name is different than who they would like the check made out to. You probably don't need to worry about the **Credit Limit** or **Billing Rate Level.**

The next tab is the **Tax Settings**.

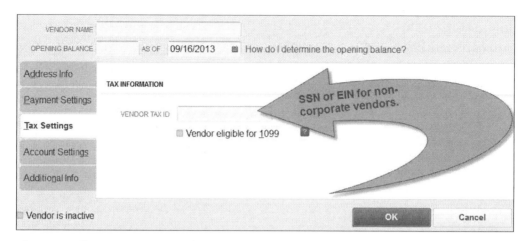

The **Vendor Tax ID** is where you will store the Employer Identification Number (EIN) or Social Security number for any non-corporate vendors you spend more than $600 a year with. I'll explain this in more detail in Chapter 15 on year-end procedures.

Now go to the **Account Settings** tab.

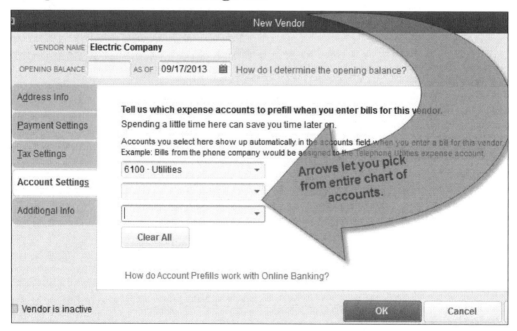

Instead of using the screen above, use the **Automatically Recall Information** option under **General Preferences**. When you choose that vendor in the payments area, the system will automatically show the expense accounts last used. The **Account Settings** tab will always bring up all of the line items you designate even if you only need one of them.

The last tab is **Additional Info**. You will notice it looks like the **Additional Info** tab in the **Add New Customer** screen.

You can use the preset vendor types or set up your own if you think you'll ever need to run reports with this information. If your governing board wants to know how much a year is spent on consultants, this could be useful. But do not bother to use the **Vendor Types** if you do not have a need for them.

2. Vendor Custom Fields

The **Custom Fields** shown are the same that you set up in **New Customers**. If any of the fields are useful for vendors, select them. You may also add any fields that will be helpful for your church. Perhaps you want to know how long you have been doing business with a vendor. You could have a *Vendor since* field to track the first time you purchased from them. Like the customer option, you can select up to seven fields.

Select *OK* and you have now saved your first vendor. After you have input your vendors, go back to the **Vendor Center**, and you will see the list of vendors and screens similar to the **Customer Center**. There you can attach documents, assign tasks to the calendar, etc. just like you did with the members.

The next chapter explains how to import names and addresses from your email contact base or from a spreadsheet. Feel free to skip it if it is simpler for you to enter the data with the method discussed in this chapter.

VII. Inputting Members & Vendors from Files

A.   Getting Members from Email Contacts

QuickBooks offers a program that will synchronize your email contact base with your customers and vendors within QuickBooks. When you update a member's information in QuickBooks, it will also instantly update in the email contact database and vice versa. You can limit the synchronization to only one direction (QuickBooks into email or email into QuickBooks).

As with any synchronization process, there are inaccuracies when the contacts are not entered consistently. For example, if I enter a company as ABC, Inc. in QuickBooks, but have it as ABC in the email database, there will be synchronization issues. Intuit (the maker of QuickBooks) also recommends limiting street addresses to two lines in both systems.

If you want to use the synchronization function to input your members and vendors, realize this will import the names and contact information, but you will still need to edit the members' files in QuickBooks for the other information such as type and options. The QuickBooks **NAME** for the member will default to first name, last name. If you have a different naming protocol, you will need to edit each of these imports. Additionally, the other non-contact information such as **Sales Rep** or custom designed fields will need to be adjusted manually. Considering the adjustments you will have to make, you must first decide if your contact database is close enough to the QuickBooks requirements to make this process worthwhile.

Another way to move your contact information into QuickBooks is by exporting a CSV (comma separate values) file from the email program into an Excel spreadsheet. This approach has the advantage of allowing you to type in the extra data via columns on one spreadsheet instead of having to edit **Customers** individually in the QuickBooks screens. If you are proficient with spreadsheets, you'll like that approach best. If not, use the email sync approach. I'll explain how to do each. But also remember, if working with computers makes your head spin, or you have a small membership, you can stick with the manual entry described in the last chapter.

1.   Adding Contacts From Synchronization

To add members and vendors from the email contact database, select *Utilities* from the *File* menu, then *Synchronize Contacts*.

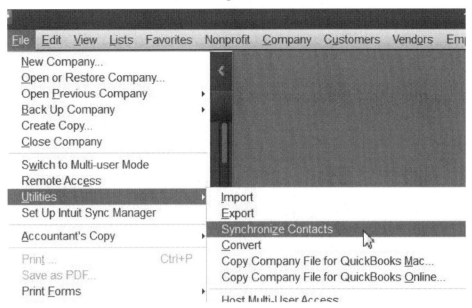

A pop-up box will ask if you would like to have *QuickBooks Contact Sync* installed on your computer. Select *OK* and the following window will open.

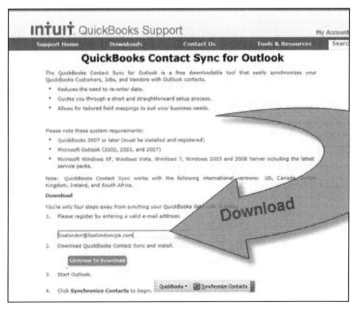

You will need to enter an email address and select *Continue to Download*. A warning might pop up; go ahead and select *Run*. A dialog box showing the status of the download will appear and possibly some warning screens. Select *Run* or *OK* as needed. Select *Next* when you see the following screen.

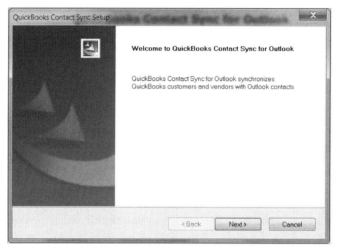

There will be some introductory screens and the license agreement to approve. Continue through these screens until you see this one.

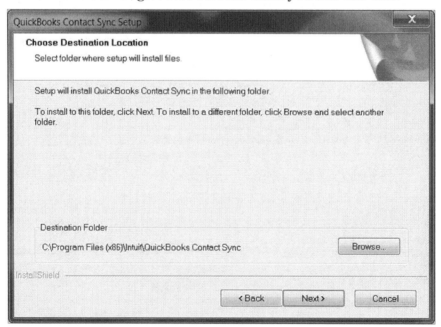

This box shows where the files will be saved. Unless you have a particular preference for another folder, just select *Next*. A status box will be displayed. Click *Finish* and don't forget to backup your church file before you go on.

2. Using Contact Sync

The program has been installed. If you have a Gmail or Yahoo account, it will take you to their website and request you to log in. If you are using Outlook, open it and see the following:

Select *Get* Started. A *Begin set up* box will appear. Select *Next* and you will be taken to a screen to decide which Outlook folder to use. Choose the one that has the contacts you want imported and hit *Next*. Now select the types of contacts.

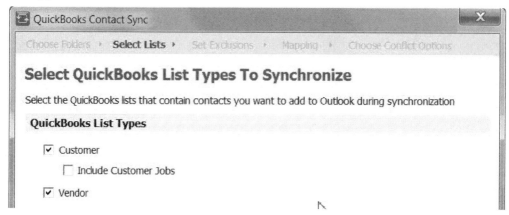

From there, it is time to determine which of your contacts can be excluded.

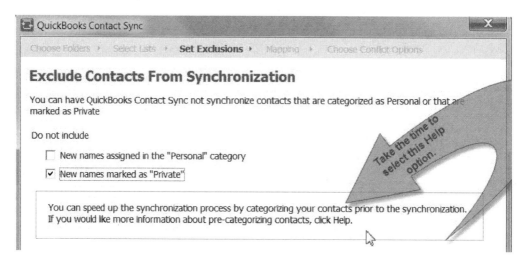

Check the appropriate options above so none of your personal contacts are loaded into the system. If you have more personal contacts in the database than members and vendors, you may prefer the manual method described in the last chapter. The *Help* option at the bottom of the screen will explain how to pre-categorize your contacts. I highly recommend reading this to save work later on.

3. Mapping Data Fields

Next we need to map the fields from the email database to the QuickBooks fields, which simply means telling the transitions software which fields from the email will go into which fields in QuickBooks.

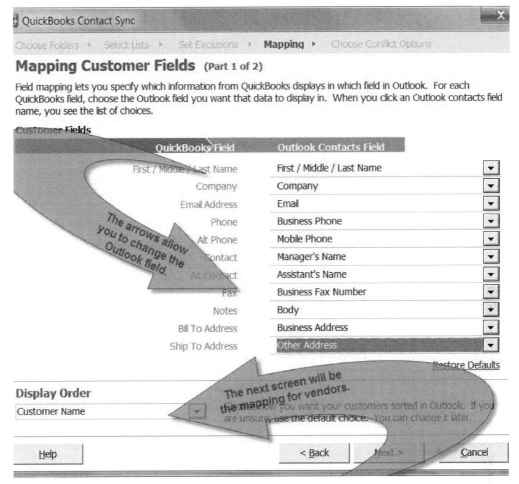

Look at the drop-down arrows by each of the fields if you would like to change the mapping. For example, if you would like the phone number to be the member's home number, select the arrow next to **Business Phone** and select **Home Phone** in its place. Once you are happy with the settings, select *Next*.

4. Solving Synchronization Conflicts

The next screen lets you decide how to settle conflicts. Remember that this system will continue to update your data files any time a member or vendor is changed.

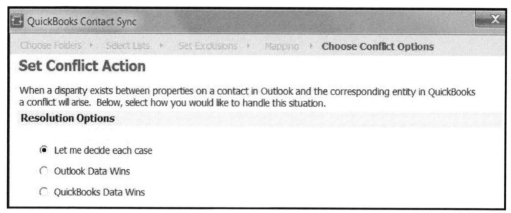

For example, if you have John Smith in QuickBooks with a 123 address, but Outlook says the address for John Smith is 122, you have to designate which is correct. If you don't have any data yet in QuickBooks, select Outlook Data Wins. Otherwise, select *Let me decide each case*.

Once you have gone through these screens, some informational screens will appear. Select *Sync Now* when it is offered, and you will then see a message similar to this one:

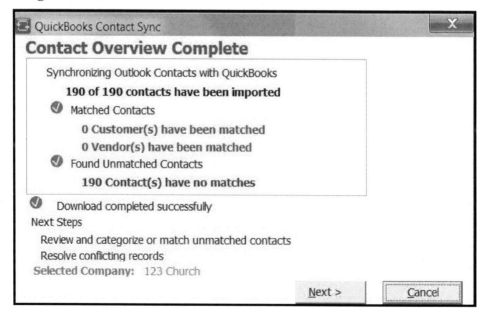

Don't let the unmatched contacts above worry you. The contacts were imported, but because there weren't already names in the system, none were matched. The next screen will allow you to categorize the names as either Customers (members) or Vendors.

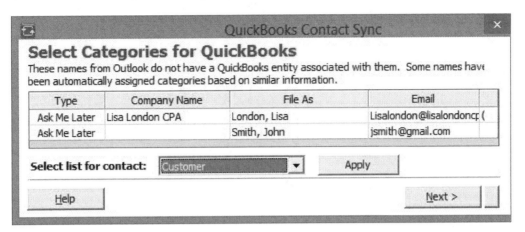

If all the lines on the screen are members, highlight them and hit *Apply*. This will change the **Type** to *Customer* instead of *Ask Me Later*. The arrow by the **Select list for contact** will allow you to change the type to Vendor or Ignore. Each line can be highlighted and changed individually or in groups.

The next screen will ask you to accept the changes, and then you should receive the following message:

Though the synchronization is complete, you aren't finished yet. To manually update the information that was not in your contact database, go to the **Customer Center**.

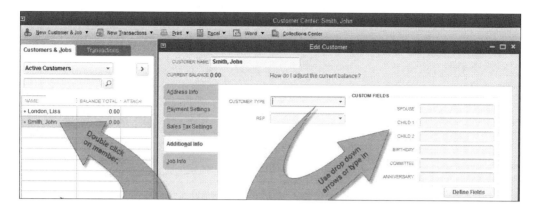

Double click on a member's name. This will bring up the same screens you used in manually setting up a member in Chapter 6. Input the additional data into the appropriate places and select *OK*.

B.   Spreadsheet Method: Importing w/Multiple List Entries

It may be easier to enter the data in the **Multiple List Entries**. First we need to see if your version of QuickBooks will allow for multiple list entries. From *Lists* on the menu bar, look at the last option.

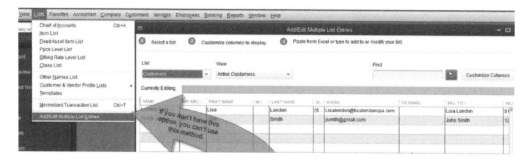

If you see *Add/Edit Multiple List Entries*, you will be able to update the additional information by columns. If not, you will need to manually enter any additional data for the member.

1.   Editing & Inputting Members Using a Spreadsheet

Part of the reason I wanted you to set up a member manually was so you could see which fields you wanted to use and which were okay to leave blank. You will be designing a spreadsheet with columns for each of the fields used. Let's start by taking a look at the entry form.

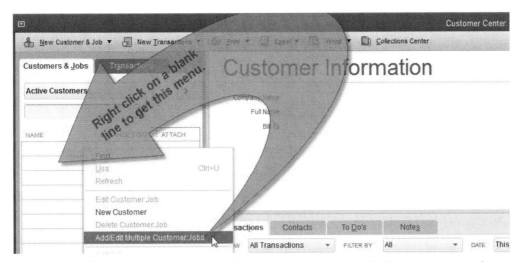

You can pull the **Add/Edit Multiple Customer Jobs** screen up from the Customer Center. The **Add/Edit Multiple List Entries** screen appears.

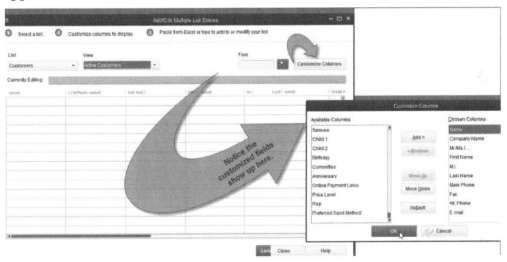

Begin by selecting *Customers* under **List**. The headings on the columns default to what the system thinks you will want to enter. Press *Customize Columns* and a popup box with all the options will appear. Notice the **Chosen Columns** on the right are the headings in the order of what appears on your **Add/Edit Multiple List** Entries screen. By selecting and adding the headings from the **Available Columns** on the left, you can change what columns are shown. If you highlight a heading in the **Chosen Column**, you can move the heading closer to the front or the back using the **Move Up** and **Move** Down buttons. This allows you to rearrange the screen to better fit how you want your columns imported.

Add or remove columns for things you would like to track. If you had set up custom fields earlier, they will be included. If you have your member list in a text file or a download from a different computer program, look at the column order and mimic it as best you can.

Once you've decided which columns you want to use, press *Save Changes*. I like to do that before I start entering the data so if I'm pulled away and have to come back to it, I don't have to remember which columns I wanted.

> *Move your cursor to the line in between columns and it will change to a +*
> *sign. This allows you to change the size of the column so you can fit more on*
> *the screen.*

Now you have your columns set. If you have already imported the names, addresses, and phone numbers from your email contacts, you can type in the additional information in this screen. Some of the columns will have a drop-down arrow which will give you options based on what you have set up. For example, if you had set up **Members** as a **Customer Type**, then the arrow beside **Customer Type** will give you a menu that includes **Members**. Likewise, if you have set up people designated to be **Reps** or have **Preferred Send Methods**, you will see the appropriate drop-down arrows. These drop-down menus save entry errors.

> *Whether you are inputting the data into QuickBooks directly or through a*
> *spreadsheet, remember the naming and date protocols you designed*
> *earlier. With custom fields, the system does not realize that 1/1/13 is the*
> *same as 01-01-2013.*

2. Converting Data into a Spreadsheet

If you chose not to import your email contacts, you can copy any or all of the columns from an Excel spreadsheet. I've found that a computer literate teenager is very handy about now. He can probably download your Word® or other software file that has all the members' names and addresses into a CSV file (that stands for Comma Separated Values). Excel can then open the CSV file and put the data into columns. You may or may not have all the information that you have columns for. Before you put the data into QuickBooks, I'd recommend finding as much of this information as possible and typing it in the spreadsheet. That way there is one less thing to have to follow up with later.

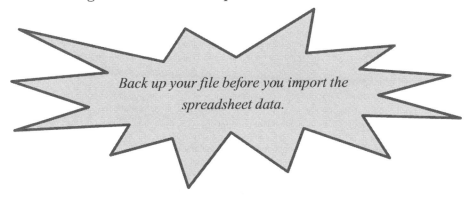

Back up your file before you import the spreadsheet data.

Here is an example of a spreadsheet set up to facilitate copying into QuickBooks.

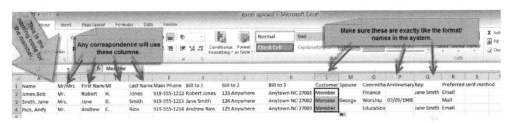

Notice that all of the columns do not have to be filled in. Some members may not have email addresses or spouses. Any information in the columns must be in the format or with the naming protocol set up for the system.

Once you are happy with the data in your spreadsheet, you can then copy it into QuickBooks one column at a time.

> *It is possible to copy all of the lines into the system at the same time, but if there are any empty fields, they are filled with the data from the previous column. Therefore, it is safer to copy one column at a time.*

3.   Potential Errors

I copied the spreadsheet above with all the columns to show you what some errors may look like.

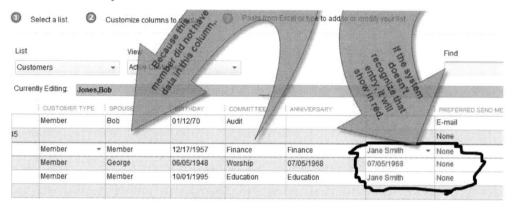

As you can see, anywhere I had a blank space in a column, the system filled it with the previous column's data. This would not have occurred had I copied the data in column by column.

The area circled in black would be colored red as the system did not recognize it. I did not have the **REP** (Sales representatives) types already set up, so Jane Smith was not recognized by the system. Additionally, I had spelled E-mail as Email, so the system did not recognize it. Luckily, I can select *Close* instead of *Save Changes* and none of these will be recorded in the system.

4.   Column by Column Copying

If you input your data by column, you eliminate the first of the errors and make it easier to correct the other errors as they occur. To input by column, copy the first column of your spreadsheet (without the heading).

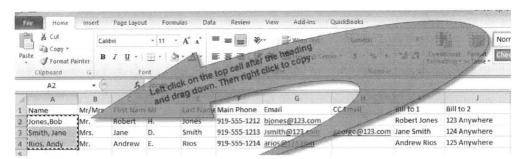

Left click on the top cell after the heading and drag down to cover the data in the column. Right click and select *Copy*.

Now you will go to the **Edit Multiple List Entries** screen in QuickBooks and paste the data in the first column. Select a blank line and right click. Select *Paste*.

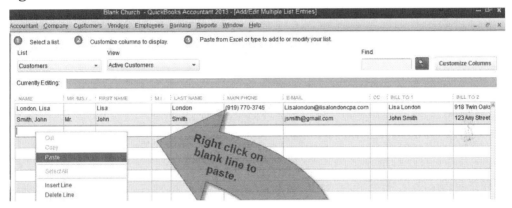

This will paste the highlighted names from your spreadsheet into the name column of the entry screen.

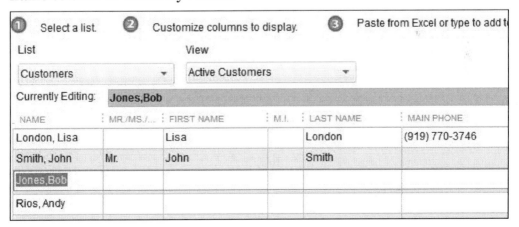

Continue doing this for each of the other columns. I like to play it safe and hit *Save Changes* after each column is pasted. That way, if I mess up a column, I can simply leave the screen and come back and try again without losing the previous columns. If the columns with the drop-down arrows give you any problems, just click on the arrows manually for each member. When you are finished, select *Save Changes* and then *Close*.

Now that you have all of your vendors and members in, be sure to back up. I'm certain you don't want to have to redo all your hard work again!

VIII. Items—Tracking the Transactions

We are almost done setting up the system. The last thing I want you to focus on before we go to transactions are the list of **Items**. By using items, QuickBooks does the accounting for normal recurring transactions without you having to remember the account numbers. In a business, the items would be the goods or services it has to sell or to purchase. For a church, the items will be donations, grants, designated programs, capital campaigns, etc. This is how you will track the money coming in. You will also be setting up items for your recurring purchases and to track volunteer hours.

There are several different item types, most of which you won't need to use. I'll give you a quick summary so you know what they are before we focus on the most important ones for churches.

1. **Service**—this is the type you will use for most of your receipts including your donations, grants, and funds collected for other organizations.
2. **Inventory part**—if you sell pamphlets or things that you buy to resell, and need to keep track of the amount on hand, you would use this type.
3. **Non-inventory part**s—use this type if you sell things you don't need to inventory.
4. **Other charge**—this can be used for fines or service charges. You probably won't use this much.
5. **Group**—I'll show you how to use this for allocations.
6. **Subtotal & Discount**—probably won't use these. They are used by businesses to total the items on an invoice and then apply discounts.
7. **Payment**s—record a payment you receive when you prepare the invoice.
8. **Sales tax item & Sales tax group**—if you are selling goods that your state requires you to collect sales taxes on, you will need a sales tax item.

A. Types of Services

Let's focus on **Service** items. Like the chart of accounts, items can have sub-items. If we have an item labeled **Donation**, we could establish sub-items such as **Pledges**, **Plate Offerings, EFT,** and **Donations**. I've included a small list of potential items in the appendix. Use these as a starting point. Don't worry about entering all possibilities. It is easy to add more items as you enter transactions.

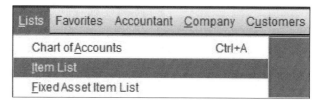

*There should be an item set up for every revenue line item on your chart of account. If you would like to track additional detail, use **Sub-items**.*

B. Setting Up New Items

Let's set up a service item. First, go to *Lists* on the menu bar.

From *Item List*, you will see the list of items on a screen like the one below.

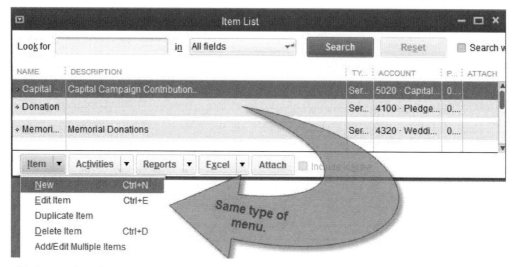

Click on the down arrow next to **Item.** Select *New* to bring up the input screen.

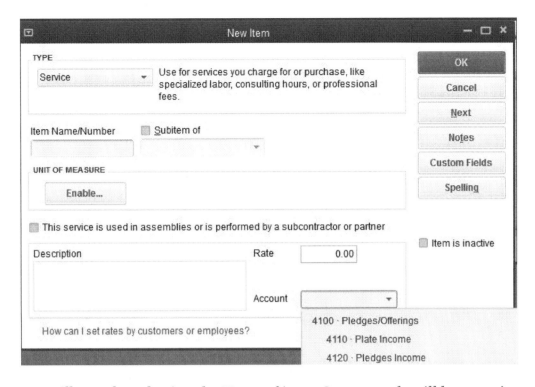

You will start by selecting the **Type** of item. Our example will be a service item. Assign the item a **Name,** and if it is a **Sub-item**, mark it here. **Units of measure** are used by businesses, so don't worry about it. Items allow you to designate a flat **Rate**, say $15 for the weekly flowers or $500 to perform a wedding. If the item you are entering has a standard rate, input it here. The invoice screens will allow you to override this amount for exceptions. Any parent account should have a rate of $0. **Account** is a drop-down menu showing you the chart of accounts. Select the income account number you would like the receipt to go to.

You may have noticed a redundancy in the items and the chart of accounts. If you do not need your financial statements to list the different types of donations, you can set up one donation account with lots of items that record into it. Read Chapter 13 on Reports and ask your governing members what level of detail they would like to see.

Custom Fields are available for items, but not necessary. To set them up, select *Custom Fields*. On the first box, select *Define Fields*. Now input any label you would like and check the *Use* box if you would like it used on this item.

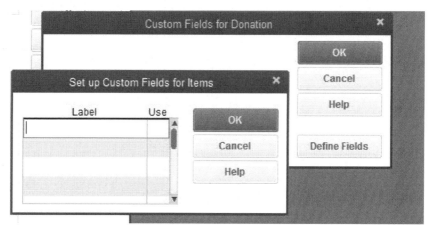

C. Using Items to Allocate Expenses

When paying bills, you may also want to use items. In Chapter 10, I'll explain how to set up items to facilitate allocation of expenses.

D. Tracking Volunteer Hours through Items

Items are also a useful tool to track volunteer hours by the type of help. By setting up the types of volunteer work (i.e. nursery, accounting, grounds maintenance) as items, you can run reports showing the volunteer hours given by your members. See Chapter 16 to learn how to use the timesheet function with items to track volunteer hours.

E. Fixed Asset Item List

There is a separate item list called the **Fixed Asset Item List**. It is used to track individual assets, like computer equipment, vehicles, and artwork. Access it from the menu bar as shown on the next screen.

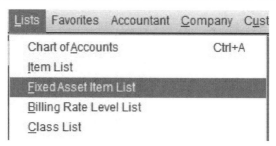

Once you click on *Fixed Asset Item List,* you will see:

Select *New* to see the entry screen.

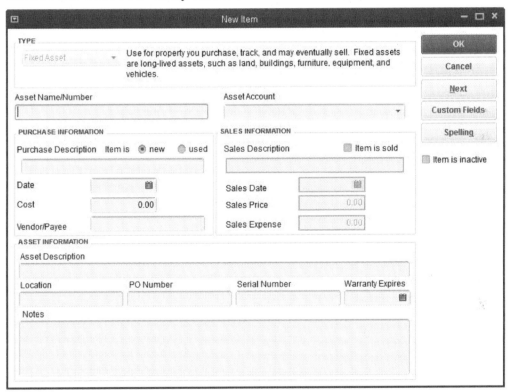

There are fields for the asset name or number, the chart of accounts number it is to be recorded in, descriptions, and costs. Examine this screen and compare it to what you are currently using to track fixed assets. Then decide if you would like to use QuickBooks to track your fixed assets.

Before we move onto Chapter 9, I would like to clarify the difference between using classes and adding new accounts or items.

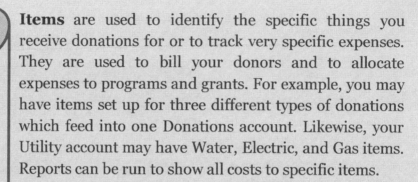

Items are used to identify the specific things you receive donations for or to track very specific expenses. They are used to bill your donors and to allocate expenses to programs and grants. For example, you may have items set up for three different types of donations which feed into one Donations account. Likewise, your Utility account may have Water, Electric, and Gas items. Reports can be run to show all costs to specific items.

Account numbers are used to track revenues, expenditures, assets, and liabilities to show on your financial statements. Each item is linked to an account number, but each account may have more than one item.

There will be quite a bit of redundancy between the account numbers and the items. You can limit the number of accounts by putting the details in Items. If you need to see how much you spent on electricity, a report on the Item *Electricity* can be run without having to have a separate account on the financial statements.

Classes can be used as separate general ledgers to track the money received and spent for a particular program or fund. Account numbers are assigned classes when a transaction is recorded so the amounts can be compiled together as individualized financial statements for each of the programs and funds.

I'll show you an example of using the Items, Account Numbers, and Classes.

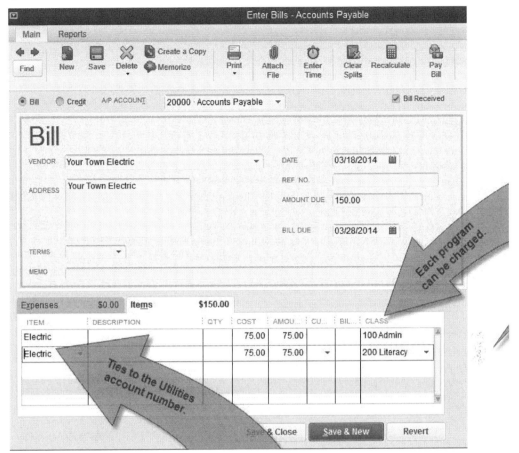

If you wanted to charge a literacy program for 50% of the electric bill, you would code the expense to the *Utilities account* using the *Electric item* and the *Literacy class*. A Class report would then tell you how much of the electric bill was charged to a program, but not what your total electric bill was.

Clear as mud, right? Just remember:
Items=*Details for invoices & bills and are linked to Account Numbers*
Account Numbers =*Make up the Financial Statements*
Classes=*Assign to Account Numbers when recording a transaction to show revenue and expenses by programs or funds*

IX. Money In—Recording Donations & Revenues

In order for your church to continue to do its good works, money needs to come in the door. As good stewards of your members' donations, you must implement accounting procedures and systems that will allow you to record and track the dollars while keeping the money safe. Before you learn how to enter the money received, I'll walk you through some basic internal accounting controls.

A.   Accounting Controls for Receipts

If you keep in mind two basic guidelines, most of the controls I recommend will make sense. First, no one should have access to cash and checks without other people observing them. Secondly, if a person has access to the accounting system (in this case, QuickBooks), he should not have access to the money. The treasurer MUST be a different person than the bookkeeper. Most thefts happen when the person handling the money can adjust the books to hide their tracks. I highly recommend going back to Chapter 1 to reread the **Case for Internal Accounting Controls** and **Points for the Governing Council.**

> *Don't start shaking your head and saying, "But we are too small to have those kinds of controls." No organization is too small to protect both their volunteers and employees from suspicion and entrust their funds from mismanagement. As a church, you probably have a governing board of volunteers to pull from as well as the congregation.*

In order to design controls for your church, think about the way money is received. A collection basket is passed around during the service; checks are received in the mail; electronic payments are made through the website; etc. Take time to walk through any scenario in which you receive money and design procedures that will not conflict with the two guidelines above. Here are some basic steps for the most common ways of receiving money.

1.   Money Received During Services

Most churches will pass the plate or a basket for donations during their weekly services. This money is often brought to the front of the sanctuary for the remainder of the service or is taken to another area in the church. If it is taken to the front of the sanctuary in full view of the congregation, it will need to be collected after the service by two people. These are usually the people that will also be the "counters," i.e. they will count the money and record on a piece of paper or deposit slip how much was received. Until the amount of money is recorded, there should be two people with eyes on it. I also recommend not allowing married couples or people living in the same household to be the counters together as there is more likelihood of collusion. Collusion is the term for working together to steal.

I like to have the members of the governing board rotate as counters with other volunteers. It allows the board members to keep an eye on the day-to-day workings of the church.

The counters, neither of which is the bookkeeper, will count the cash and make copies of the checks or record each of them manually. A summary form should be filled out and signed by the counters. The deposit will then be driven to the bank and put in the night deposit. One person can do this as there is a record of the receipts at the church. When the bookkeeper comes to work later that week, he will have a record of what was deposited to input into each member's account.

If the money was placed out of sight of the congregation during the service, there should always be two people keeping an eye on it until it can be counted.

2.   Remote Imaging Scanner

If your church receives a large number of checks, you may wish to ask your bank about an RID—Remote Imaging Device scanner. This allows you to quickly scan the checks and print out a report for your files. The scanned file is automatically sent to the bank, so the deposit can be made immediately rather than waiting on a volunteer to drive to the bank later in the week. Once the bank has the scanned image, it does not need the physical check.

The original checks can be marked with a highlighter to show they were scanned and filed for future reference. The scanner will not let you send the same check twice. Beware though. If you accidentally try to deposit the scanned checks at the bank, a deposit correction fee will be charged.

By scanning the checks immediately after the service, there is less likelihood of someone taking them and depositing them into their own account. The scanner also is less likely to make math errors.

> *Banks usually charge a fee for the RID scanners, but the time savings and control features are often worth the additional expense.*

3. Money Received Through the Mail

Often members or other donors prefer to mail in their donations rather than bringing them to the church. It is a good idea to have a post office box. This keeps anyone from stealing the checks out of your mailbox. You don't want your bookkeeper to be the one to pick up the mail. Theoretically, he could steal some checks but make the member's account look like it was received. Designate someone without access to the accounting system to go to the post office, and then, back at the church, have him open the mail in front of a second person. Each check should then be recorded and the summary signed by the two observers. If you have an RID scanner, scan the checks immediately, and then give the deposit report and the marked checks to the bookkeeper.

4. Electronic Payments Received Through the Website

Now that so much is being done on the web, many churches have found it advantageous to add a donation button to their website. This can be activated through many different services.

The most important thing to do with electronic payments is to safeguard the link to the bank account. Many online credit card processors will require signed corporate resolutions stating you are a legal organization and the check signers have authorized the funds to go to that account. Others, like PayPal®, simply use an email/password combination. This is potentially a problem as the person who has the password could reroute the appointed deposit bank account to their personal account number.

A PayPal® employee told me of a women associated with a small nonprofit that had set up its PayPal® account. She had a falling out with the organization and refused to tell them the password to collect the money.

To keep this from occurring with your church, I would recommend the account be linked to an email address administered by your church (xxx@yourchurch.org) and assigned to someone who has no access to the members' records. This person would have the authorization to change the bank deposit account and permit transfers from the PayPal® account to the bank.

PayPal® does allow for a secondary user with limited rights that can only see reports, not change bank accounts. You will want this to be your bookkeeper so he can reconcile the receipts PayPal is reporting to the cash posted into the bank. Any discrepancies should be investigated immediately.

We've covered some basic steps to protect your people and your money in the most common ways donations are received. Now make a list of all the other ways money is received and ask yourself—for each case, how you can get it to the bank and recorded in the financial statements while providing good stewardship of your gifts and your volunteers and employees?

These are the minimum steps to take to safeguard receipts. If your church already has more complete procedures, please follow them.

B. **Entering Donations**

1. **Pledge, Plate, and Other Simple Donations**

Most of your receipts will be simple donations. By simple, I mean that the member does not expect to be invoiced or even given a receipt. This is also the easiest way to enter receipts into QuickBooks.

Before entering any receipts or donations, go to the main menu bar and select *Edit, Preferences, Checking, My Preferences*.

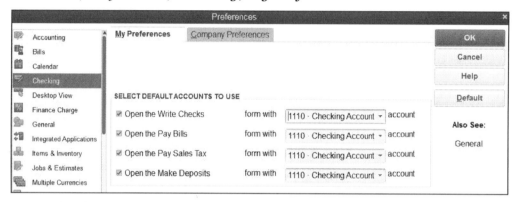

Using the drop-down arrows, select the correct bank account for each of these categories and hit *OK*. For most churches, this will be the basic checking account.

From the **Home** screen of QuickBooks, you will see an icon labeled **Create Sales Receipts**. If you have the more expensive, non-profit version, it will be labeled **Donations.**

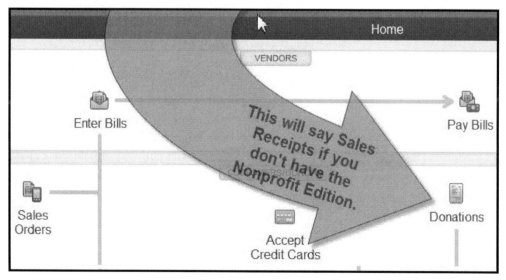

Alternatively, you can select from the top menu.

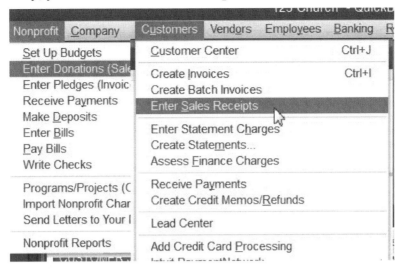

Or through the Customer Center.

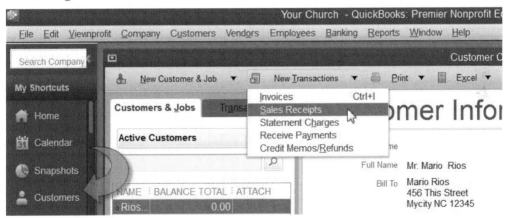

A screen titled **Enter Sales Receipts** or **Donations** will appear.

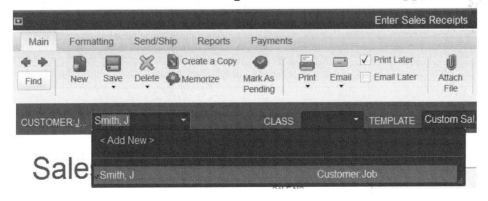

In the box marked **Customer**, you may type in the member's name (or code, if you didn't use last names), and the system will try to guess which name you want. In this example, I had only typed an "s" and the system brought up all the names that started with "S". If you had used the Customer Center to pull up the sales receipt screen, it would default to the first member name or one you had highlighted on the list.

2. Entering Checks Received

You are now ready to enter the money received. Across the top is the member name and the default class you would like the money to go to. This class will be automatically filled in for the line items below.

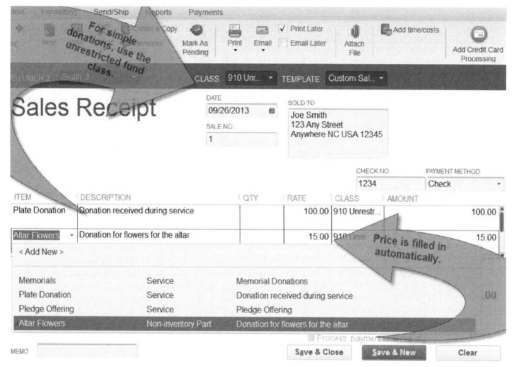

The date will default to today or the last date entered, depending on the preferences set up under Customers. The **SALE NO** is automatically generated, and unless you have a donation numbering sequence you would like to use, ignore it. Input the type of receipt (check, cash, credit card, etc.) and the check number if applicable.

> *Unless the donation is for a specific program or fund, use the unrestricted fund class.*

In this example, I have a check numbered 1234 for $115 from Joe Smith. He put it in the collection basket with a note that $15 was for flowers for the altar and the rest was his normal weekly offering. In Chapter 8, you set up items for each type of income you expect to receive. These are the items you will be allocating the donations to. In the item setup, you were given the option to assign a rate. With Plate Donation, we left the rate blank because people donate different amounts. In this example, I had set up Altar Flowers with a rate of $15 as the standard amount. This can be changed for a single transaction on the sales receipt screen, but it saves keystrokes if that is the common price.

Select *Save & New* and a blank sales receipt or donation screen appears ready for you to add the next donation.

3. Acknowledging the Donation

QuickBooks has a convenient feature which allows you to customize the sales receipt and email it directly to your donor. I'll walk you through the process in Chapter 15. This isn't necessary for the weekly donations but is useful for donations that need an immediate acknowledgement. In Chapter 12, I'll show you how to send out annual or quarterly donation reports for regular gifts.

After entering the donation, select the *Email* icon.

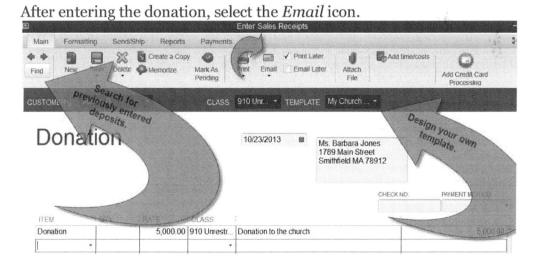

If you don't have Outlook on your computer, you may receive a screen asking you to set up and use QuickBooks email. If so, follow the steps in the dialog boxes to set up.

If you want to send all the emails at once, select *Email Later*, otherwise leave blank. The default email is very generic and will need to be changed. To do this, go to the main menu under *Edit, Preferences*, and select *Send Forms, Company Preferences.*

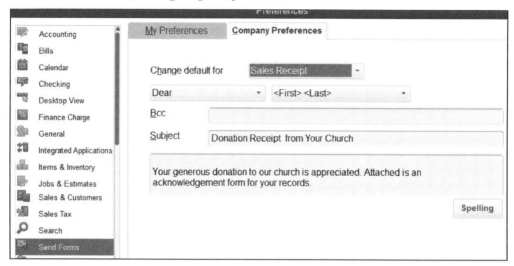

Change the **Change default for** menu to *Sales Receipt.* You will see a very generic "Your sales receipt is attached" type message. Erase this message and type in what you would like the basic message to say to your donors. If you are emailing one donor at a time, you can also edit the individual donor's message on the email screen before you send it.

Press *Email* and a screen similar to this one will appear.

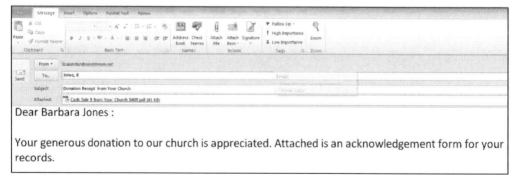

The email will attach the basic sales receipt form unless you design something different.

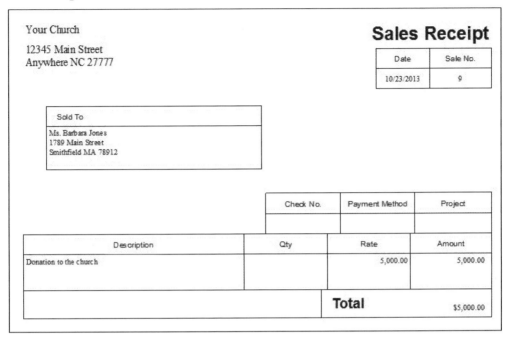

I'll discuss how to customize forms and reports in Chapter 15.

C. Entering Cash Receipts

Let's set up a member called **Cash.** You can add new members from the sales receipts screen. Select the drop-down menu and then highlight *Add New*.

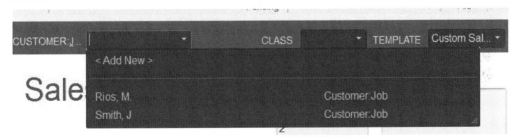

Now make the **CUSTOMER NAME** *Cash.* You do not need to input any addresses, but under **Additional Info** you can select the **CUSTOMER TYPE** to *Member* if you like.

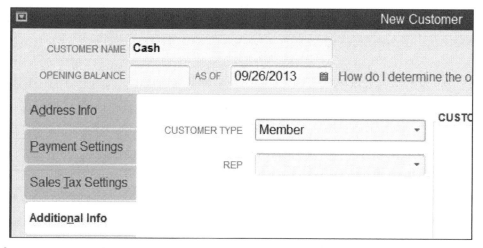

After you save the Cash member, you will be back at the Sales Receipt screen with Cash in the Customer box.

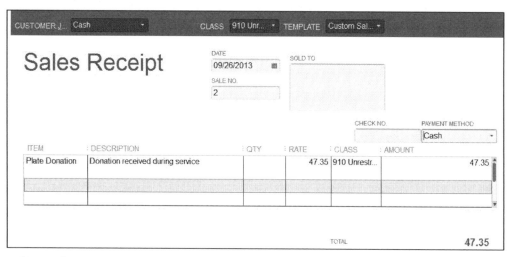

Select **Class** to be *Unrestricted*, the **Payment Method** to be *Cash,* and the **Item** to be *Plate Donation.* Input the amount (it can go under **RATE** or **AMOUNT**), and *Save.*

D. Entering Donations from a Separate Donor Base

You do not have to track your members through QuickBooks. Many organizations use Internet-based donor record systems. These databases offer more flexibility in analysis and in correspondence with the donors. Some offer a download file that can then be imported into QuickBooks. Others will require you to make a manual entry.

Without knowing which database you are using, I can't walk you through that step, but the database company will have instructions for you. I can, however, show you how to enter it manually. Start by setting up a new member called Donor Database.

Next you will run a report from your donor database that totals the donations. You'll need these donations grouped to match the donations deposited. For example, if you received 10 donations throughout the week and went to the bank to deposit them two different times, you will need the report to list the donations based on the day deposited. This is important as you need the amount of the donations to match the related daily deposit.

Bring up the **Sales Receipt (Donation)** screen.

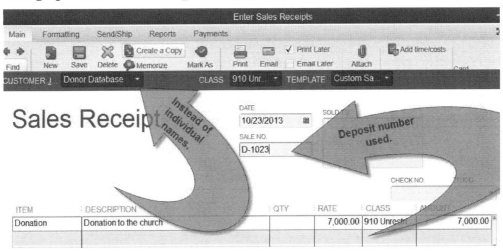

Select the customer **Donor Database** and choose the correct class (unrestricted for regular donations). Input the day these donations were deposited in the **DATE** box.

The **SALE NO. (DONATION NO.)** should be the deposit number. You will not need to input a check number or payment method. Designate the items and amount of one of the daily deposits from the donor database report and then select *Save &New*. Continue entering the amounts of the deposits from the report.

E. Pledges Made and Paid

1. Recording Pledges as Receivables

If your church asks it members to make pledges annually or for a project, QuickBooks can help you track them. When the system uses the word **Invoice** as it relates to **Customers**, I want you to think instead **Pledges** from **Members**.

The Home screen has an icon called **Create Invoices**. The same phrase is used under the Customer's menu along the top bar. From the Customer Center, you will find it under **New Transactions**.

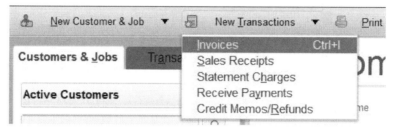

The invoice screen is then shown.

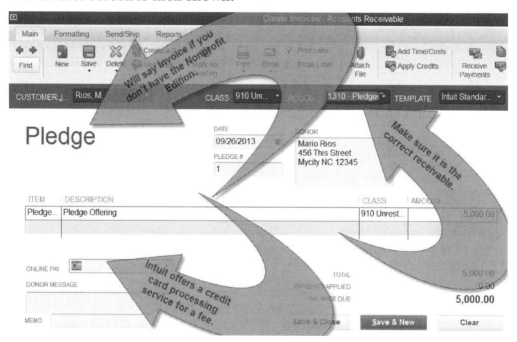

Enter the member's name, and, as this will be a pledge for normal operations, select the unrestricted fund under **Class**. The next option is the **ACCOUNT.** This will have a drop-down menu of all the options. Select *Pledges Receivable.*

TEMPLATE is the next option. If you have the nonprofit edition, there is a template labeled **Intuit Standard Pledge** that will appear. Otherwise, it will come up labeled **Invoice**. Unless you plan on sending a copy of this pledge invoice to the member, don't worry about the labels. We will design a pledge statement to send out later in this chapter.

At the bottom of the screen is the **ONLINE PAY** option. It should be selected if you choose to use Intuit's processing. I won't be covering that in this book as the Intuit professionals will need to set you up with this service. The **DONOR (CUSTOMER) MESSAGE** option would only be used if you were to send the pledge invoice out to the donor.

Once you select *Save & New*, you will be directed back to the empty invoice screen. Continue entering pledges and close. If you are entering pledges received for the following year, date the pledges on January 1 of the next year, otherwise keep today's date. You may receive the following warning, but that's okay.

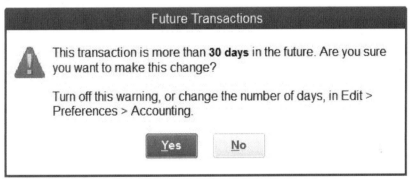

2.   Entering Beginning Receivable Balances

If your church had open receivables as of the start date, you will need to enter them as invoices dated in the previous accounting year. For example, assume you had three members with outstanding pledges of $1000 each as of December 31, 2014, and you are setting up QuickBooks with a start date of January 1, 2015. For each member, enter an invoice dated in 2014 for $1000. This will make your beginning balances as of January 1 correct and will give you invoices to apply payments to when the pledges are received in 2015.

3. Receiving Payments on Pledges

QuickBooks makes receiving payments on pledges easy to record. Once again, go to *New Transactions* from the Customer Center, then *Receive Payments.*

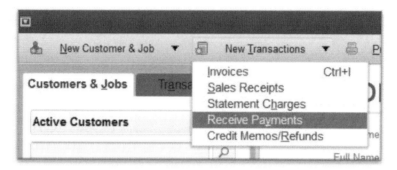

This will then bring up the **Customer Payment** screen.

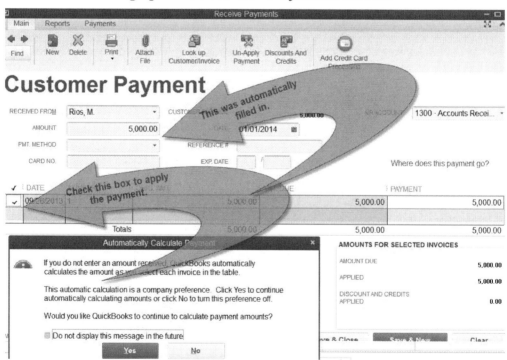

When you input the member's name, any outstanding balances will appear. Just click on the small box to the left of the **DATE,** and the system automatically assumes the entire balance is being paid. A warning box then appears to make certain you wanted to do that.

If a partial payment on the pledge was made, fill in the **AMOUNT** box before selecting the checkbox near **DATE**. This will apply the amount against the balance.

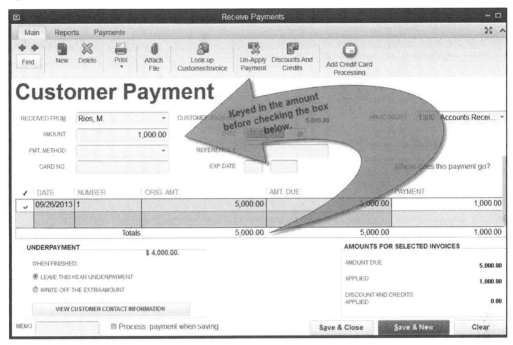

F.   Receipt of Restricted Funds

When you receive money that has been restricted by the donor, you must designate the **Temporarily Restricted Class** or the **Permanently Restricted Class.** Go back to the sales receipt or donation screen.

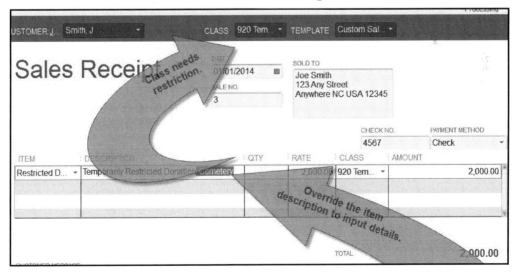

Select **CLASS** to *Temporarily or Permanently Restricted*. If it is a grant or contract that you will need to report the related expenses, it will be set up as a job. Let's first assume you do not need to report back to the donor.

The default descriptions from the items can be changed by typing over them. The more detail here, the easier it is to look up information later. Remember, you can attach documents detailing the restrictions to the member's account through the Customer Center. If this was an endowment or other permanently restricted donation, you would select the **Permanently Restricted Fund** as the class.

Perhaps your church has received a grant or contract that requires specific steps and accounting. For example, a member has decided to donate $50,000 to the church to help train welfare recipients in the skills needed to be hired. She would like the money spent on training materials for the volunteers and on day care and clothing for the attendees. The church will need to submit a report after one year detailing the costs and the success or failure of the program.

First you will need to add a job to the donor's file. From the Customer Center, select *New Customer & Job, Add Job*.

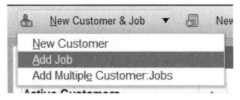

The New Job screen will open.

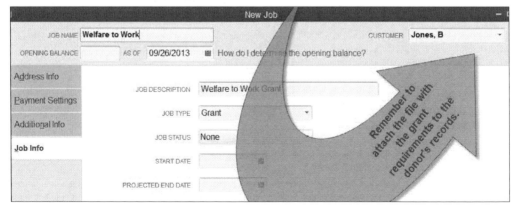

Under the **Job Info** tab, assign a name to the grant or contract and select the member donating the money under **Customer**. Fill in the description, designate a job type, and the start and end dates if desired.

Select *OK* and you will be taken back to the Customer Center with this job highlighted. Use the attach files button on the top right corner to save the related grant documents. Now go back to *Sales Receipts* under *New Transactions* and enter the check.

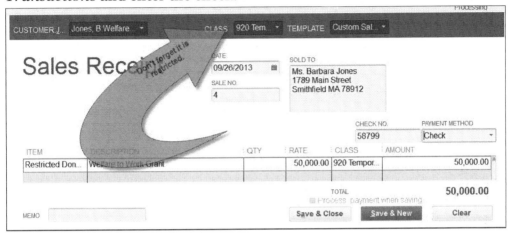

G. Miscellaneous Receipts

1. Receipts not related to a particular donor

For miscellaneous donations not related to a particular donor, you will need to have items set up to link them to the chart of accounts. They can be entered through the **Sales Receipts** screen. Leave the customer blank or set up some generic customers (i.e. Carnival Fundraiser, Pamphlet Sales, etc.) and enter them the same way you did cash or check receipts above.

An even easier option is to go to the deposit screens.

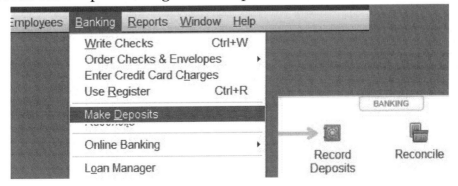

Go to the **Record Deposits** icon on the Home page or the *Make Deposits* option from the *Banking* menu at the top. If there are outstanding deposits to be made, a **Payments to Deposit** screen will appear. If so, select *Cancel* to see the next screen, **Make Deposits**.

On the **Make Deposits** screen, you can enter the non-donor related income without setting up customers.

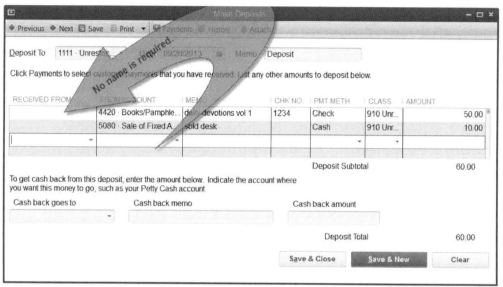

DO NOT enter individual donor information on this screen. Donations must go through invoices or sales receipts or you will not be able to generate accurate reports by donor.

2.   Insurance settlements

Sometimes things happen at a church that require an insurance report. If your church receives a settlement for such occurrence, you may wish to compare the amount received with the related expenses. For example, if a hail storm ruined the roof, you may wish to see how the expenses to repair the roof compared to the dollars received from the insurance settlement.

The easiest way to track this would be through the **Customer:Jobs** area. The insurance company is set up as both a customer and a vendor because it is someone you both received money from and pay money to. Set the insurance company up as a customer with a job (called Roof Repair). To record the payment you received, under **Enter Sales Receipts**, select the insurance company name:job and record the check.

Or, if you know the check is coming, you may record it as an invoice and then use **Receive Payments** when the check arrives. The insurance check can be coded to an "*Other Miscellaneous Income*" account or directly as a credit to repair cost if you don't want to show the check separately.

When the bills from the repair come in, go to the **Enter Bills** screen. there is a column called **Customer: Job** that has a drop-down menu. As you pay for the roof repairs, charge the expense to *Repairs* and select the insurance company name:job. You can then run a Job report showing how much of the insurance money was used.

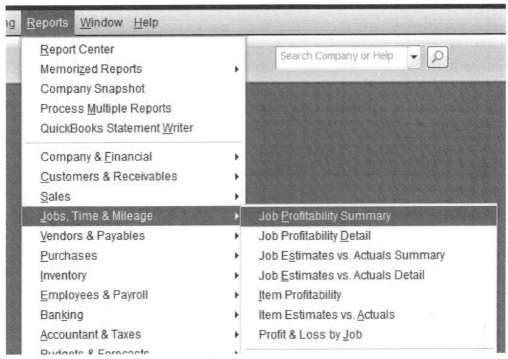

H. Pass-Through Collections

Your church may take up collections for other organizations, like a local food bank or Habitat for Humanity®. A check will be sent to the organization for the amount of the donations, so you will need to record them a little differently.

First, you will want to set up an **Item** with **Service** as the type called *Pass-Through Donations* (or something similar). It should be linked to an **Income Account** in the revenue area (*Outreach* or *Pass-Through*

Funding, perhaps). When money is received, choose *Sales Receipt* (or *Donations*).

If you are receiving the donations through a fundraiser or cash not from a particular donor, set up a **Customer** named for the other organization (i.e. Food Bank). If the money is received from a donor, use their name instead. The class is unrestricted as the payment will be made to the organization on a timely basis.

Enter the donations as you normally would, but set the **Item** to the *Pass-Through Donation*. If you are collecting for several different organizations, set up **sub-items** to track by organizations. If you have a description in the item, it will appear. You can delete it or add any additional information under the **Description** line. Enter the *Amount* and select *Save & Close*. After all of the donations are entered, run a **Sales by Item** report for the time period of the donations to see the total dollars owed to the receiving organization.

You will now set up an **Item** with **Service** as the type called *Pass-Through Payments* linked to an **Expense Account**-*Payments of Donations to Others* or *Pass-Through Donation*. Set up any sub-items for any multiple organizations to match the ones you set up above.

Next, go to the Vendor Center and set up the receiving organization as a Vendor. It cannot be the same as the Customer name, so simply add a "v" after the organization's name. Enter a bill for the amount of the donations (from the **Sales by Item** report) and charge it to the *Pass-Through Payments* item or related sub-item. The check can then be printed as explained in the next chapter.

If you are using an RID scanner, scan all of the pass-through checks for an organization together as one deposit, and then record it as one entry instead of the individual checks. This makes it easier to keep the funds separate.

This method assumes churches want to track their outreach donations for management purposes. If you need to have GAAP compliant financial statements, accounting principles may require you to treat this as a liability, not a contribution. If so, you will set up the **Pass-Through Donation** item linked to an **Accrued Liability** account instead of an income account. When you pay the receiving organization, use the same **Pass-Through Donation** item on the write checks screen. This will bring the liability account to zero once the organization is paid.

I.   Undeposited Funds

Once you are back at the Customer Center, the middle column will list the members and the amount of pledges outstanding.

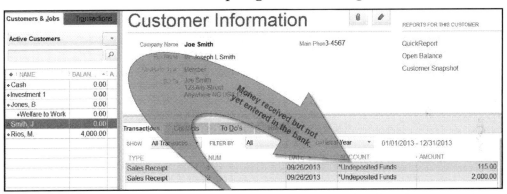

If you highlight a member, you will see the list of related transactions. The sales receipt from my earlier example for Joe Smith appears but shows up as **Undeposited Funds** instead of money in the checking account.

I hate to talk like an accountant, but I need to explain what QuickBooks is doing behind the scenes. QuickBooks records the money coming in as revenue based on the account numbers you assigned to the items. In the accounting world, there must be two sides to each entry, so instead of recording the money straight into your checking account designated in the chart of accounts, it is posted in *Undeposited Funds*. The system assumes that after you recorded the money coming in, you put it in a safe or bank bag along with other checks to be deposited. Think of *Undeposited Funds* as the stack of checks and money you have in that bank bag.

> *If you do not see **Undeposited Funds** by the sales receipts transactions, you do not have your preferences set correctly. Go to the top menu, select Edit, then Preferences. Scroll down to Payments, Company Preferences and chose the **Use Undeposited Funds as a default deposit to account**.*

When you are ready to deposit the money or record the deposit that was made after the Sunday services, including those through an RID scanner, go to the *Make Deposits* screen from either the top menu or the deposits icon. You will see two screens like this.

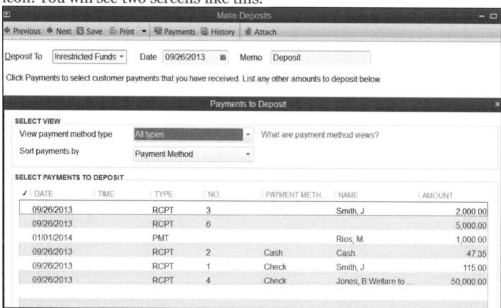

All of the cash and checks recorded are listed. Assuming the church is tracking their checking account with the three subaccounts (unrestricted, temporarily restricted, and permanently restricted), the bookkeeper will need to record three different deposits. For this example, the church is going to deposit all of the non-restricted money into the unrestricted portion of the checking account, the grant into an investment account, and Mr. Smith's $2000 restricted gift into the restricted portion of checking. If you are depositing all of the money into your checking account without the subaccounts, you will only need to make one deposit. I'll step you through the more complicated subaccount approach as it includes the one account method plus two additional steps.

The first deposit is the unrestricted gifts.

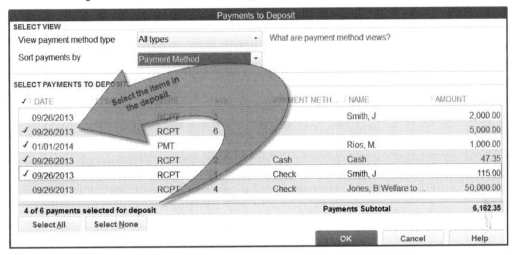

Select the items that will be deposited together in the bank. If you used an RID scanner, select all that were transmitted together. Hit *OK* and this will bring up the **Make Deposit** screen below.

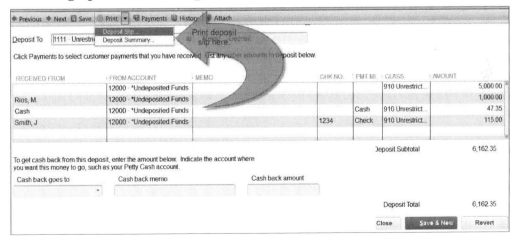

The **Deposit Total** should be the amount of the total deposit made from unrestricted money. If you hadn't already made the miscellaneous deposit discussed earlier, those items could be added to this deposit.

Select the *Print* button to print a deposit slip and summary. When I did that, I received an error message that all deposits must have a Cash or Check payment method.

This is QuickBooks way of letting me know I forgot to enter some data. If you look back at the deposit screen, you will notice that I forgot to identify whether the money was cash or check on two of the lines. I also noticed a class was missing. Now I can go back to that screen, fix it with the drop-down arrows, and then print my deposit summary.

However, I still have money to deposit. The next deposit needs to be made into one of the investment accounts. Select the restricted grant from the **Payments to Deposit** screen and click *OK*.

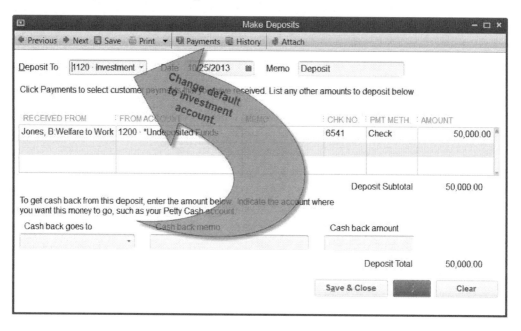

The deposit will be made directly into the investment account. Point the **Deposit to** box to *Investment account* and select *Save& Close*.

> *Using **Undeposited Funds** makes reconciling your bank account so much easier. It summarizes the receipts deposited together so the total matches the deposit amount on your bank statement. Otherwise you would have to select individual customer checks on the bank reconciliation screens until they added up to the total deposits. (This will be more clear in Chapter 12.)*

J.   Recurring Donations from Credit Cards

Churches are increasingly encouraging members to use credit cards to pay their pledges monthly. This gives the church a better handle on cash flow and allows the member to pay his full pledge even if he misses church. Churches encouraging their members to enroll in an automatically recurring donation program have seen a significant increase in the amount of pledges received and the consistency. For example, if Mr. Smith pledges $100 per month but goes out of town for the summer and forgets to send in payments, the church would only receive $900 instead of the expected $1200. Usually, the additional cost of processing the credit card transactions are more than offset by the increased revenue.

Credit card receipts can be set up for online payments through a third party or through a service within QuickBooks for a fee. You will need to research the fee structure and reports available to determine which makes the most sense for your church. If you use a third party, you would input the receipt as we discussed above but change the **Payment Method** to the type of credit card. At month end, you would then need to record the credit card charges through a journal entry. I'll explain how to do that in Chapter 12.

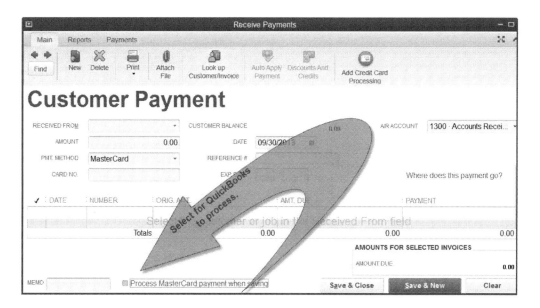

If you use the QuickBooks service, it has a synchronization option that allows you to enter the donation as an invoice, sales receipt, or payment.

QuickBooks processes the credit card and will record the donation and the receipt into your records. The synchronization process makes it much easier to reconcile the money deposited in the bank to the amount recorded in QuickBooks.

> *I've gone over how to record the contributions, but there are numerous IRS rules covering acknowledging them, including very specific wording for different types of donations. My book, **Church Accounting: The How-To Guide for Small & Growing Churches**, explains these in detail. You can also link to the IRS webpages for these rules through my website, accountantbesideyou.com/irs-forms/.*

X. Money Out—How Do I Pay the Bills?

A.   Cash vs. Accrual Methods

Now that you know how to record the money coming in, it's time to work on the money going out. Before we get started, I'm afraid I'll need to throw a little accounting terminology at you.

There are two methods to account for expenses and revenues in the accounting world—Cash and Accrual. The cash method is the simplest. The cash is recorded in the financial statements when it is physically received and when the checks are written. The accrual method requires dating the transaction when the income was earned (i.e. when the grant was awarded) or the expense item was purchased, not when cash changed hands or the check was written.

For businesses or organizations that pay taxes or are publically held, the difference is significant. Churches can use either depending on their governing boards and other requirements. Fortunately, QuickBooks allows you to report the information either way. Assume you receive an invoice from a contractor who did repairs on the church dated July 31, but you didn't write him a check until August 15. If you enter the invoice with a date of July 31, you can run financial reports for July showing the expense by selecting the accrual method. If you were to run the report using the cash method, the expense would not appear in the July statements.

In case you are wondering why I'm telling you this, I'm going to have you input your bills on the accrual method so you have both options for reporting.

*The **accrual method** gives you the most accurate financial picture of your church right now; showing money you have earned and expenses you have incurred. The **cash basis** gives you a better idea of when the money has come in or gone out. By allowing you to run the reports either way, QuickBooks gives you the best of both worlds.*

B. **Internal Accounting Controls for Paying Bills**

Fraud, theft, and mistakes are as much of a concern with the money going out as they are with the money coming in. Procedures and controls need to be in place to keep phantom employees or fake vendor invoices from being paid. To assure good stewardship over your church's money, you will need strong accounting controls in place as it relates to the money paid out.

> *Remember the basic rule. If someone has access to the money, he should not have access to the financial records.*

The bookkeeper must not be an authorized check signer. I know this sounds nearly impossible for a small church, but, here again, you may need to utilize the members of the governing body or other volunteers.

Bills should not be entered into the system without documentation and approval from someone other than the bookkeeper. This could be the pastor or treasurer. Sometimes the documentation is as simple as the bill from the utility company or a handwritten note asking the supply organist be paid $100. If the expense is to be charged to more than one program, the approver should also notate this. But most importantly, all bills to be paid must be approved. Petty cash expenditures will be addressed later in the chapter.

The bookkeeper will enter and code the bills into the correct expense categories and programs or grants. He will then print the checks, match them up with the approved documentation, and give them to an authorized check signer. The check signer should assure himself that the payee, address, and amounts agree to the approved documentation and sign the checks. The checks can then be mailed and the documentation filed or scanned. I recommend you use a voucher-style check. This allows a space for the payee to see what invoice was paid.

Your portion of the voucher should be stapled to the approved invoice and filed under the vendor's name. The check signer should never sign a check made out to him. A different signer is required for that.

*From the File menu, select **Print Forms** and **Labels** to automatically make file folder labels for each of your vendors and donors. You can also print mailing labels. Play around with the options and get organized!*

You will want at least two authorized signers. Besides not allowing a signer to sign his own check, a signer may become unavailable and the church will still need to pay their bills. Requiring two signatures over a certain dollar amount is another control, but be aware, with electronic scanning; banks no longer check for two signatures on the checks.

Don't forget about physical controls. Checks must be kept in a locked drawer, not just a locked office. A member of a cleaning crew once stole some checks from a client and forged them.

C.   Controls for Electronic Payments

Paying bills online is a very convenient process. No more tracking down envelopes and stamps and running to the post office. However, the convenience makes it necessary to implement controls to assure all payments are recorded in the financial statements in a timely manner and no unauthorized payments are made.

> *The bookkeeper should enter the online payments into QuickBooks before the church's authorized user submits the payments through the bank account or website. The bookkeeper can then give the list of payments to the authorized signer to submit. This is an especially important step to assure the cash balance is sufficient for the payments.*

You may process payments electronically through QuickBooks. This means one person can set up the vendor, enter the transaction, and send the payment electronically. While this is convenient, it does not separate the person making the entry from the person sending the money. Separate users with limited access will need to be established in the system. I'll explain how to do this in Chapter 16.

Your bank may offer bill payment through their website. If so, you will need to set up separate logins and passwords for the bill payment area and the reporting and downloading area. This is because you want to allow the bookkeeper to see the transactions and download them, while not having access to the money. Additionally, you do not want the person authorizing the payments to be able to manipulate the financial statements. Because each bank or service is different, you will need to work with their professionals to establish your logins and passwords.

If payments can be made directly through a vendor's website, the login and password combination must not be known to the bookkeeper. The bookkeeper will record the payment in QuickBooks, but an authorized check signer should have the login and password combinations.

D. **Entering Bills**

It's time to pay some bills. The mail has been opened, the bills approved and coded, and you are now ready to start entering. As you have noticed in the other areas, there are several ways to access the bill paying area.

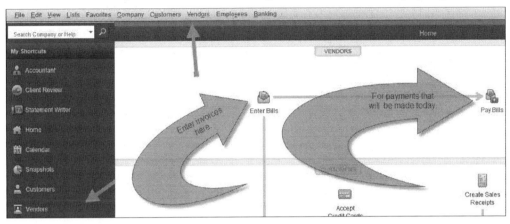

The **Enter Bills** icon will take you directly to a screen to start entering the bills. Both the top and side menus will bring you to the **Vendor Center**. The Vendor Center looks similar to the donor list in the Customer Center. All vendors previously entered are along the left side and you can enter transactions through the **New Transactions** menu.

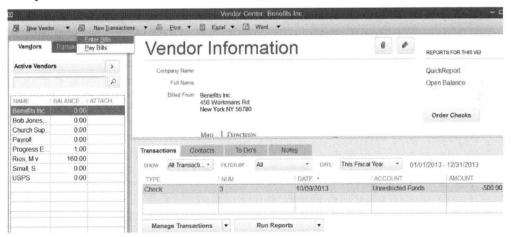

An entry screen for **Bills** will appear whether you go through the icon on the home page or the *Enter Bills* under *New Transactions* in the Vendor

Center. If you highlight a vendor from the Vendor Center, that name will appear on the entry screen.

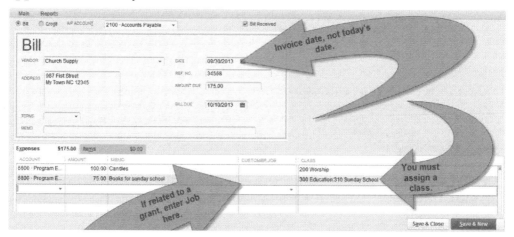

Once you have selected the **VENDOR**, the address is automatically entered. Input the **DATE** of the invoice next. This is important in order to run reports on an accrual basis. The **REF NO** should be the invoice number. If there is no invoice number, I like to use the date. **AMOUNT DUE** is the total amount of the bill. If you had assigned **TERMS** when you set up the vendor, QuickBooks will calculate the **BILL DUE** date automatically. If you didn't, you can use the drop-down arrow beside **TERMS** and select the appropriate date. Having an accurate due date helps the management of the cash flow.

The bottom half of the screen is where you will enter the individual line items of the invoice. There are two tabs: **Expenses** and **Items**. You will primarily be using the **Expenses** side. **Items** are used more for manufacturing and business.

In the first line under **Expenses,** select an account for the first item on the invoice to be charged to. Start to type in the word and the drop-down menu will give you options. Next, input the dollar amount of that purchase and in the **MEMO** area type a description of what it is. If it was purchased for a grant or contract that needs to be tracked, select the **CUSTOMER:JOB** from the drop-down menu. The **BILLABLE** option is only needed if there are reimbursable expenses that can be billed back to a donor. The last column is the **CLASS**. There should be a class (think program) designated for every expense item.

If there is more than one item on the invoice, just go to the next line and key in the data. The system will input any amount remaining on the next line until the full amount is fulfilled. You may wish to charge a percentage of the bill to one class and a different amount to another.

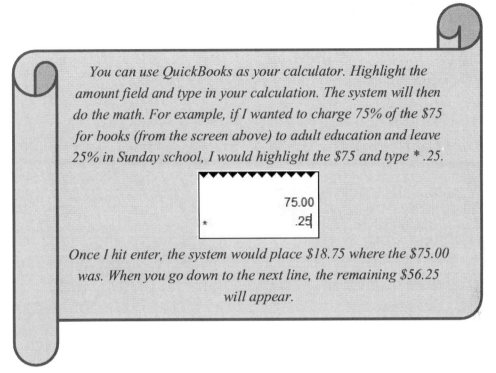

*You can use QuickBooks as your calculator. Highlight the amount field and type in your calculation. The system will then do the math. For example, if I wanted to charge 75% of the $75 for books (from the screen above) to adult education and leave 25% in Sunday school, I would highlight the $75 and type * .25.*

Once I hit enter, the system would place $18.75 where the $75.00 was. When you go down to the next line, the remaining $56.25 will appear.

Now, go to the **Class** field and enter *Adult Education.* If you have more invoices, select *Save and New,* and you'll get a new **Enter Bills** screen. If not, select *Save and Close.*

E. Copy/Paste Line Items

Another enhancement started in 2014 is the ability to copy items from one line on an invoice or bill down to the next line. This is useful if you are charging the items on a bill across several programs.

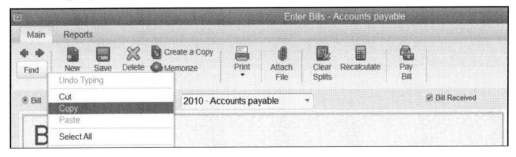

After typing in the item, right click on the name and choose *Copy*. Go to the next row.

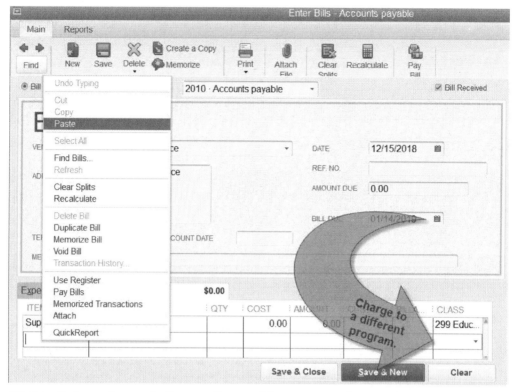

Right click again and choose *Paste*. Then enter the program you would like to charge the item to and fix the amounts between the programs.

There are also improvements to customize which account balances are shown under **View Balances** on the left menu.

If your church has used the accrual method of accounting, you may have a balance in your accounts payable as of your start date. If so, each of the vendor invoices need to be entered into the system with an invoice date of the prior year. For example, if your beginning balance includes a $200 bill from a printing company from December of the prior year, enter it as a bill with a December date. This will allow your beginning balance to reflect the correct amount in accounts payable.

F. **Recurring Bills**

Your church probably has some bills that need to be paid each month, like rent, utilities, etc. QuickBooks allows you to set up recurring bills, and then reminds you to pay them. Pull up the **Enter Bills** screen.

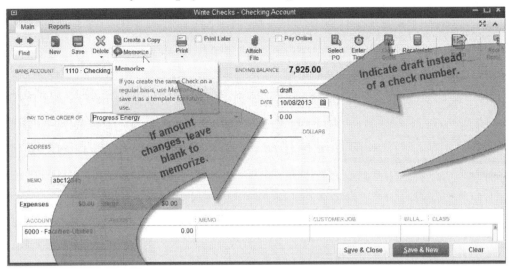

Input the vendor's name, but do not include an amount unless it stays the same each month. If you pay the same rent each month, then go ahead and input the amount of rent. But for bills that vary (water or electricity, for example), leave the amount blank. Enter a line item for the expense account and the class.

Near the top of this screen is a blue button that says **Memorize**. Select it to see the following screen.

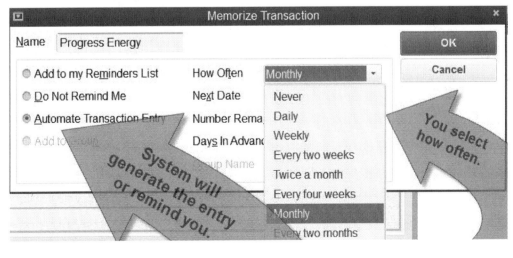

The name of the vendor will be at the top. There are three options relating to reminders. The first will add it to a reminders list that will pop up when you open the system. The second option allows you to set up the memorized transaction but not remind you. This is used for items without a set schedule. The third option is the handiest. It will automatically enter the bill into your accounts to be paid.

As our example is for a utility bill, I have selected *Monthly*.

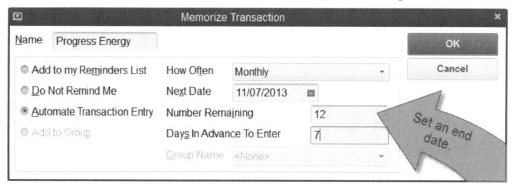

I now need to let the system know the date of the next invoice, how many times I want it to generate this invoice, and how many days in advance to put it in the system. By selecting 12 under **Number Remaining**, I am telling the system to keep generating these bills monthly until 10/1/2014. I can also leave this blank, and it will keep generating the monthly invoices until I tell it to stop. The **Days in Advance to Enter** should be determined by how often you pay bills. If your church pays weekly, seven days should be sufficient.

The memorized transactions will not be recognized until QuickBooks has been closed and reopened. If you close the system every day, this will not be an issue, but if you regularly keep the system up, you will need to close it and reopen.

After selecting *OK*, you will be back at the Enter Bills screen ready to input this month's utility bill. Enter the amount and select *Save & Close*. This takes you back to the Vendor Center. All of the vendors with their open balances are listed. By highlighting a vendor, you can see their transactions.

G.   Editing and Deleting Invoices

When Progress Energy was highlighted, I noticed I had booked the October electric bill twice.

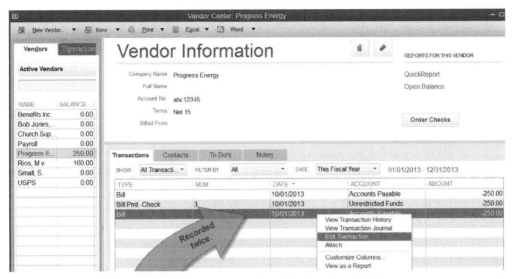

To remedy this situation, I need to highlight the bill input in error and right click. This will bring up a drop-down menu allowing me to *Edit Transaction.*

The bill will pull up as it was entered. I can now edit the amounts, expense accounts or classes, but as this was a duplicate, I need to delete it. At the top of the screen is a blue X marked **Delete.**

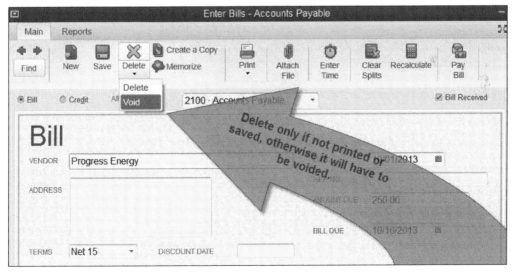

The bill can now be deleted or voided. As a duplicate that has not been saved or printed, I can delete it. If you need a record of the invoice, select *Void* instead. A warning box asking if you are sure will appear. If you are, select *Yes* and you will be back at the bills screen.

H. Bills Entry Main Menu

I'd like to go over the top menu of the bills screen with you.

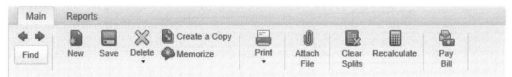

The **Find** arrows allow you to scroll through your entered bills by date. **New** brings up an empty **Enter Bills** screen. Select **Save** to assure that any changes to the bill are logged. **Delete** and **Memorize** were reviewed above. **Create a Copy** duplicates a bill but does not offer reminders. **Print** is self-explanatory. **Attach File** allows you to upload a document relating to this bill. If you scan your invoices, you could attach the file here. **Clear Splits** erases all the line items you had recorded for this bill if you change your mind after allocating the expense. **Pay Bill** will take you to a screen allowing you to print the checks.

I. Paying Bills

You have entered all the bills and are now ready to cut the checks. All the bills are not due at the same time, so you will go through the **Pay Bills** screen to select the ones to pay. Access the screen from the **Pay Bills** icon on the home page, from the button on the bills entry menu, or from the vendor menus.

This screen will list all bills due by a certain date or, if you prefer, all bills. There is a default accounts payable account that should not need to be changed. The **Filter By** option allows you to show all vendors or just one. The **Sort By** option gives you the choice to see the listings by vendor name, amount, or due dates.

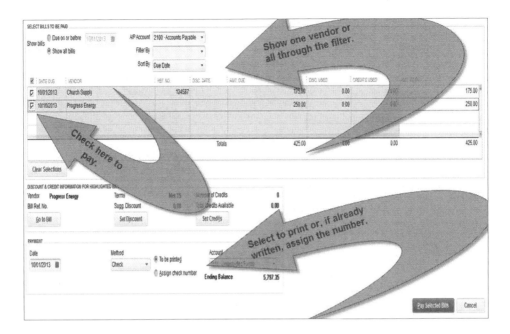

Select the bills to be paid by clicking on the small box next to the bill. Toward the bottom of the screen, the payment date is then chosen, and you will designate whether the check is to be printed or not. Choose the *Assign check number* if you have already written the check manually and need to enter it into the system. The default account is the one you designated in the payment preferences set up in the beginning. This can be overridden using the drop-down arrow.

If you have purchased this invoice item using a credit card, select *Credit Card* under **Method**. The account will then need to be linked to a credit card account in the chart of accounts. Later in the chapter, I'll explain the different ways to enter credit card charges.

Once you have selected the bills you would like to pay, click on *Pay Selected Bills* and a dialog box summarizing the selections will appear. Select *Print Checks* and you will see the following screen.

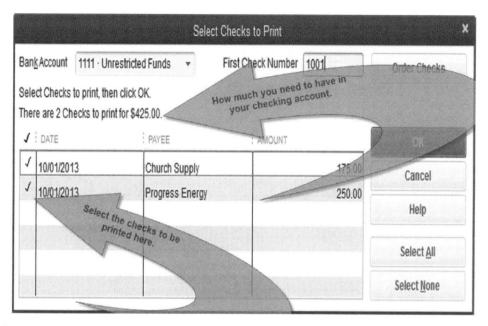

The system will tell you how much money will be required. You can select all or some of the bills to pay. The **First Check Number** will default to the next check in the series from any previous printings. Once you are happy with the selections, press **OK**.

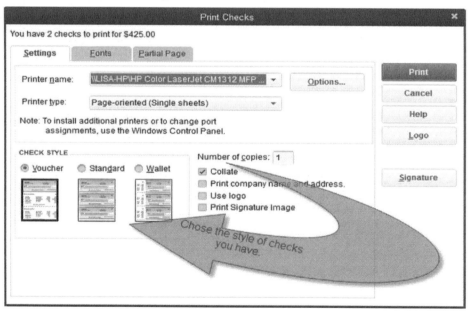

You will select which printer and the style of your checks and select *Print*.

*QuickBooks offers the option to store an electronic signature to have printed on the checks (**Print Signature Image**). Do not use unless you have a multi-users setup with passwords; otherwise the check signer could also have access to the transactions, or the bookkeeper would have access to the cash.*

The system will bring up a dialog box asking to verify that the checks printed correctly.

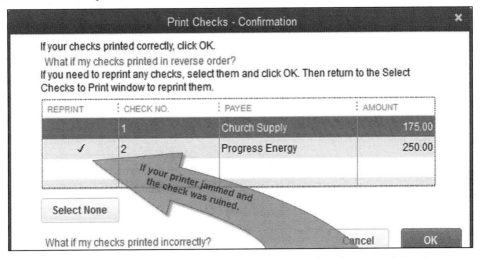

If all the checks were printed correctly, do not check any of the items and chose *OK*. If the printer jammed and the last check is unreadable, QuickBooks makes it easy to reprint the check. Simply select the check that needs to be reprinted and hit *OK*. You can then go back to the **Select Checks to Print** window through the **Print Checks** icon on the home page and reprint.

J.   Tracking Amounts Owed to Parent Organizations

Many churches are associated with a larger organization and are required to share a portion of their donations. It may be an annual allocation based on a previous year's receipts or it may be a percentage of each month's receipt.

Set up your parent organization as a vendor and select *Enter Bills*. If it is just one annual amount you need to pay, chose the *Expenses* tab. Select an expense designated as the amount to send; the sample chart of accounts calls it 6700 National Church Allocation Exp. It will then be reflected as a liability in **Accounts Payable** until you pay it.

If you are calculating it weekly or monthly from your receipts, I would recommend you *memorize* the bill and then adjust the amounts for each period. If you need to track the percentage of plate offerings or tithes separate from the percentage of other donations, I would use **Items**. Add new expense items for each percentage type. At the end of each week or the month, go to the *Enter Bills* screen. Select *Items* tab, enter the first item, amount, and class. Then enter the next percentage item. *Memorize* this bill and you can easily update it as needed.

Your *Profit & Loss* statements will reflect the amount each month due from that month's donations. Either way, when you are ready to write the check, simply go to *Pay Bills* and select all of the weeks or months you'd like to pay for the parent organization and write the checks.

K. Online Banking Payments

If you utilize online banking through your bank's website, you will still enter all the bills and select bills to pay as mentioned above. But at the bottom of the **Pay Bills** screen, you will need to select *Assign check number*. Once you select *Pay Selected Bills*, the following screen will appear.

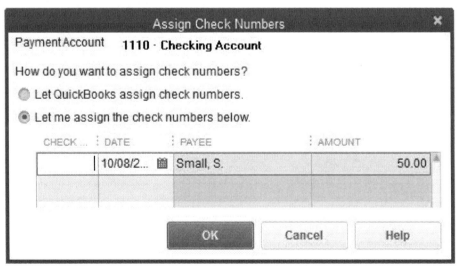

Enter a number that tells you it was an online banking withdrawal (perhaps X01, X02, etc.) and select *OK*.

L. **Write Checks**

All of your bills have been paid. But your organist just stopped by and needs a reimbursement for some sheet music. Rather than enter this as a bill that then needs to be paid, you can go directly to the **Write Checks** option from the home page or under **Banking**.

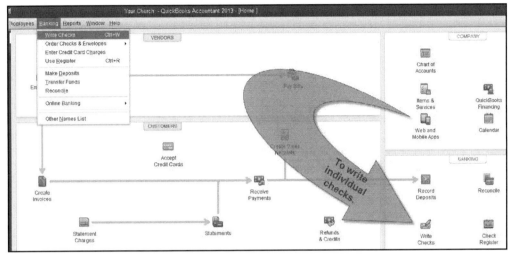

A screen will appear that looks like a check.

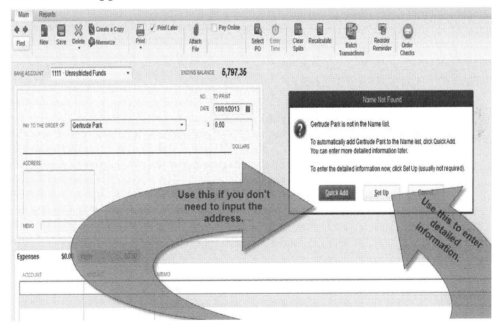

Today's date will default, and there will be a box by the **PAY TO THE ORDER OF**. The options under this drop-down include all vendors, customers, and employees who have been set up. (Under **Bills**, only vendors are listed). When I input Gertrude Park, a warning box appeared that she is not already in the system.

Two options are available to set Gertrude up in the system. The first one is **Quick Add**. This puts her name in the system and you can add other information later if you like. Use this option if you want to get names in quickly and don't need all the additional information that is tracked for vendors or members.

Set Up takes you to the entry menu for a new vendor, donor, or employee and allows you to key in all the related information. If the check will be mailed, you need to use the Set Up option.

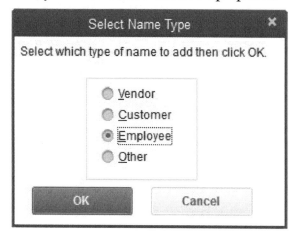

Once you decide which setup to use, the above screen will appear. If you used the Set Up option, the system will then take you to the related entry screen, or, if you chose Quick Add, back to the check.

Once back at the write check screen, enter the amount and the line items. You'll notice the screen looks like the Enter Bills screen. To print the check immediately, make certain the **Print Later** is not selected.

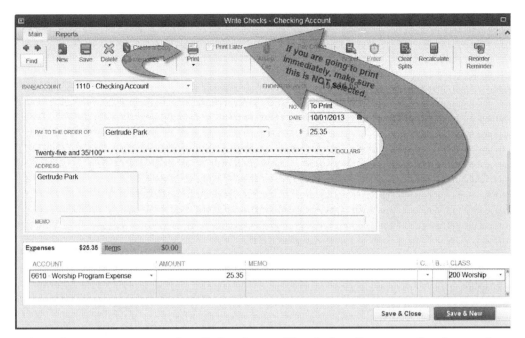

Select the *Print* icon and a dialog box will ask for the next check number. Put the check in the printer, type in the check number, and select *OK*. The remainder of the screens follow the same sequence as before for printing checks.

> *If you would rather enter employee and member reimbursements through the Enter Bills screen, you will need to set up vendor accounts. If you try to use the same name as the donor account, you will receive an error. One option is to put a small "v" after the name to differentiate (i.e. **Smith, J** is the donor and **Smith, J v** is the vendor account).*

M. Handwritten Checks

Sometimes you may need to write a check by hand and enter it into the system later. You will do this through the **Write Checks** option. The difference between what we just covered and a check that was already written is to enter a check number manually.

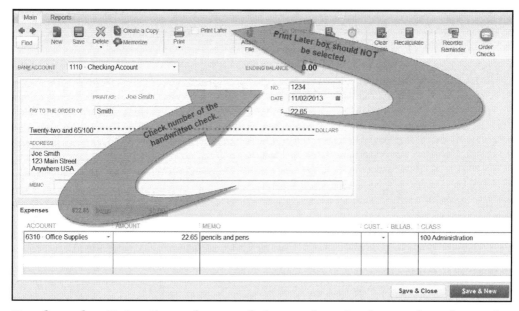

Deselect the *Print Later* box and input the check number from the handwritten check. The rest of the information is entered as before. Then *Save & Close* and the check is recorded.

N.   Bank Drafts

If you have regular bank drafts, it is easiest to memorize them through the **Write Checks** screen. From the home screen, select the *Write Checks* icon.

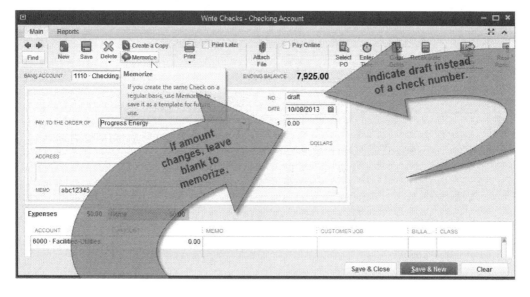

Make sure the **Print Later** box is unselected and type *draft* in the check number area. If the amount is the same for each month, go ahead and enter it. If not, leave the amount blank. Fill out the rest of the form and then memorize it just as you did for the bills. If an amount was entered, the system will deduct it from the cash account. If not, you will edit this check when you receive the bank statement for the amount charged. Finish by selecting *Save & Close*.

O.   Entering Credit Card Receipts

Some of the church employees may have a credit card in the church's name. The charges need to be supported by receipts, entered into the system, and the bill paid. There are two basic approaches to handling credit card charges.

The first option is to hand the employee a copy of the bill when it arrives and require them to fill out an expense report detailing what the expenses were for. The receipts should be attached to the expense report and submitted to a supervisor for approval. The approved expense report is then entered as a bill.

The second option is to have the employee hand in receipts for approval as they use the credit card. The treasurer then knows how much cash will be needed to pay the bill when it arrives.

In QuickBooks, credit card charges are handled a little differently than other bills. Instead of entering the charges through the Vendor Center, go to the menu bar and select *Banking, Enter Credit Card Charges.*

A screen will open which looks like the pay bills screen. If you had set up an account in the chart of accounts with a type defined as Credit Card, you will select it for the **CREDIT CARD** box.

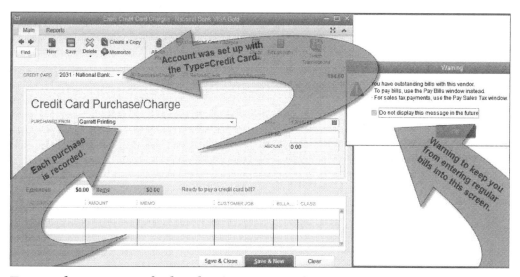

Enter the name of the business on the credit card receipt into **PURCHASED FROM**. If you already have outstanding bills with that vendor, QuickBooks asks you to be certain you want to enter it in this screen.

Put in the amount of the purchase and break down by line item under the **Expenses** tab.

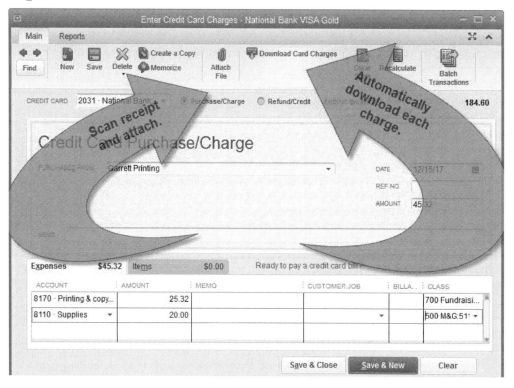

Continue to manually enter the receipts as you receive them. You can also scan the receipt and attach it to the file for support.

If you would prefer not to manually enter each receipt, the system will connect with your credit card account online under **Download Card Charges**. In the next chapter, I will show you how to reconcile bank accounts. You can use the same function to reconcile your credit card account.

> *If you use the download function, you must still receive the receipts with approvals.*

P.   Credits Received from Vendors

Your church may return an item or receive a notice that they were overcharged by a vendor. The vendor will issue a credit to the account. You will need to enter this credit before you pay the vendor. To do this, go to the **Enter Bills** screen.

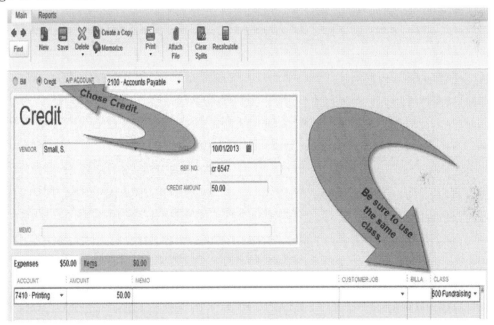

Near the top is a small circle next to **Credit**. Select it and a screen similar to the one above will open. Enter the vendor's name, the credit number or invoice number it is to be applied against, and the amount. The line under expenses will populate with the last expense used for that vendor, but you need to update the correct class. Select *Save and Close*. To apply this credit against an **already entered bill**, go to *Pay Bills*.

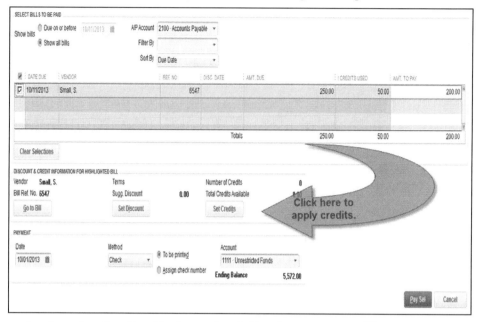

By selecting the *Set Credits* box, the following screen will activate.

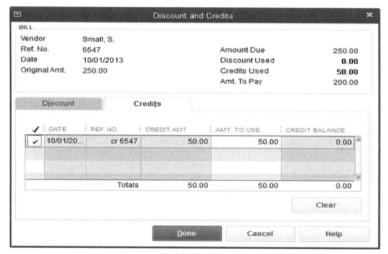

Chose the credit you wish to apply and then click *Done*. This will bring you back to the previous screen with the credit in the column marked **CREDITS USED**. You may then click *Pay Selected Bills,* and the check will be generated for the amount of the invoice less the applied credit.

Q. **Automatic Allocation of Expenses**

Accounting programs dedicated to nonprofits usually offer an automatic allocation of expenses option, such as distributing the cost of electricity across all programs that use the church building. This allows the user to define percentages or amounts by program and have the overhead expense automatically calculated and posted for any vendor or transaction. QuickBooks does not do this. However, I will show you a work-around option. It will take some time to set up, but if you wish to allocate expenses, it will save you time later.

To set up the allocations, you will utilize the items function. Go to the menu bar and select *Lists, Item List, Item, New.* Set up a new **Service** item for the expense. In this case, I set up Electric.

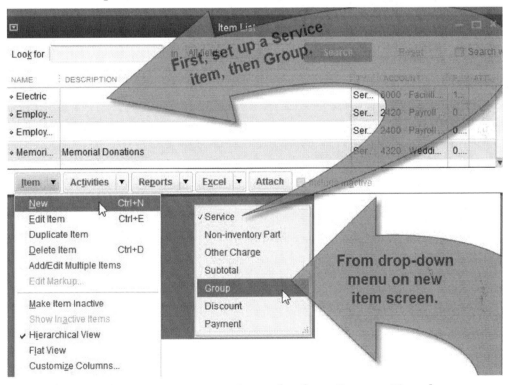

Bring the new item menu up again and select *Group.* Give the group a name that will make it easily identifiable. Under **ITEM**, select the related expense item. In the **QTY** column, input the percentage of the bill for each program as a decimal. You will be entering the program classes later.

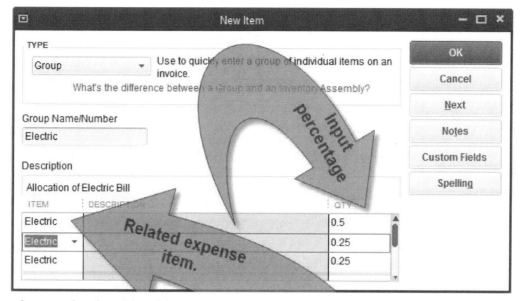

The totals should add to 1.00. In this example, I am assuming the worship program uses 50% of the electricity, administrations uses 25%, and education uses 25%.

Click *OK* and bring up the **Enter Bills** screen.

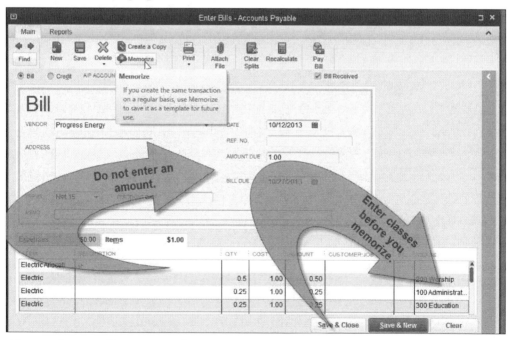

Enter the vendor name, but not an amount or reference number. You will be using the **Items** tab instead of the **Expenses** tab. Under **ITEM,**

select the group allocation. The quantities will show the percentages saved for that group, but the classes will be blank. Enter your program information under **CLASSES** and then *Memorize* the bill. Do not select *Save & Close* at this point or you will see a bill for $1.00 on your payables list.

When you are ready to pay your utility bill, go to the menu bar and select *Lists, Memorized Transaction List*. A list of all memorized transactions will display. Select the utility bill and the following screen will appear.

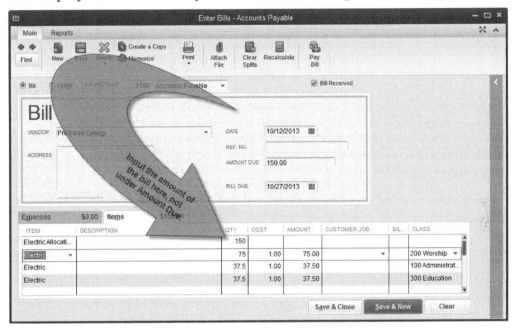

Select the Items tab to see the allocation percentages. Instead of entering the amount of the bill under **Amount Due**, you will enter it under the **QTY** column. The system will make the calculation for you. Double check the system-assigned date of the bill. Select *Save & Close* and you are ready to pay the bill.

This same process can be done on the **Write Check** screen. Additionally, you can set up groups for payroll or donation items to save time in allocations.

> *If you allocate expenses across programs, you will love the amount of time saved breaking out invoice costs.*

XI. Entering Payroll

There are numerous ways churches prepare their payroll. Most use an outside service that takes care of the tax and reporting requirements and allows for direct deposits. Some use an accountant to handle it for them. Others prepare their payroll themselves. In this book, I will first walk you through the most common approach of how to record the payroll from an outside service into QuickBooks, then we'll cover how to handle a small payroll in-house. For additional information about payroll, consider my book, *Church Accounting: The How-To Guide for Small & Growing Churches.* There are three chapters covering payroll, including the intricacies of minister's payroll, how to calculate payroll, and how to file the reports.

A. Recording Payroll from a Payroll Service

1. Using Journal Entries to Record Payroll

Recording payroll can be done via a journal entry or through the **Write Checks** screen. First I'll explain the journal entry option. If you will recall, you used the journal entry approach to record your beginning balances. You will now use it to record each period's payroll.

> *Look at your bank statement to see how the payroll service pulls the money out of the account. This way you can design your journal entry to match, which will make reconciling the bank account easier. For example, if the payroll service charges your checking account with three amounts each month—net pay, employee withholding, and payroll taxes—you will want to assure that your journal entry credits (reduces) the bank account with those three numbers separately, not one complete payroll number.*

The first thing I like to do is design a spreadsheet for the journal entry. This is an extra step, but it assures that once I have all of the allocations completed, the entry will balance.

Your Church				
Payroll Entry				
10/31/2014				
Description	**Account**	**Class**	**Debit**	**Credit**
Total Gross Pay-Clergy	Clergy Salary Expense	Worship	5,000.00	
Total Gross Pay-Admin	Admin Salary Expense	Admin	3,000.00	
Employer Liability Exp.	Payroll Tax Expense	Admin	229.50	
Benefit Contribution Withheld	Other Withholdings Liability	Admin		100.00
Non-Direct Deposit Check	Cash	Admin		2,220.50
Net Pay Allocations	Cash	Admin		5,000.00
Employee Tax Withholding	Cash	Admin		679.50
Employer Liability Due	Cash	Admin		229.50
Totals			$ 8,229.50	$ 8,229.50

Starting from the bottom, this entry assumes the payroll service has electronically pulled the net pay ($5,000), the employee withholdings ($679.50), and the employer liabilities ($229.50) out of the cash account in separate amounts. It also reflects a check written to an employee that did not use direct deposit ($2220.50). This is important to list separately as it will clear the bank as a check. The Benefit Contributions Withheld ($100) went into a liability account as the church will need to write a check to the benefit company for that withholding.

The tax expenses did not have to go to a liability account because the payroll service has already withdrawn the money. If your payroll service does not pay the taxes on your behalf, you would need to record those into liability accounts and then write the appropriate checks.

The gross pay needs to be allocated to the correct accounts and classes. If some of the payroll time should be charged to a grant or contract, input that amount under the **Customer:Job** column. If the reports from your payroll service do not group the employees by program, ask your payroll representative if that can be changed. This works well if people are charged in total to a program. Having their reports already total the dollars by program makes entering the journal entry much easier.

> *All expense items must have a designated class. This is how the expenses are allocated to programs.*

Under the **Company** menu, select *Make General Journal Entries*. This will bring up a screen allowing you to key in your entry from the spreadsheet we just completed.

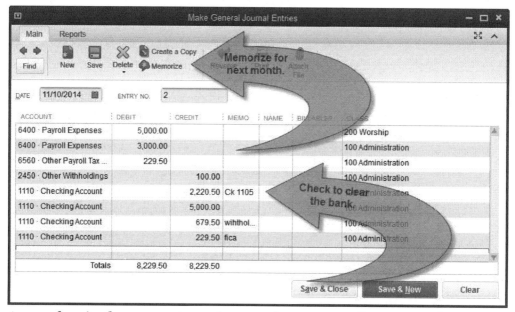

As you key in the account numbers and amounts, please note the system does not require you to use the lowest subaccount on this screen. You will need to be extra careful that you are using the correct account, especially if you are using subaccounts to track restricted cash.

For any payroll that will not be direct deposited, record the check number to make reconciling the bank account easier. If your payroll is fairly consistent, consider memorizing the entry and having the system record it automatically each month. You will need to edit the entry for the actual data, but it will save data entry time. Journal entries are memorized in the same way as the invoices discussed earlier in this chapter.

2. Entering Payroll through the Write Checks Screen

The other way to enter payroll from the outside service is through the **Write Checks** screen. This is in lieu of the journal entry. You must be very careful that each draft is treated as a separate check. Set up a vendor called Payroll and record the first check for the net pay.

Under the **Expenses** tab, you would need to record the gross pay levels by class. Employee withholdings would be coded to the Payroll

Withholdings account with a negative sign in front of the amount. This is to make the check equal the net pay the employees actually received.

Using the example above, you would then write three more checks—two for the other drafts and one for the non-direct deposit amount. If your payroll stays fairly consistent, memorize these checks and edit them for the following pay periods.

3.   Paying the Benefit Contribution

There is one more thing to do before we finish up the payroll. We need to pay the benefit contribution that was withheld. You will do this through the Write Checks screen.

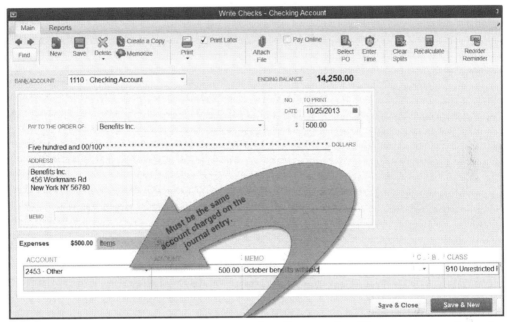

Enter the name of the benefit provider, but under **Expenses**, select the liability account charged in the payroll entry. Select *Save & Close*. This should now zero out the liability account.

B.   **Preparing Payroll In House**

QuickBooks strongly encourages its users to use an outside service, preferably their own. In fairness to them, payroll can become very complex, so an outside service takes some of the stress and risk off of the church's bookkeeping staff. But if you would like to calculate payroll yourself and track it through QuickBooks, I'll take you through the steps.

1. Setting up the payroll

If you only have a few employees without unusual items, you can save money by calculating your own payroll and using QuickBooks to print the checks and keep track of each employee's earnings. First you have to find out how to access the manual payroll area.

I warned you that QuickBooks wants you to use an outside service. In order to even get started with manual payroll, you must go to the **Help** menu on the top bar and select *QuickBooks Help*.

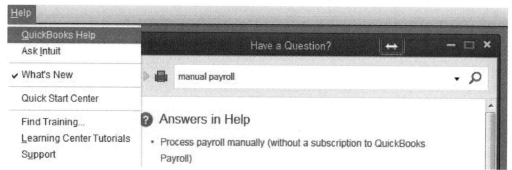

In the search box, type in *manual payroll*. Select *Process payroll manually (without a subscription to QuickBooks Payroll)*. You will see the following information.

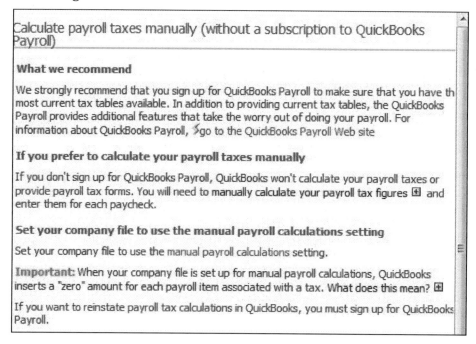

After trying to convince you again to go to the payroll service, they ask you to select the *manual payroll calculations* link. This will pop up another box with some warnings.

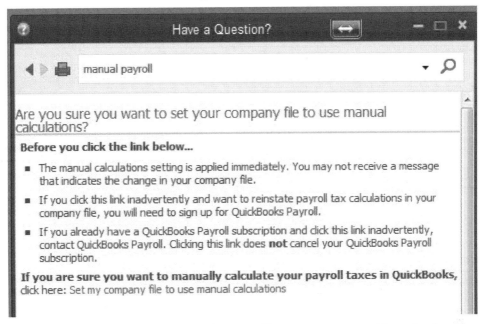

After reading the information, if you still want to manually calculate your payroll, click the *Set my company file to use manual calculations* link. More information is given to you.

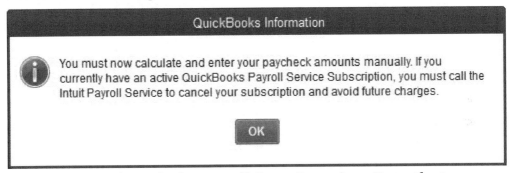

It is time to go through the Payroll Setup Interview. Go to the top menu and select *Employees, Payroll Setup*.

An introductory box will appear.

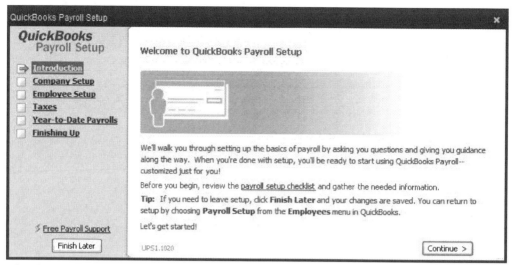

The link to **payroll setup checklist** is very valuable and even includes hints for finding information if you are switching from another payroll provider. Download the checklist and gather the necessary materials before you go on.

Once you have the company, employee, tax, and historical paycheck information, you are ready to get started. Select *Continue*.

This screen allows you to say how you pay your staff. If everyone is salary, only the **Salary** box needs to be checked. Churches typically don't have commissions, tips, or piecework, so I'm leaving those blank.

Throughout this example, I will choose the more common selections a church may have. You can change these options later. I recommend you click on the blue links in the system for more information, as there are too many options for payroll for me to cover in this chapter.

Select *Finish* to see a list of your compensation types.

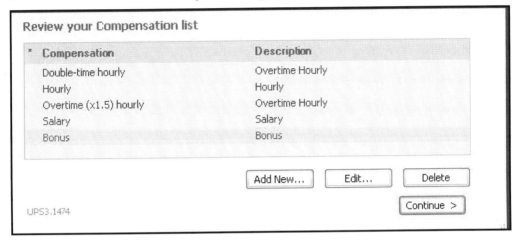

If you don't need to add to or edit this list, select *Continue* to see a page introducing the **Employee Benefit** set up. Press *Continue* to set up the insurance benefits.

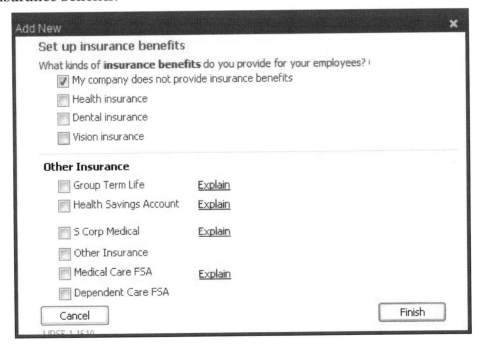

You will select as many of these as apply. For each one you select, QuickBooks will ask if the company pays for all of it or if it shared by the company and employee. It will also ask if the payment is deducted after taxes or before taxes. Check with your plan administrator if you do not know.

The next screen allows you to set up the payment schedule for the insurance.

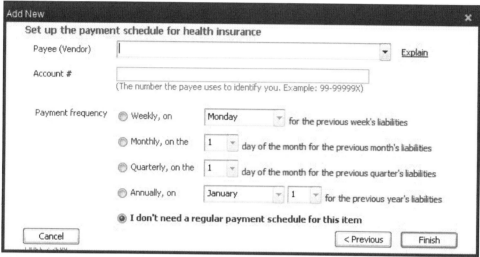

Once you have completed that page, the system will continue down the insurance benefits list with similar screens. Enter all that apply and select *Finish*. A summary of the insurance benefits list will appear.

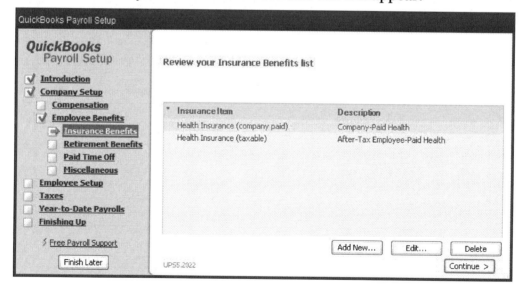

You can edit from this screen or select *Continue* to set up **Retirement Benefits**.

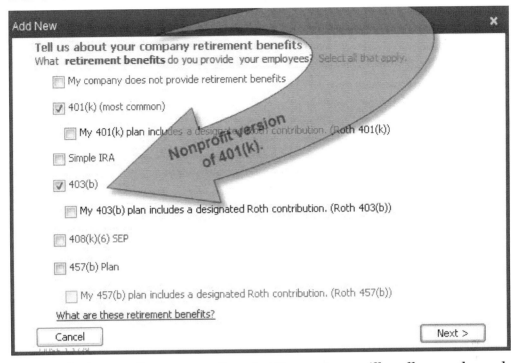

Select all that apply to your church. The system will walk you through screens similar to the insurance benefits, allowing you to set up payment schedules for each item selected. When you are finished, a summary list similar to the insurance benefits will be shown.

Select *Continue* to set up paid time off.

After selecting all that apply, select *Finish* to see a summary page. Select *Continue* to set up **Miscellaneous** additions and deductions.

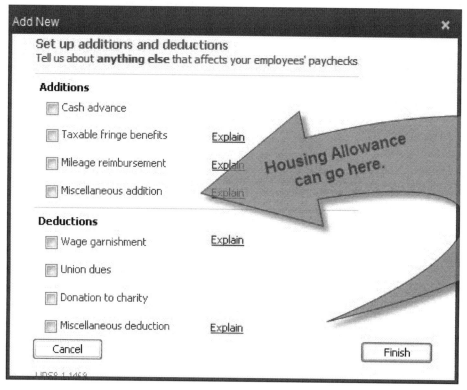

These are used to add money to or deduct money from the employees' paycheck. Your minister may receive a housing allowance that does not have to be added to his taxable earnings, but you would like to have it paid with his salary. If so, set up a **Miscellaneous addition** for the monthly amount. The **Deductions** include an option to donate to charity. Your staff may wish to have their tithe come directly out of their paycheck monthly.

Once you have selected the additions and deductions you'd like to set up, select *Finish*. A summary screen will appear. Don't worry about the names, we'll edit them later.

Select *Continue* to see the **Employee Setup**.

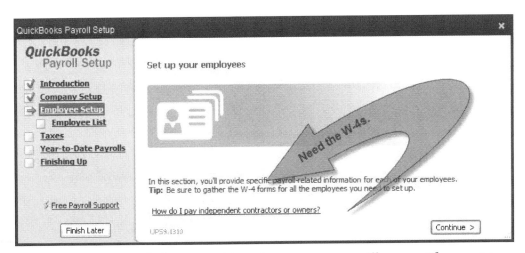

Select *Continue* and the **New Employee** screen will open. The next two screens will request the name, address, hiring date, SSN, etc. for the employee. Enter the employee's information and select *Next*.

This screen asks how you will be paying the employee, including how often and hourly versus salary. If it is an hourly employee, be sure to include the overtime rateas well.

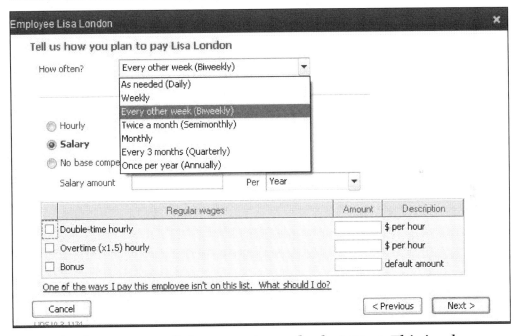

Enter the frequency and the pay rates and select *Next*. This is where you will find the **Miscellaneous Additions** and **Deductions** you set up earlier.

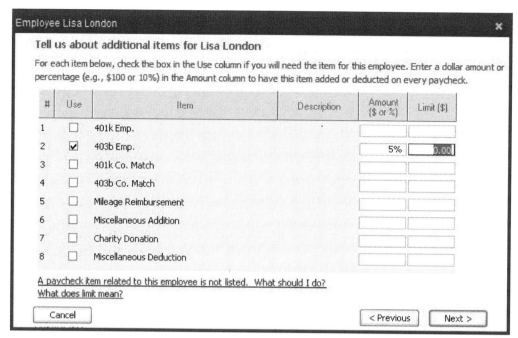

Enter the percentage or dollar amount for each item this particular employee uses and chose *Next* to set up the state and federal withholding for the employee.

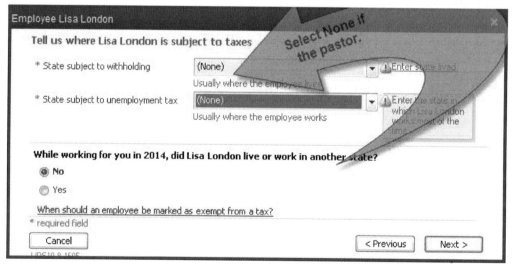

For most employees, show the state the church is located in. Pastors, however, are treated differently than most employees and federal and state withholding is usually not required. The above example assumes I am the pastor. The system gives several warnings that I should select a state, but still allows me to move on once I select *Next*.

*For detailed information on how to handle pastor compensation, see my book, **Church Accounting: The How-To Guide for Small & Growing Churches**, available at www.AccountantBesideYou.com and Amazon.com.*

The federal tax information from the employee's W-4 is entered next. If the employee is the pastor, do NOT select the boxes under **Withholdings and Credits.** Qualified ministers do not have Social Security and Medicare withheld from their paychecks.

For your regular employees, select *Subject to Social Security*. The **Medicare Addl Tax** option is for highly paid employees. Churches are not required to pay **Federal Unemployment (FUTA)** taxes on any of their employees, so do NOT select that box.

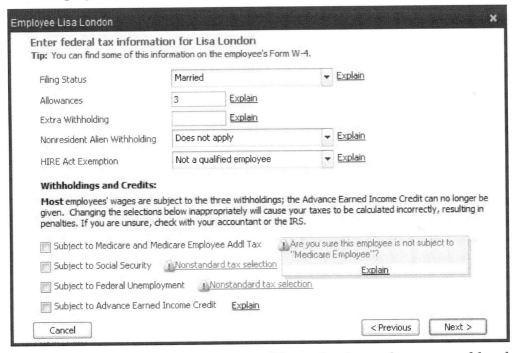

Once you are finished, select *Next* to fill out the forms for state and local taxes.

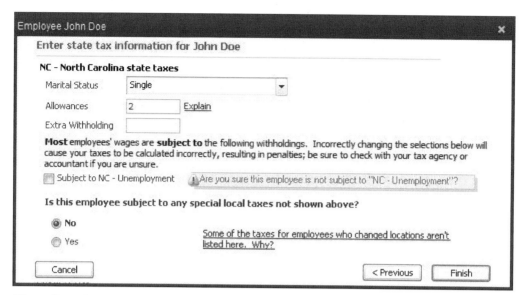

Churches in most states are not subject to state unemployment taxes (SUTA). There is a linked list of websites for all states' department of revenue for your convenience at AccountantBesideYou.com/state-weblinks. After completing, select *Finish*.

Enter each of your employees. Once finished, review the summary page and edit if necessary. Press *Continue* to be taken to the **Taxes** set up.

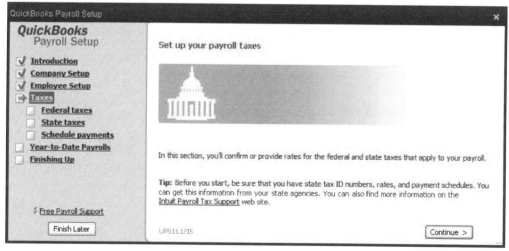

At my website, I've added links to the various IRS web pages with payroll information, including Circular E. Circular E details the federal tax withholding rates each year. See the list at accountantbesideyou.com/irs-forms.

The system will set up the basic taxes for you.

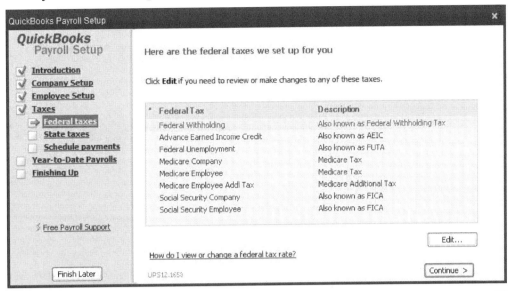

Press *Continue*. A screen asking for your state unemployment rate will appear.

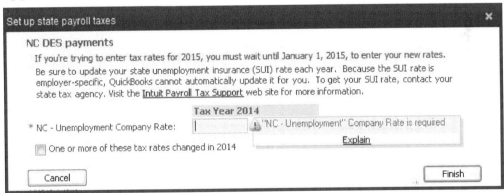

If your state does not charge churches SUTA, leave blank and select *Finish*. The next screen sets up the FUTA schedule.

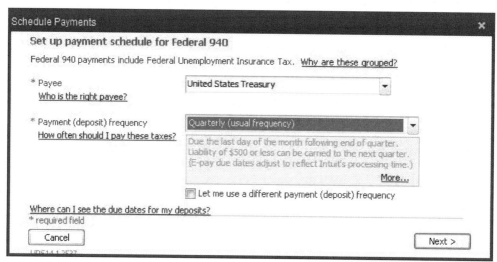

As churches don't pay FUTA, simply select *Next* to set up the federal withholding schedule.

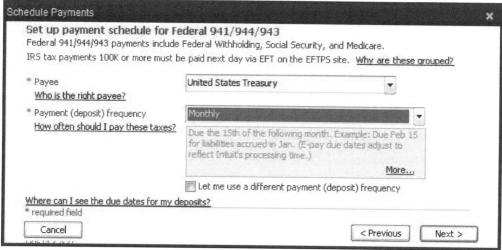

Your payment frequency is based on the amount of payroll and taxes withheld. Refer to the IRS guidelines or your tax professional if you are unsure of your filing frequency.

The next screen will ask for information regarding the state unemployment filings. If required, complete, otherwise, select *Next*. Payments are scheduled for the state tax withholding on the next screen.

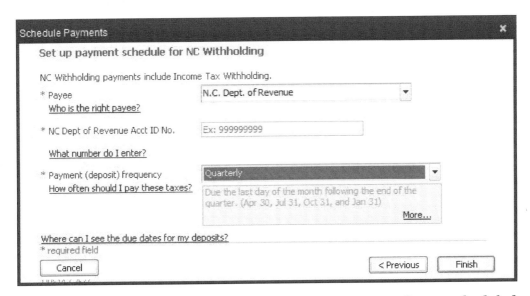

Once that is complete, select *Finish* to see a summary of your scheduled tax payments. After reviewing it, select *Continue* to enter **Year-to-Date Payrolls**.

From the **Year-to-date payrolls** introductory screen, select *Continue*.

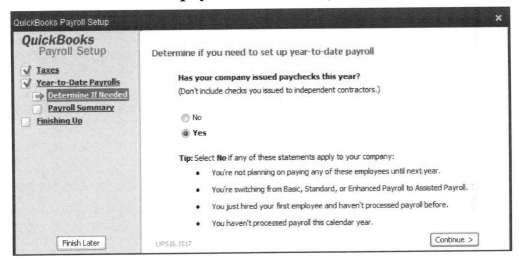

If you have issued paychecks this year, select *Yes* and *Continue*.

Ideally, you want to start a new payroll program on January 1. But that isn't always feasible. If you have already paid employees in this year, you will have to enter the individual paychecks, taxes deductions, and contributions that have been paid. This is to assure the W-2s are correct at year end.

A screen will appear with lots of columns. These can be removed or added using the **Customize Columns** button.

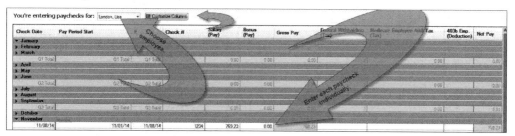

I realize this screen shot is difficult to read, but it gives you the basic idea. Select the first employee from the drop-down menu. Enter each paycheck individually by date so the quarterly totals agree to the filed 941s. *Save* and continue for each additional employee.

Once you have completed all the employees, you will see the following screen.

Select *Go to Payroll Center* in order to run the payroll and pay the taxes. Employee information may also be edited there.

2. Generating Payroll

From the top menu, select *Employees* to find the **Employee Center. It** lists the employees and each of their paychecks.

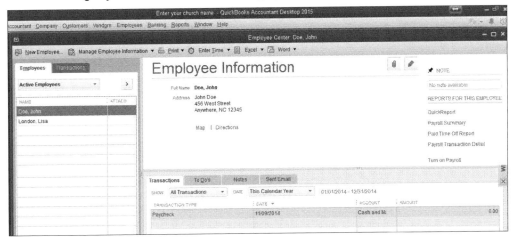

You can add new employees or edit existing employees' information. I won't go through the process of adding in detail as it is similar to the Add New Customer and Vendor screens you've already seen. Similarly, you can attached scanned documents via the paperclip icon and add notes.

From the top menu, select *Employees, Pay Employees.*

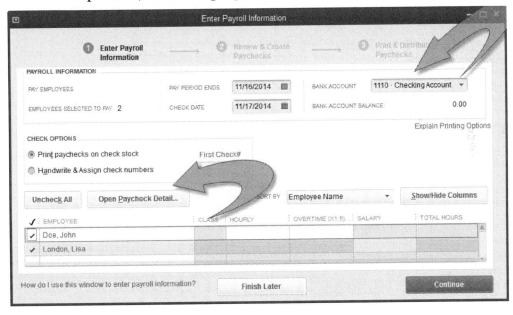

Be certain the correct bank account is selected as well as the ending date of the pay period. Check each of the employees you wish to write a check for. Select *Open Paycheck Detail* before continuing.

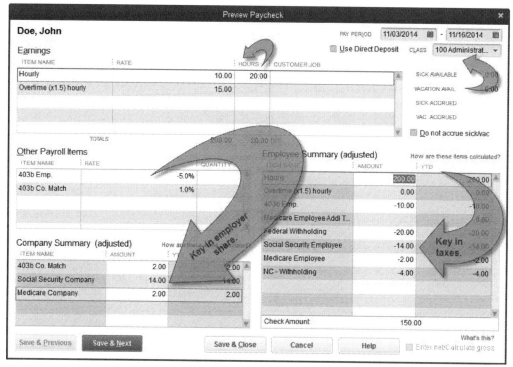

Start at the top and make sure the pay period is correct. Add the appropriate class and then enter the hours for the employee. Notice that the federal withholding, Social Security, and Medicare amounts are zero. The system does NOT calculate the withholding. You will need to do this manually and input the amounts into this screen. The company portion of the payroll taxes must also be entered manually.

Once the correct withholding amounts are entered, select *Save & Next* to enter taxes for the next employee. If entering data for a salaried employee, enter the class and any withholding but don't worry about the hours.

> *Remember: Do NOT withhold federal income or Social Security and Medicare taxes from a qualified minister.*

Once you have closed the window on the last employee, you will be back to the **Enter Payroll Information** screen. Select *Continue* to review and create the paychecks.

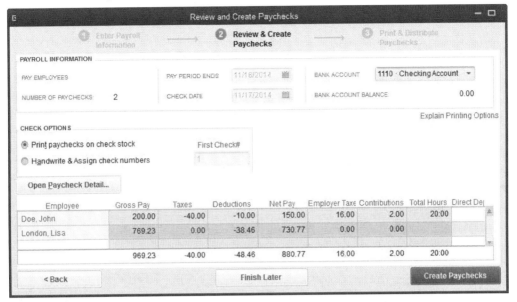

Review the screen for accuracy and select *Create Paychecks.*

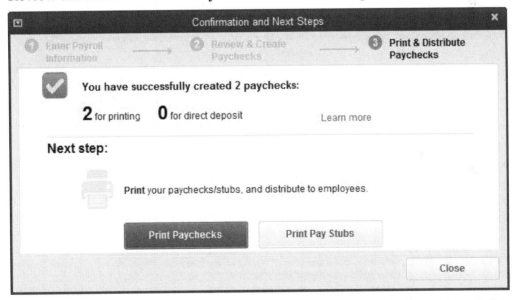

You have the option to print the pay stubs or the paychecks. Select *Print Paychecks* and a dialog box will appear allowing you to select which paychecks are printed and to assign check numbers. There is also an area to put a company message on all pay stubs.

After you print the paychecks, you will be brought back to the screen above to print the pay stubs. Select *Print Pay Stubs*.

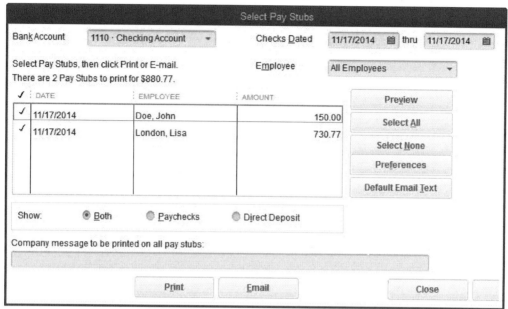

This screen gives you the option to email the pay stubs or print. If you choose email, the following message will appear.

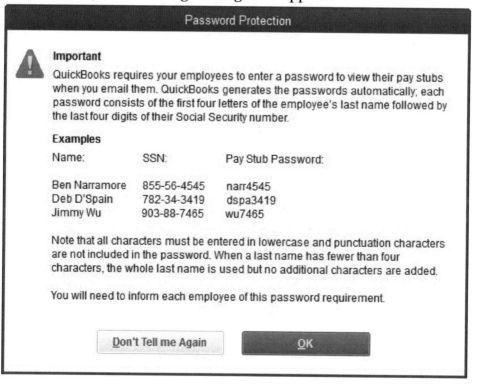

Follow the dialog boxes to email or print as desired. You will then be taken back to the Employee Center where you will see the paychecks recorded in the employees' files.

3.   Payroll liability payments

When the system recorded the payroll checks, it also recorded the related liabilities into the payroll liability accounts. When the amounts are due to the taxing and benefit agencies, go to the top menu and select *Employees, Payroll Taxes* and *Liabilities, Pay Payroll Liabilities.*

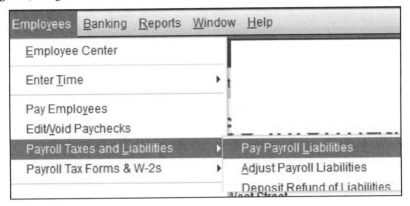

A screen showing all the outstanding payroll liabilities appears.

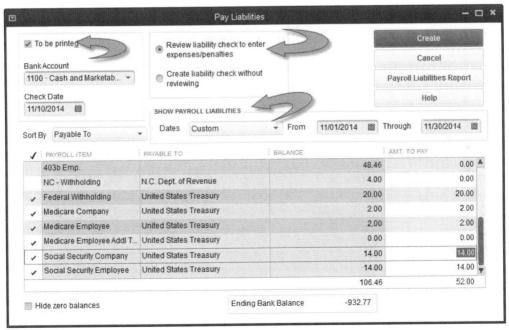

Select *Review liability check to enter expense/penalties* for a review before paying. For the items that need to be paid by check, mark those you would like to pay. If you had not yet set up the vendor information for the items, the system will give you a warning and take you to a screen to input the data. If you are printing the payments, select the box in the upper left corner. Once you have chosen the items you wish to print, select *Create* and a check will appear for you to review and print.

Federal payroll tax deposits need to be paid through the Electronic Federal Tax Payment System (EFTPS). Information on this system can be found at www.eftps.gov or in *Church Accounting: The How-To Guide for Small & Growing Churches*. Once you have filed the tax deposits electronically, come back to the **Pay Payroll Liabilities** screen, select the items paid and deselect the **To be printed** option. This will record the payment in the system, but not issue a check.

4. Quarterly & Year-End Payroll Filings

Beside paying the deposits, quarterly or annual filings need to be made. Again, I will refer you to the IRS website for details on the filings. QuickBooks has an option from the top menu under the *Employees, Payroll Tax Forms & W-2s* to *Process Payroll Forms* and *Tax Form Worksheets in Excel.*

When you select *Tax Form Worksheets in Excel,* an Excel spreadsheet opens and the following options appear.

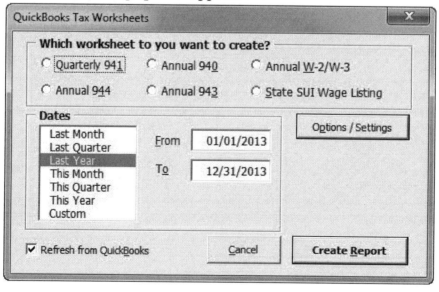

Select the report you would like to run. Choose the appropriate time frame and *Create Report*. An Excel workbook appears which summarizes the payroll data from QuickBooks into the line items needed to complete the reports. Print out the report and use it to fill in the electronic reporting requirements or to manually fill out the forms.

After the end of the year, you will need to give each of your employees a W-2. The system will generate the information you need, but you will have to manually fill out the IRS approved forms.

*This basic chapter explained how to use QuickBooks to pay your employees and the related payroll liabilities. For more information on the complex issues of ministerial compensation, please consider reading my book, **Church Accounting: The How-To Guide for Small & Growing Churches** or consulting a CPA or a payroll service.*

XII. Bank Reconciliations & Other Reconciling Issues

You have spent the month receiving donations and paying bills. Now it is time to reconcile the bank accounts. But rarely is there a month with only donation receipts and normal bill paying. You may have transferred cash between accounts, received an insufficient funds check from a donor, or voided a check you had written. These will all affect your bank reconciliation. So I am going to step you through a few things to do before you start.

A. Internal Controls & Bank Reconciliations

The bank statements should be received and opened by someone beside the bookkeeper. This person should review the checks paid and question any payments made to the bookkeeper or an unknown vendor. If the bank does not send copies of the scanned checks, this person should have access to the online banking program to view the checks. Paying fake vendors is a very common way to steal money, so any unusual or double payments should be investigated. After verifying accuracy of the requested payments, the reviewer should initial the statement and give it to the bookkeeper to reconcile. The reconciliation should never be performed by anyone who has access to the cash.

B. Cash Transfers

Most churches have a separate investment account from the checking account. If you deposit all donations into the checking account, you will want to transfer any excess cash into the investment account. When you need the funds, you will then transfer the appropriate amount from the investment account back into the checking.

There are two ways this is usually done. A check may be written from one account and deposited into the second account. Or the transfer is made through the bank or investment company's website or customer service associate. I'll walk you through how to record each of these ways in QuickBooks.

1. Transfers without Writing a Check

If the transfer is done electronically without writing a check, go to the menu bar and select *Banking, Transfer Funds*.

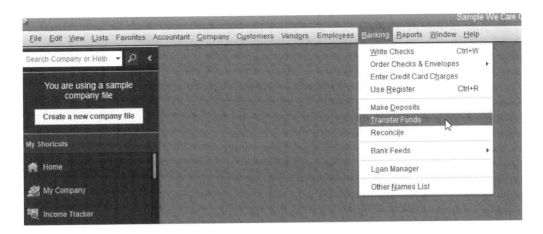

This will bring up a screen which looks somewhat like a check.

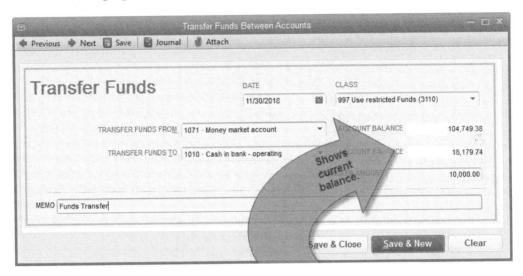

Enter the date and class. Select the account you want the money to be taken from. The system will show you the balance before the transfer. Next, select where the money should go. Enter the amount to be transferred and any memo. If there is a document you would like to be associated with this transfer, you may attach a file at the top of the screen. Select *Save & Close,* and your transfer has been recorded.

2. Transfer Cash via Check

If you transfer cash between accounts by physically writing a check, you will take a different approach. Select the *Write Checks* icon from the home page or from the **Banking** option on the menu bar.

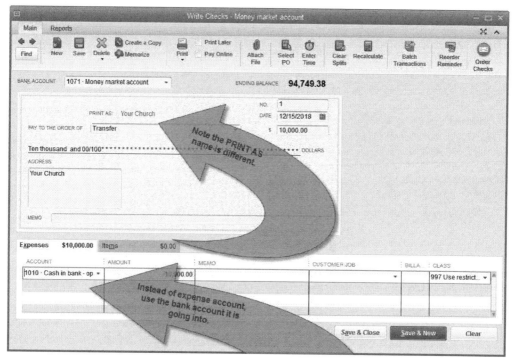

From the **BANK ACCOUNT** box, choose the account you are writing the check from. For the payee, you will need to set up an Other Name called *Transfer*. From the payee drop-down menu, select *Add New*, and you will see the following screens.

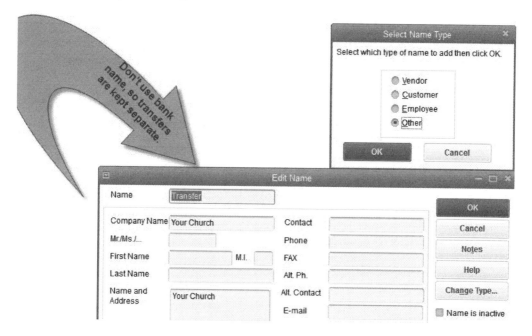

Choose *Other* to keep this separate from any vendor or customer. Enter the name as *Transfer*, but in the **Company Name** box, enter the name to be printed on the check. Select *OK* and you will be returned to the write check screen.

If you look back at the illustration of the write check screen above, you will see the **Name to be Printed** is Your Church. Enter the amount of the transfer. Now go to the bottom under **Expenses**. Even though the screen says **Expenses**, the drop-down menu includes the complete chart of accounts. Select the cash or investment account this check will be deposited into, enter the related class, and *Save & Close*.

When you physically deposit this check, put it on a separate deposit slip. Recall that your other receipts go through Undeposited Funds and are therefore grouped together by deposit record. This transaction will not be in the undeposited funds, so it should not be grouped with the others.

C.   **Returned Checks**

Every so often you may have a check returned by the bank because a member did not have sufficient funds in his account. You will need to take this out of the checking account in the system, record the bank fee for processing the bounced check, and invoice the member for the original amount plus the fee.

1.   **2014 version and later**

QuickBooks added a bounced check feature in the 2014 version. Select the *Receive Payments* window.

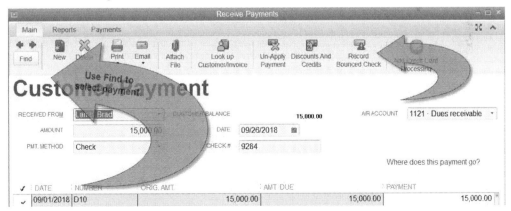

Use the **Find** arrows to go back to the check which bounced. Then select *Record Bounced Check*.

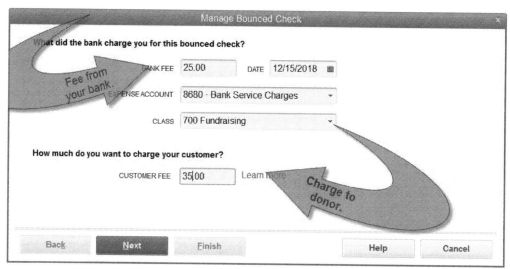

Input the fee charged by the bank and the related class. Also input the fee you would like to charge your donor for handling the returned check. Select *Next*.

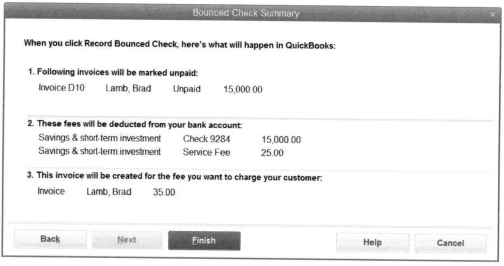

QuickBooks shows you how it is going to record the transaction. Select *Finish*. The donor's payment now highlights the fact that a check has bounced and has recorded an invoice charge for the returned check fee. This allows you to easily send an invoice to the donor with the service charge included.

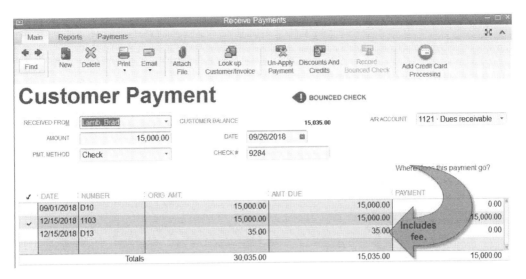

2. Earlier Versions

For earlier versions of QuickBooks, you'll have a different approach. When you receive the notice from the bank, first make a journal entry to correct your bank accounts. Go to the menu bar and select *Company, Make Journal Entries*. A blank journal entry screen will appear.

If this was a regular receipt (not invoiced), enter the donation account number where the income was originally charged. You will debit the income and credit the bank account. I like to put the returned check number and name in the memo line for a reminder. If you type it in before going to the next line, the system will automatically fill in the next line with the same memo.

If the money was received as a payment on an invoice, the first line will be the accounts receivable account. To the right on this screen is a place to input the customer name. Put J. Smith in that column to adjust his accounts receivable balance.

The related bank charge also needs to be recorded. Debit your bank service charge account and credit the cash account for the amount charged. After making certain the journal entry balances, select *Save & Close.*

The member will need to be informed of the insufficient funds and the related service charge. You can invoice him for the original amount plus the charge. You will need to add a service item entitled **Insufficient Funds Charge** or similar. See Chapter 8 for adding items and Chapter 9 on how to invoice.

> *If the member had been invoiced originally, you do not need to reinter the donation amount. It should now show as an open invoice in the member's account. Simply add the service charge and resend the invoice.*

D. Voiding a Check

There will be times that you need to void a check. Perhaps it was lost or was made out for the wrong amount. It is easy to void a check in QuickBooks. If you realize the mistake while you are in the write checks screen, you can void it there.

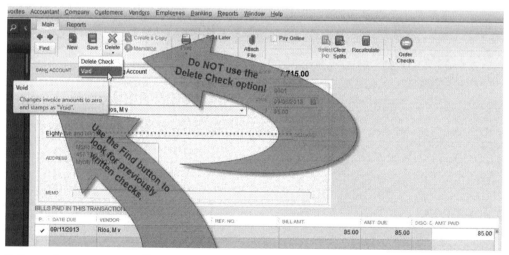

Select the arrow under the **X Delete**. This will give you the option to **Delete Check** or **Void**. Never use the **Delete Check** option as it does not leave an audit trail. When you **Void** the check, it records the check number in the system with an amount of $0, so there is an audit trail. After the check is voided, the screen reappears with VOID in the memo box and the amount as 0.

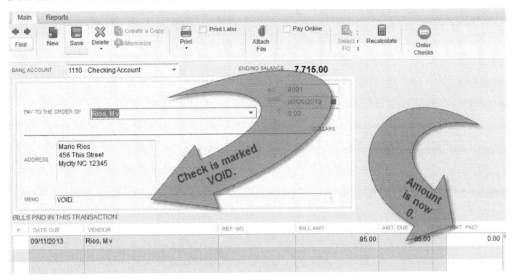

Select *Save & Close* to record the void. A warning box will appear asking you to be sure. Select *Yes*.

If we go back to the Vendor Center, we will see the bill back in the payables transactions.

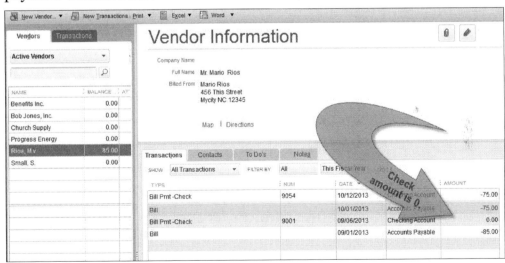

Mr. Rios is showing an open balance of $85 since the check was voided. We can go to the pay bills menu and reprint the check if it were lost. If the bill was entered incorrectly, we can double click on the bill line item and edit it.

Another way to void checks is through the check register. Go to **Banking** on the menu bar or the **Check Register** icon under **Banking** on the home screen. Select the account you would like to see on the pop-up box. In this example, I chose *Checking.*

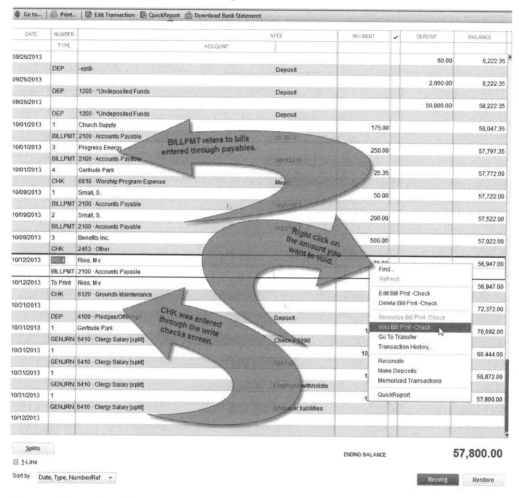

The register details every transaction in the selected bank account. **DEP** signifies a deposit; **BILLPMT** is a bill paid through accounts payable screens; **CHK** was paid through the write check entry; and **GENJRN** is a general journal entry. Right click on the amount for the check you wish to void. Select *Void Bill Payment Check* and hit *Record.* A dialog box will ask if you want to record changes. Select *Yes.*

Another dialog box may pop up and asks if you would like QuickBooks to create a journal entry in the earlier period and a reversing entry in the current period. Chose *No, just void the check.* If you select *Yes* when voiding a **CHK** entered check, the system will void the check and put a separate entry in the register with **To Print** in the **NUMBER** column.

Note also the **Restore** button at the bottom right corner. If you have selected the **Void** option, but have not yet saved the transaction, select *Restore* and the transaction reverts back. Once you have saved the transaction, it does not. Click on the small X at the top right hand corner of this screen or chose **Home** from the side menu to leave this screen.

> *The system allows you to enter transactions directly into the check register, but I would like to discourage you from doing so, especially deposits. Even though the screen allows for donor names, the transaction will not be linked to their donor account. You will get more detailed reports by entering your data through the transaction screens.*

E.   Reconciling the Bank Account

I am sure you are ready to balance your checkbook, which QuickBooks calls **Reconcile**. First, I would like you to make certain that you have recorded all of the money from undeposited funds into your checking account.

On the home screen, click the *Record Deposits* icon.

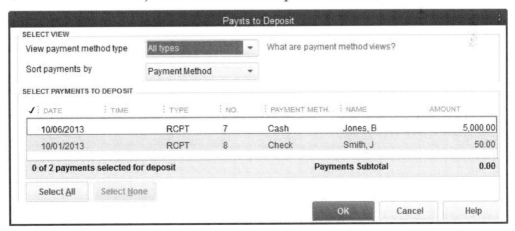

If there are any receipts listed that have already been taken to the bank (or scanned through the RID), select the receipts and press *OK*. This takes you to the **Make Deposits** screen. Be sure the total of the selected payments matches the deposit amount listed on the bank statement and select *Save & Close*. I encourage you to check this screen each month before you begin reconciling to assure all deposits are recorded. It will save time during the reconciliation.

Next, look at your bank statement for any automatic drafts or other charges. Compare those to the check register to see if all of them were entered. If not, go ahead and enter the missing charges through the write check screen as we discussed in Chapter 10.

From *Banking* on the menu bar or the banking area of the home page, select *Reconcile*.

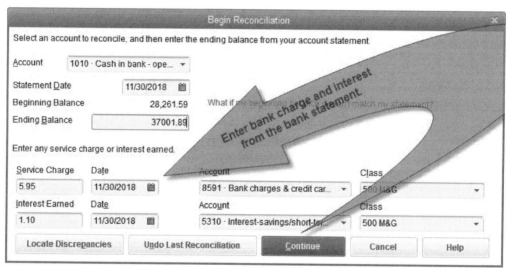

Select the appropriate bank account. If you are using subaccounts under checking, reconcile only the parent account.

From your bank statement, you will need to enter the statement date and ending balance. Additionally, look for any service charges or interest earned. These will default to the accounts you set up in the Checking Preferences. Select *Continue* and you see a screen similar to the one on the following page.

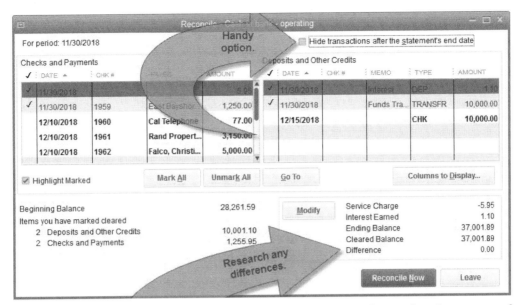

You will scroll down the checks and payments side and select any of those that have cleared the bank. Notice at the top of the screen the option **Hide transactions after the statement's end date**. This option displays fewer transactions on the screen to have to scroll through.

After you have selected all the payments that have cleared, look at the bottom left side of the screen. There is an area labeled **Items you have marked cleared**. It totals the deposits and other credits you have selected above on one line and the checks and payments on the second. At this point, the total amount you have cleared under **Checks and Payments** should agree with the total checks and other withdrawals on your bank statement.

If the total payments match, you are ready to go to the deposit side. If they do not, check to see if a payment has cleared the bank that you have not entered or if you have marked a transaction as cleared that has not. If you see a payment that has not been entered, minimize the reconciliation screen and enter the missing payment in the Make Payments or Write Bills screen. When you bring the reconciliation screen back up, the new charges should appear. If not, select *Leave* and reopen the reconciliation. If it still does not appear, make certain you entered the correct date on the payment.

If you notice a check in your system was entered with the wrong amount, you can click on it within the reconciliation screen. The transaction screen will appear with the check data. Edit the amount and save. A warning will pop up. Select Yes and you will go back to the reconciliation screen.

The deposits listed on the bank statement should match those in your system due to using the Undeposited Funds option. If there is a receipt in the bank but not in your account, research the posting and record it on your side. If it is recorded on your books but not the bank, double check to be certain the receipt was not entered twice or entered with the wrong date. Otherwise you will need to track down the missing deposit.

Another possible reconciliation error relates to the beginning balance. When you first bring up the reconcile screen, the system shows you the beginning balance, but does not allow you to adjust it. The system has calculated the beginning balance based on the previously cleared entries in the cash account.

If the beginning balance does not match the bank statement's beginning balance, someone has probably voided, deleted, or changed a transaction that was cleared in a previous reconciliation.

For example, you pay Joe Smith $50 a week to mow the grass. He typically deposits the check the next day, and when you reconcile the bank account, you clear his checks. But one day he comes to you and says that he has lost last week's check. You void the check and issue him a new one. The only problem is, you accidentally voided a check from last month that had already cleared. This will make your beginning balance not tie to the last reconciliation.

Luckily, the **Reconciliation Discrepancy Report** will show any changes in the bank reconciliation since the last report. Though not in all versions, if available, this report can be accessed from the menu bar by selecting *Reports, Banking, Reconciliation Discrepancy Report*. You can then edit the incorrect transaction and reconcile your bank account.

Once you have matched everything possible with the bank statement, the bottom of the reconciliation screen should show a $0 difference. If there is a balance, you may have an error in one of your transactions. Check for transpositions (if the difference is divisible by 9, it may mean you switched two numbers around—45 instead of 54) as well as differences between the check amounts recorded by the bank and in the accounting system. If nothing works, a last resort is to select *Reconcile Now*. The system will offer to allow you to record an adjustment.

> *Only choose the record an adjustment after all other options have been exhausted. What looks like a small variance could be two large mistakes that happen to offset each other.*

If there is no variance, select *Reconcile Now*, and you will be given the option to print a summary report, detail report, or both. Select *Both* and hit *Print*.

The first report is a summary. It gives you the total amount of cleared payments and deposits and the amounts you have outstanding.

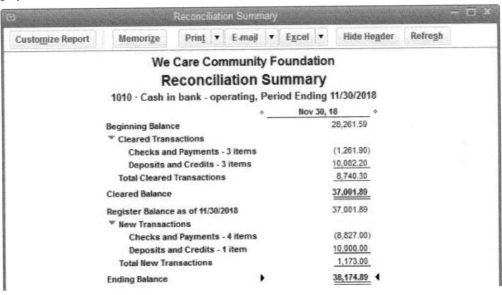

The next report is the detailed version.

<table>
<tr><td colspan="8">Reconciliation Detail</td></tr>
<tr><td>Report</td><td>Share Template</td><td>Memorize</td><td>Print ▼</td><td>E-mail ▼</td><td>Excel ▼</td><td>Hide Header</td><td>Re</td></tr>
</table>

We Care Community Foundation
Reconciliation Detail
1010 · Cash in bank - operating, Period Ending 11/30/2018

Type	Date	Num	Name	Clr	Amount	Balance
Beginning Balance						28,261.59
Cleared Transactions						
Checks and Payments - 3 items						
▶ Bill Pmt -Check	11/30/2018	1959	East Bayshore HMO	✔	(1,250.00)	(1,250.00) ◀
Check	11/30/2018			✔	(5.95)	(1,255.95)
Check	11/30/2018			✔	(5.95)	(1,261.90)
Total Checks and Payments					(1,261.90)	(1,261.90)
Deposits and Credits - 3 items						
Deposit	11/30/2018			✔	1.10	1.10
Deposit	11/30/2018			✔	1.10	2.20
Transfer	11/30/2018			✔	10,000.00	10,002.20
Total Deposits and Credits					10,002.20	10,002.20
Total Cleared Transactions					8,740.30	8,740.30
Cleared Balance					8,740.30	37,001.89
Register Balance as of 11/30/2018					8,740.30	37,001.89
New Transactions						
Checks and Payments - 4 items						
Bill Pmt -Check	12/10/2018	1962	Falco, Christina		(5,000.00)	(5,000.00)
Bill Pmt -Check	12/10/2018	1961	Rand Properties		(3,150.00)	(8,150.00)
Bill Pmt -Check	12/10/2018	1963	Rutherford Pensio...		(600.00)	(8,750.00)
Bill Pmt -Check	12/10/2018	1960	Cal Telephone		(77.00)	(8,827.00)
Total Checks and Payments					(8,827.00)	(8,827.00)
Deposits and Credits - 1 item						
Check	12/15/2018	1	Transfer		10,000.00	10,000.00
Total Deposits and Credits					10,000.00	10,000.00
Total New Transactions					1,173.00	1,173.00
Ending Balance					9,913.30	38,174.89

This report shows the check numbers and dates of cleared and outstanding payments and deposits. Review the detailed report each month to see if there are old outstanding checks or deposits that need to be followed up on. Attach the reports to the bank statements and file. Your auditors or audit committee will want to see these reports.

If you chose to have the system record the adjustment, it will automatically create a **Reconciliation Discrepancies** account to record the transaction. You will need to change this account to fit into your numbering structure in the chart of accounts. Go to *Lists, Chart of Accounts,* and scroll down until you see the new account. Highlight it and right click to edit the account. Change the account number to fit into your numbering sequence. I chose 6399 so it would display near bank charges and made it a subaccount of Administrative expenses. Select *Save & Close*.

F. **Reconciling Petty Cash**

Many churches find it necessary to keep a petty cash account. Petty cash accounts can take different forms; it may be a couple hundred dollars locked in a drawer or gift cards purchased from local businesses that are used as needed.

Your church should have written procedures and guidelines regarding the use of petty cash. One person should be responsible for maintaining the cash or cards. Receipts must be brought back to the church in the amount of the cash expended. The fund is replenished with those receipts as the support.

I'll walk you through a typical example. Betty, the receptionist at Your Church, has asked for a $200 petty cash fund. She promises to keep it in a security box locked in a filing cabinet behind her desk. People are always asking her to get donuts and coffee or office supplies at the last minute, and she doesn't personally have the funds to cover them until she can be reimbursed.

You will write a check made out to Your Church to be cashed at your bank. Instead of an expense account number, you will set up a petty cash account with type marked as **Bank**. If you look at the account after you write the check, it will show a $200 balance.

At the end of the month, Betty brings you $175 of receipts and asks if she can get more money. First, verify that she has $25 of cash left. Betty should always have a combination of receipts and cash that equal $200. You will write a check for $175 and file the check voucher with the $175 of receipts under a Petty Cash file. From the **Write Check** screen, record the receipts under the **Expense** tab. Office supplies, meeting expenses, or whatever expense the receipts are for will be the expense accounts charged.

If you have purchased gift cards or prepaid credit cards, set up an account called Gift Cards with an account type of Prepaid Expenses. Each month, you should verify that the receipts and the balance of the gift cards equal the amount of the card purchases.

> *Consider checking the balance of the petty cash and receipts at irregular intervals during the month. This discourages people from thinking they can borrow money they may not be able to replace at month's end.*

G. Other Reconciliations

Cash is not the only thing that needs to be reconciled monthly. Some churches have postage meters. The allocation of the postage expense is typically done via a journal entry.

When you write the check to purchase the postage, record the amount to a prepaid asset account instead of an expense account. At the end of the month, record postage usage by going to the menu bar and selecting *Company, Make General Journal Entries*.

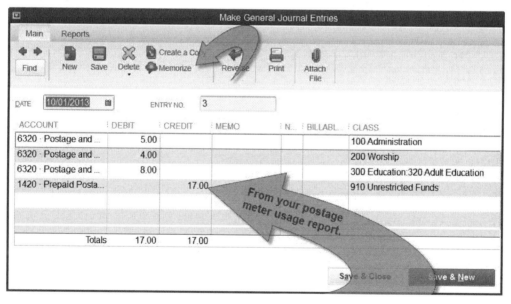

Use your postage meter usage report and allocate the postage to the appropriate classes. The total should be the amount of postage charged in your meter for the period. I recommend memorizing the entry so you will only need to change the dollar amounts each month.

To make certain the prepaid postage amount ties to the balance in your meter, go to the chart of accounts list and compare the balance in prepaid postage to your postage balance report. If you had purchased $200 of postage and used $17, the prepaid account should show $183.

Now that you've entered all the transactions and reconciled your accounts for the month, it's time to run reports. On to Chapter 13 to learn what reports are available and what information you need to most effectively run your church.

XIII.   Where Do We Stand? Designing & Running Reports

As you were working on the set up and entering the transactions, you may have been asking yourself, "Why do I have to do all this?" Being able to access accurate financial reports is crucial to funding the church's mission, and every entry you make helps paint a fuller picture. In this chapter, I will explain the different types of reports you may need, walk you through the standard QuickBooks options, and show you how to design and export customized reports.

A.   Types of Reports

At a minimum, all organizations need two basic reports—the **Balance Sheet** and the **Income Statement (or Profit and Loss Statement)**. Churches and other nonprofits call these reports **Statement of Financial Position** and **Statement of Activities**. The Balance Sheet (or Statement of Financial Position) is a snapshot of what the church owns, owes, and what is left in net assets as of a certain date. The Income Statement (or Statement of Activities) summarizes the revenues and expenses over a defined period.

So this sounds like accountant talk again, doesn't it? I'm afraid you will have to humor me a bit to assure you are comfortable with the differences and will know when to request which report.

The balance sheet indicates the financial health of your organization. If assets are greater than liabilities, you own more than you owe. What is left is the net assets. Net assets are the accumulated amount of the difference between the amount owned versus owed since the church's inception.

If you wanted to know how much cash you had in the bank this year versus last year, you would run a balance sheet as of today. The columns would include both this year and the same date last year, so you could see your increase or decrease in cash.

The income statement reflects the operations of your church. If you want to know how much money has been donated to your church this year, you would run an income statement report for the year. If you needed to know how much was donated in the last quarter, you could run the report for a three-month period.

Besides the two primary reports, you would probably like to see who your biggest donors are, who has donated how much, comparisons to budgets, how much money is expected from pledges, and how much you owe vendors. QuickBooks allows you to run reports on all of this information and more. Let's walk through the basic reports offered.

B. Navigating the Reports Center

From the Shortcuts or Menu bar, select *Reports, Reports Center.*

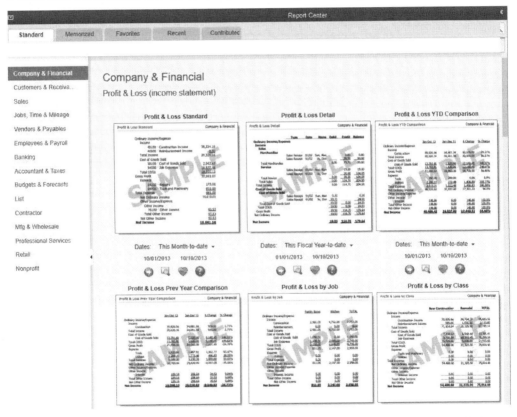

Depending on the version you are using, you will not see all of these options down the side. Across the top, there are five tabs. Think of these as file folders to help you organize your reports. The first one, **Standard,** gives you all of the options for reports in each of the categories. Scroll down the screen to see more options.

The **Memorized** tab is the folder to store the reports you have memorized so you don't have to reenter the way it is displayed. You can store reports from any of the categories into this folder.

Favorites is where I like to store the few reports I run on a regular basis. I like to limit the number here so I can just click on the reports and not have to scroll around looking for them.

The system stores the last copy of the reports you have run under **Recent**. This saves you from having to reenter the parameters on a report you closed.

The **Contributed** tab is a wonderful resource.

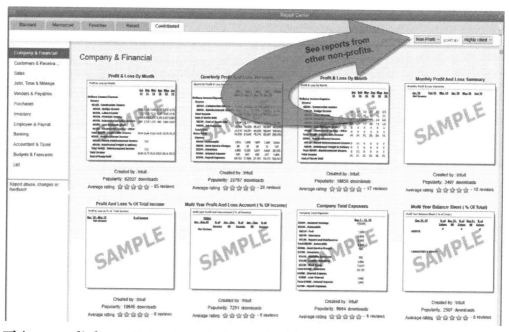

This page links to Intuit's website and allows you to download reports designed by other users. You can sort based on your industry and then download the report that matches your needs.

C.   Defining the Parameters

From the **Company & Financial** screen, select the first *Profit & Loss Standard*. If it is not the first time this has been chosen, a report may appear. In that case, select *Customize* in the top left corner to open the **Modify Report** dialog box. Options to change the information displayed, select filters for the report, to customize the headers and footers, and to change the fonts are offered.

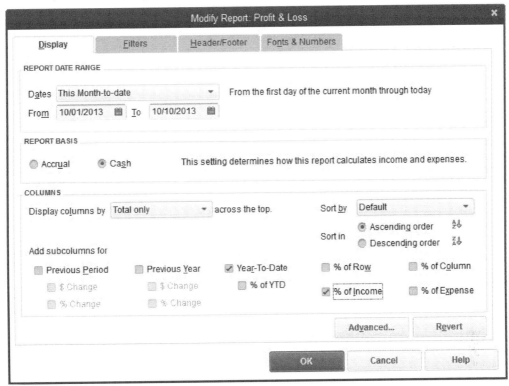

1. Display options

Starting near the top of the screen, notice the drop-down arrow after **Dates**. This allows you to select the time period, including *All, Today, Week, Week to date,* etc. The system will fill in the dates based on your selection. For greater flexibility, you can manually type over the dates in the boxes to any range you like.

The section titled **Report Basis** determines whether this report will be calculated on a cash or accrual basis. Recall from our previous chapters, the cash basis option will display only transactions for which cash has been received or paid out. If you have recorded pledges receivable for the year, but want to run a profit and loss based on the pledges actually received, select the *Cash* basis. The accrual option will display transactions based on the transaction date, not when cash was exchanged as discussed in Chapter 10.

Next you can determine what columns you would like to see on the report. The **Display columns by** menu includes everything imaginable; *day, week, customer, item,* etc. We'll stick with *Total only* for now. You can decide in what order to sort the data and which, if any, subcolumns you would like. As useful as all of these columns sound, if you select them all, you will have a very wide report. So play around, select a few, and see what you like. For this example, I've chosen to see the data for the month, year to date, and as a percentage of income.

Clicking the *Advanced* button gives you the following options.

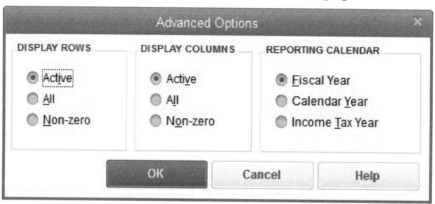

You decide if you would like all the rows and columns to display or only the active or non-zero ones. Selecting *All* may cause your report to show accounts that have no data in them. The **Reporting Calendar** is useful if your income tax year is different than the calendar or fiscal year. **Fiscal Year** is your accounting year. For most churches, this will be the same as the calendar year, but some organizations have a different year end.

2.   Filtering the report

Selecting *OK* will take you back to the Display screen, where I want you to now select the *Filters* tab at the top. The *Filters* tab allows you to select which accounts, amounts, items, etc. you want included in the report. For example, if you would like to only see transactions above $5000, you would filter the report for **Amount**. Notice there is a **Revert** option. If you have been playing around with the filters, but want it to go back to the original options, select *Revert* and the filters reset.

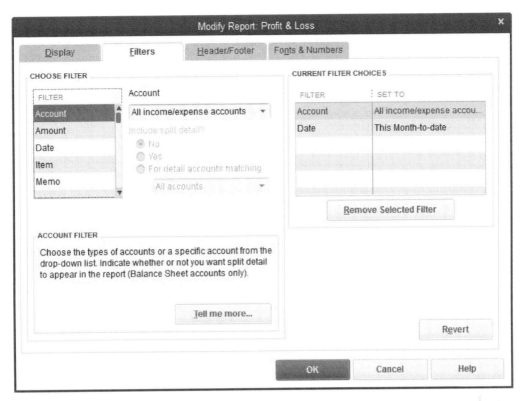

Starting in 2015, you can search the filters by typing in its name in the box instead of scrolling down the list.

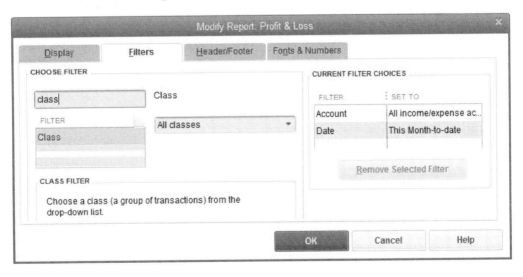

3. Labeling & formatting

Now select the *Header/Footer* tab. This screen is where you will label your report.

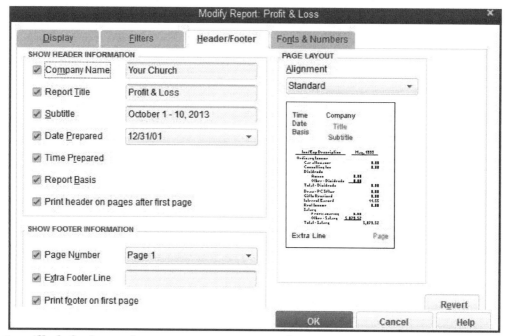

It will default to the company name and report title, but you can type anything in the grey boxes. If you do not want some of this information to show on the report, unselect the box to the left of the option. Do not select *OK* yet, as we want to go to the *Fonts & Numbers* tab.

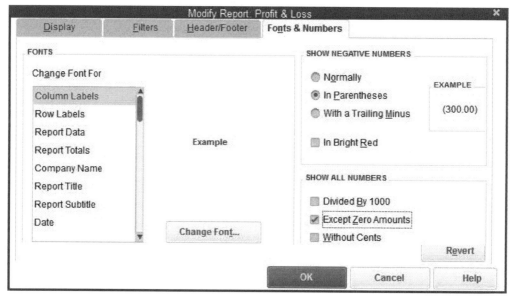

If you would like the heading font for the church's name to be different than the font used on the rest of the report, highlight *Company Name* and then select *Change Font.*

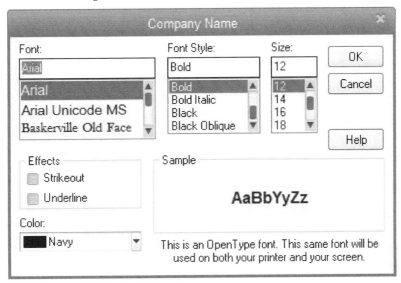

Choose the font, style, size, and colors and click *OK.* You will now be directed back to the Fonts & Numbers screen. The **Show Negative Numbers** options let you decide if negatives should be shown with a minus sign, parentheses, or in bright red. To save ink costs for printed reports, I'd recommend staying away from the colors.

The **Show All Numbers** area allows you to produce reports omitting zero balances, without the cents showing, or with the numbers rounded by 1000. Unless you are a VERY large church, I doubt you'll need to round by 1000.

4. Reviewing the report

Now you can select *OK,* and you will see a Profit and Loss report. You will see your profit and loss by income account. If you click on the small grey arrows to the left of an account, the system will display the subaccounts that total it. This is very handy to review for errors.

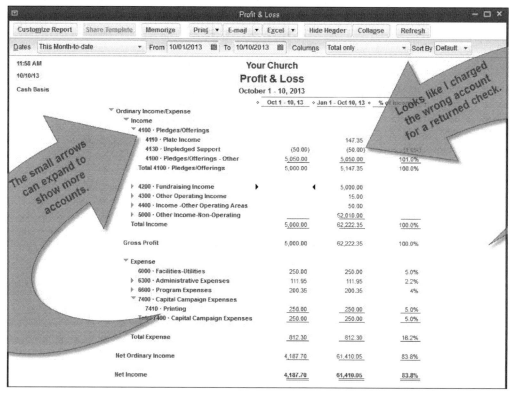

In the example above, I see a negative amount in Unpledged Support. There shouldn't be a negative amount there. If I double click on the (50.00), I will see the following:

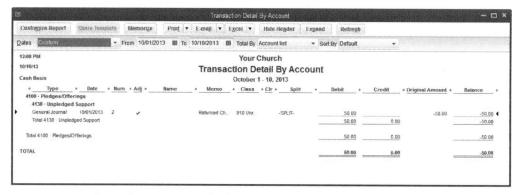

It appears that the returned check should have gone against Pledged Support, not Unpledged Support. I can double click on the transaction in this report, and it will bring up the journal entry for me to edit. Once edited and saved, the Profit and Loss will show the $50 in the correct account.

> *I'll be referring to the ability to link to the transactions from reports as **drilling down***. *To drill down, simply double click on the transaction in question.*

Let's look back at the top of the report.

The top left button labeled **Customize Report** will take you to the modify screen with the four tabs we discussed above. **Memorize** allows you to memorize all of the filters and parameters of this report and will save it under the **Memorized** tab in the Reports Center.

The **Print** button allows you to print or save as a PDF. The PDF option is convenient when you want to send reports and be certain no one will change the numbers on them. It also makes the reports easier to read for people who don't use spreadsheets.

Often when you print a report, the columns don't fit on one page. Added in 2014, there is now a scaling option. Now when you select *Print Reports*, you can choose to scale the report to a defined number of pages wide or high.

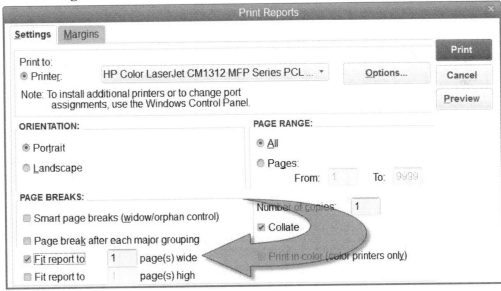

Email allows you to send the report as an Excel sheet or as a PDF. With the 2015 version, you can send multiple reports in a single email by creating a **Report Group**. To do this, go to *Reports, Memorized Reports, Memorized Report List.* This will bring up the current list of memorized reports.

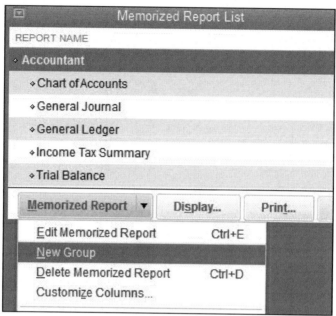

From the drop-down arrow next to **Memorized Report,** select *New Group.* Name the new group and select *OK.* Then save the reports you would like to send together to this new group by pulling up the reports and memorizing each of them into the new group.

Go back to the top menu bar and select *Reports, Process Multiple Reports.*

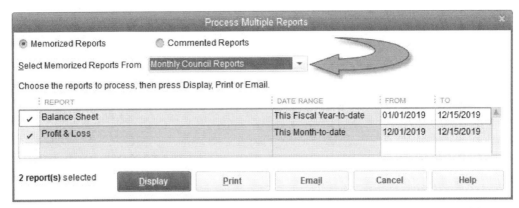

Select the name of your group and chose which reports you'd like to email or print.

The **Excel** option will create a new spreadsheet or update an existing one. As QuickBooks is designed for businesses and not churches, many churches prefer to export reports to a spreadsheet and then change the terminology to their own. The **Update an existing spreadsheet** option allows you to set up a template and then simply change the numbers each time you run the report. After you become more familiar with the reports in the system, this will be an area you may wish to play around with. (I'll walk you through how to do these techniques later in this chapter.)

Hide Header removes the descriptive header from the report. **Expand** or **Collapse** shows or hides the subaccounts from the report. The report on the facing page has been collapsed. You could select individual accounts to expand, or the **Expand** button at the top will show all of the subaccounts.

Refresh will update the numbers for any changes in the transactions since the report was generated. Below the top bar is an area to change the date range and the columns to be shown.

> *Though QuickBooks has numerous types of reports, you will navigate around them and change the parameters in the same way.*

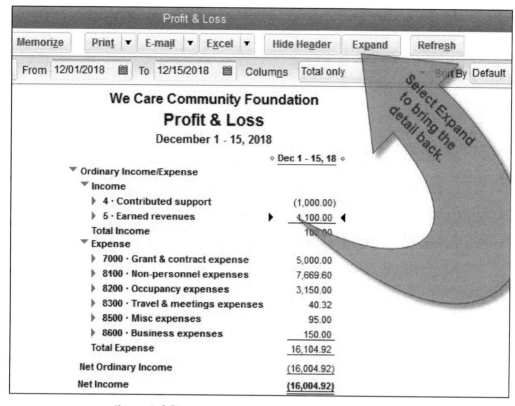

5. Adding comments

The 2015 version has added a comment function. This is a wonderful way to write yourself notes or send additional information to another user.

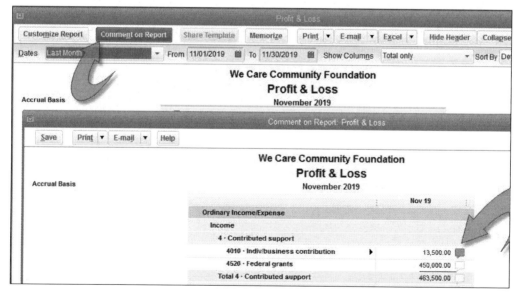

Select *Comment on Report* and a separate screen with the report will pop up. Click the box to the right of the line you wish to comment on.

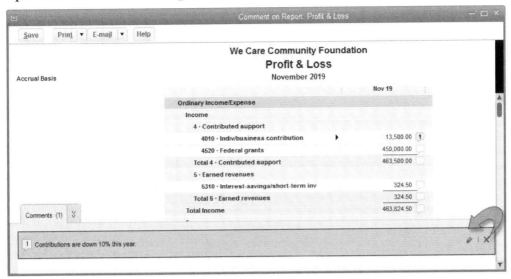

Type in your information and select *Save*. It can be edited later by selecting the small pencil icon in the right corner of the box. Add comments for as many line items as you like. The comments will be automatically numbered.

After all of your comments are entered, click on the *Save* button at the top left corner to save the report. You will need to enter a new name. The report can then be retrieved by selecting *Reports, Commented Reports*.

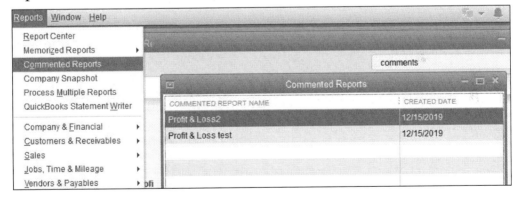

D. **Most Useful Reports**

Go back to the Report Center and review what types of reports are available under each of the categories. As you do, I'll explain some of the most useful reports so you can look them up and see if they meet your needs or what would need to be changed. If you have the Nonprofit version of QuickBooks, there is a category titled **Nonprofit**. Select it and you will see options for the various reports.

Report Name	Description
Biggest Donors/Grants	Lists members/donors in order of donation size. (Customers)
Budget vs Actual by Donors/Grants	Compares donations and grants and their related expenses to the budget. (Jobs)
Donors/Grants Reports	For an individual grant, summarizes the related income and expenses. (Jobs)
Donor Contribution Summary	Lists donation subtotaled by members. Use this list to develop year-end giving statements. (Customers)
Budget vs Actual by Program/Projects	Individual programs compared to budget. (Budgets for a Class)
Program/Projects Report	Details expenses for individual program. (Profit & Loss for a Class)
Statement of Financial Income & Expenses	Profit & Loss by program. (Profit & Loss by Class)
Statement of Financial Position	Balance sheet. (Balance Sheet)
Statement of Functional Expenses	Expense summary needed if you file a 990 tax return.

If you do not have the nonprofit edition, don't worry. I've put in parenthesis the corresponding report in the regular versions. You will need to change the headings or export the file to a spreadsheet to rename the items to nonprofit terminology. You may also want to look through the contributed reports tab in the Report Center for a good match.

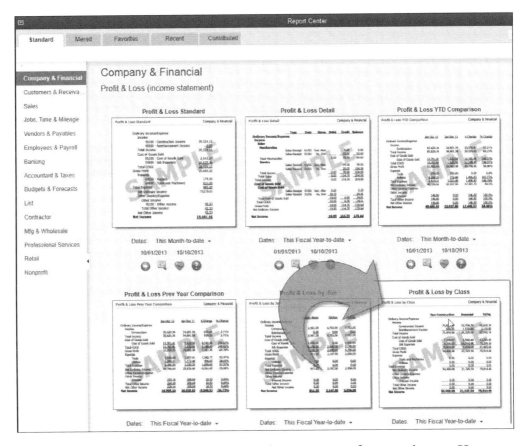

At the bottom of each report is a date area and some icons. You can change the date range before you pull up the report. When you click on the icons, they will do the following:

> Green circle = displays report.
> Magnifying glass = explains what the report is used for.
> Red heart = saves the report in the Favorites tab.
> Blue circle with ? = brings up a help window.

You will choose the data for each of these reports as we discussed before. I'll walk you through the selections for **Statement of Financial Income and Expenses** as an example. I chose this report as it will give information by each of the programs.

The screen shots will be from the sample nonprofit company, so you can follow along. (Close your church and open the sample nonprofit organization.) For those using the nonprofit edition, select *Statement of Financial Income & Expenses* from the **Nonprofit** area. The rest of us will go to the **Company & Financial** option and select *Profit and Loss by Class.*

Either the modify dialog box will appear or the report. If the dialog box appears, select *OK* and the report will display.

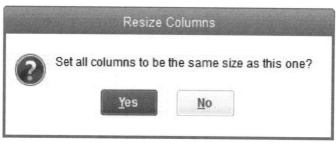

As we learned earlier, you can change the date range, header, etc. by using the menus across the top of this screen. The **Collapse** button will hide the detail accounts. Additionally, you can change the size of the columns by hovering your mouse over the little diamonds between the columns. When the cursor changes to a +, slide it to the right to make the column narrower or to the left to make it wider. You will then see the following dialog box.

Choose your preference and you will see the report resized.

Above, I collapsed the data so the report would not be so long. Looking down this report, you see for each program the income, operating expenses, and an ordinary income line. This tells you how much you have received from regular donations and grants and the related expenses. Below the Net Ordinary Income line is the non-operating income and expenses. These are the unusual things that may occur at your church.

With all those columns, the print would be very difficult to read on a print out. The report shows all subclasses as well as regular classes, but I would like a report that just summarizes the top-level classes. To do this, I'll need to export the data to a spreadsheet.

E.   **Exporting Reports to a Spreadsheet**

I must warn you, this section assumes you know Excel well enough to do basic formulas, adding worksheets, and formatting. As an accountant, I'm afraid I assume everyone uses the program as much as I do. But if you are not familiar with the spreadsheet program, you may wish to ask for help from someone who is as you go through this section.

Select *Excel, Create New Worksheet* from the top of the report.

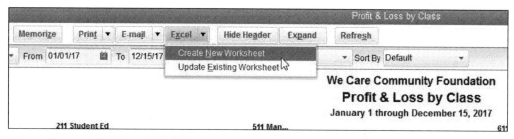

Next there will be a dialog box.

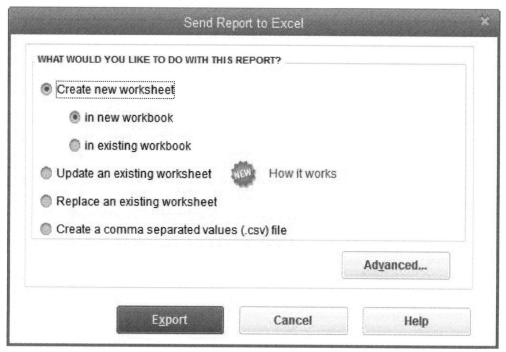

Choose *in new workbook* and click *Export*.

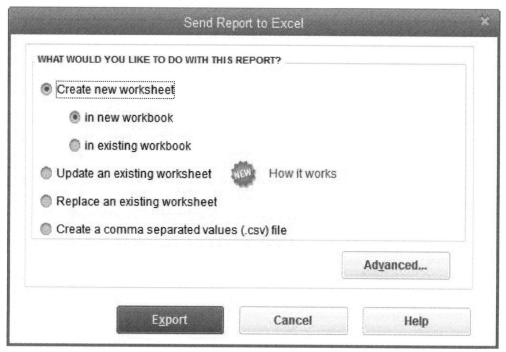

This worksheet has all of the data from the QuickBooks report. As we would like this report to only show the top-level classes, highlight any columns with subclasses, right click, and select hide as shown below.

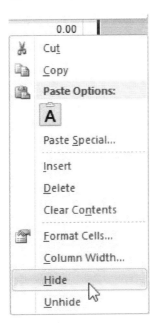

Continue doing this until only the parent classes are showing.

Now you will want to make the remaining columns smaller. Use the **Wrap Text** option at the top of the menu bar. This will allow the headings to make the cell taller when you reduce the width.

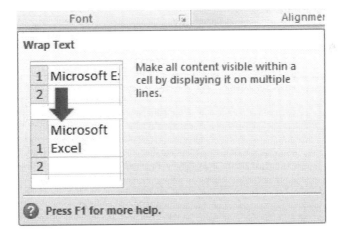

Rounding to the nearest dollar instead of showing the cents will also save space.

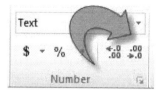

Highlight the entire worksheet and click on the small arrow pointing to the right twice to remove any numbers after the decimal.

Now you are ready to reduce the columns to the narrowest size possible while keeping the numbers legible. Holding your cursor at the line between columns will change it to a bold +. You can then move the edge of the column to the right or left. Do this for each of the columns until you are happy with the result.

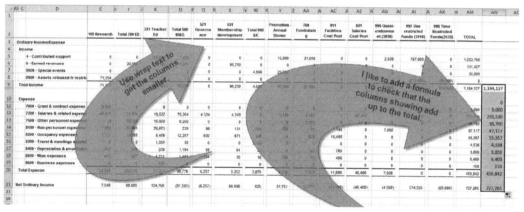

As an extra precaution, I add a temporary column with a formula summing all the columns that are showing. If the amount is different than the total on the worksheet, I know I have either left a subclass showing or hid a parent class. These formulas should be deleted before it is printed or saved.

You can also add headings, logos, change the fonts, etc. to make the report look exactly like you want. Save the worksheet and note the name and place.

Go back to the report we have been working with in QuickBooks. Now change the date parameter to this month. Notice that all of the numbers have changed in the report. If you would like to use these numbers but in the format you designed previously, select *Excel, Update Existing Worksheet.*

This time when the dialog box appears, you will choose *Update an existing worksheet.*

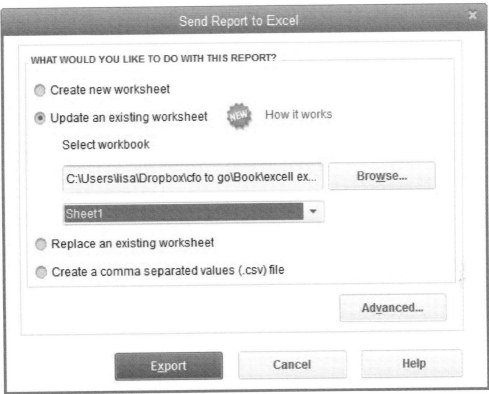

Use the *Browse* button to find the file and select the name of the sheet. If it is a large workbook, you will want to rename the individual sheets for information. Choose *Export.*

You will see a warning and then the updated spreadsheet will open. If there are errors, QuickBooks will alert you to these and offer tips.

This will not save all of your changes, but does keep you from having to redo your headings and labels each time. Here is the exported spreadsheet for just the month.

	100 Research	221 Teacher Ed	521 Governance	531 Membership development	700 Fundraising	911 Facilities Cost Pool	996 Quasi-endowment (3030)	TOTAL
y Income/Expense								
Income								
4 · Contributed support	0.00	0.00	0.00		(1,000.00)	0.00	0.00	(1,000.00)
5 · Earned revenues	0.00	1,100.00	0.00		0.00	0.00	0.00	1,100.00
Total Income	0.00	1,100.00	0.00		(1,000.00)	0.00	0.00	100.00
Expense								
7000 · Grant & contract expense	5,000.00	0.00	0.00		0.00	0.00	0.00	5,000.00
8100 · Non-personnel expenses	0.00	485.00	70.60	114.00	0.00	0.00	7,000.00	7,669.60
8200 · Occupancy expenses	0.00	0.00			0.00	3,150.00	0.00	3,150.00
8500 · Misc expenses	0.00	95.00			0.00	0.00	0.00	95.00
8600 · Business expenses	0.00	150.00			0.00	0.00	0.00	150.00
Total Expense	5,000.00	730.00		114.00	0.00	3,150.00	7,000.00	16,064.60
Net Ordinary Income	(5,000.00)	370.00		(114.00)	(1,000.00)	(3,150.00)	(7,000.00)	(15,964.60)
Net Income	(5,000.00)	370.00		(114.00)		(3,150.00)	(7,000.00)	(15,964.60)

It is substantially smaller as not all of the programs had activity in that month.

Most of the reports in QuickBooks can be exported to a spreadsheet with your customized headings and formatting. Take a few minutes and try some other reports with the sample company. Also, use the spreadsheet program to change the fonts and practice exporting. You will find this a handy tool.

F. Other Miscellaneous Reports

1. Pledges Receivable, Member, & Vendor Information

There are several other reports you will want to keep an eye on. If you have entered pledges as invoices, you can run the **A/R Aging Summary** or **Detail**. This report lists the members and how much they still owe on their pledges.

In the Reports Center, select *Customers & Receivable*. The first report offered is *A/R Aging Summary*. Choose today's date and you will see what is owed the church as of today. The *A/R Aging Detail* is the same report but lists the individual invoices entered by member.

Further down in the Customers & Receivables section of the Report Center is the **Customer Phone List** and the **Customer Contact List**. These lists can be printed, exported to Excel or PDF formats, or saved to text files to import into other software.

*If you need mailing or filing labels, go to the main menu bar, select **File**, **Print Forms**, and **Labels**. Choose **Customer Type** and click **OK**. You can then select your label format and print the labels.*

If you have been entering your bills as they are received, but not yet paid, you can go to the **Vendors & Payables** section of the Report Center and select **A/P Aging Summary**. This is the accounts payable report which shows all the bills that have been entered but not yet paid and when they are due. It is a useful tool for cash-flow management. The vendors section also allows you to run reports on all transactions for a particular vendor using the **Transaction List by Vendor**.

2. Deposit Detail

The Banking area of the Report Center has the **Deposit Detail** report. This report shows every deposit made and the bank account it went to along with the individual transactions that made up the deposit. If the deposits on your bank account do not tie to the deposits listed in your accounts during your bank reconciliation, refer to this report to see if you put the money in the wrong account in QuickBooks.

3. Accountant Reports

If you have the Premier or Nonprofit versions, you will see a section titled **Accountant and Taxes**. I'll explain more about these in Chapter 15.

The final section is **Budgets & Forecasts**. In the next chapter, I'll show you how to input your budgets and best utilize this powerful tool.

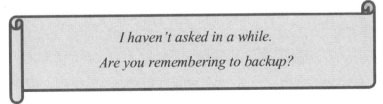

I haven't asked in a while.
Are you remembering to backup?

XIV.   Am I Meeting My Targets? Budgeting

Planning for the future is crucial for any organization. Preparing an annual budget requires a church to consider the priorities of their congregation and the best way for the organization to respond. Because there is a limit to the donations expected to be received, there is also a limit to the services that can be offered.

> *Approach the budgeting process as a way to get consensus around the priorities of your church.*

A.   The Budget Process

Budgets are typically done on operating income and expenses. Income and expenses outside of normal church operations (non-operating income and expenses, like the receipt of a bequest or repaving the parking lot) only need to be budgeted if they are substantial.

The budget process will have several steps. First you must consider if you need budgets at a top level (total church only) or program by program. Budgeting at the program level will take more time, but will also give you more information.

You may also wish to budget by grant. QuickBooks allows you to input class (program) budgets separate from the whole church budget. If you prepare program budgets for all areas (including administration), this will summarize to a total church budget.

Next, you will need to determine what donations and other revenues you are expecting. If your church membership and donations have been fairly consistent over the years, you can use historical trends and tweak them for any likely changes.

For example, if pledges have consistently been close to $100,000 for the last five years, you are probably safe budgeting $100,000 for next year. But if a large donor moved to another state, consider reducing the expected pledges by their usual donation.

Some churches prefer to ask for the annual pledge commitments before they begin the budgeting process. This gives the treasurer a fairly accurate idea of the minimum amount of donations that will be received. The difficulty with this approach is simply the timing. If you start asking members for their commitments in October, it may be late December before you have them nailed down.

A hybrid approach is to use historical data and update it with known pledges before you finalize the budgets. This incorporates the best of both worlds and also allows the treasurer to do what accountants call a "smell test." A smell test really means "does it make sense?" If pledges committed are 50% less than last year's, but membership is stable, you either have an entry error or need to follow up with your members to see what has changed.

Non-pledged donations are usually budgeted at historical rates. This would include money received in the collection plate, memorials, rent, etc. Investment income can be budgeted based on expected returns of the investments. If you have $100,000 in a money market account that is currently paying 2% interest, you would budget $2000 of investment income.

For the expense budgets, I like to get buy-in from the heads of the programs. Start by printing out a report showing the directors of each program how much money they have spent this year.

Select the **Profit & Loss Standard** report and filter it for class. (You learned how to filter the reports in the last chapter.)

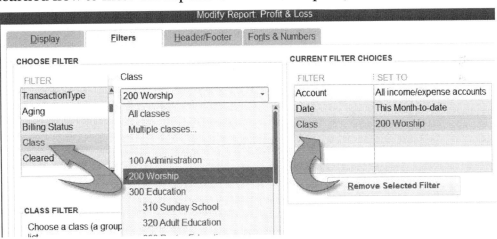

Then, ask your program heads to submit their budget proposal of expected needs for the next year, and if it is substantially different than this year, an explanation should be included. I refer to this as the wish list. Be sure to remind the directors it is not part of the budget until approved by the finance committee or governing board.

Preparing their proposal and explanation encourages the program directors to think about what they would like to do differently. The written documentation is a good resource for the governing board as they deliberate on how to divide the budget dollars. This also gives you the information to put in a class (program) budget in QuickBooks.

Besides program expenses, your church has facilities and other overhead expenditures. These can usually be calculated based on historical information or contracts. If you are allocating this expense across the programs, save yourself time by waiting until all of the direct program costs have been budgeted. Then you can do a one-time calculation based on percentage of space used, number of employees, or percentage of total costs to allocate the overhead.

For example, use a spreadsheet to estimate all of your building expenses. If you have three programs, Administration, Worship, and Education, you would add one third of the expected building expenses to each of these three budgets. You can do the same thing for salaries if you allocate people over more than one program. Some churches use different allocation percentages for facilities costs versus supplies and administrative costs.

> *Consider exporting last year's actual overhead expenses to a spreadsheet. You can use formulas that add an inflation percentage and then allocate by program. The allocation would be input into QuickBooks' budget by account.*

B.   Entering Your Budget

Once you have compiled all the information from the program directors, pledge cards, historical information, and anywhere else, it is time to put it all together in a budget. You will probably go through several iterations before your board decides on a final budget, so don't worry if you don't have all the information you would like.

From the menu bar, select *Nonprofit, Set Up Budgets* or *Company, Planning & Budgeting, Set Up Budgets.* If a budget had been previously set up, you will see a different screen. If so, select *Create a New Budget.*

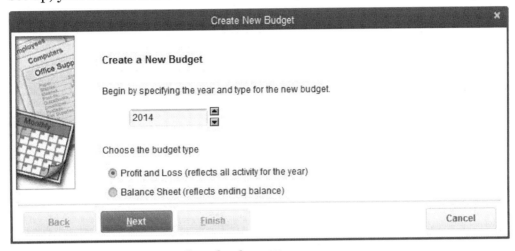

Change to the year desired and select *Next.*

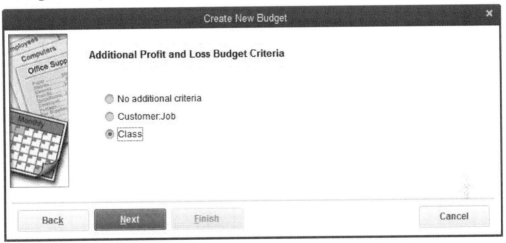

The **No additional criteria** allows you to prepare a budget without budgeting programs separately. **Customer:Job** is used to budget grants. Select **Class** to budget by program.

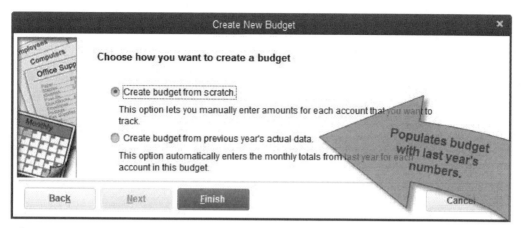

This screen allows you to start your budget without any data already inserted or to have the system populate the data with the monthly amounts by account. If you are primarily using an historical approach to budgeting and have last year's data in the system, the second option is a time saver.

For our example, select *Create budget from scratch* and hit *Finish*.

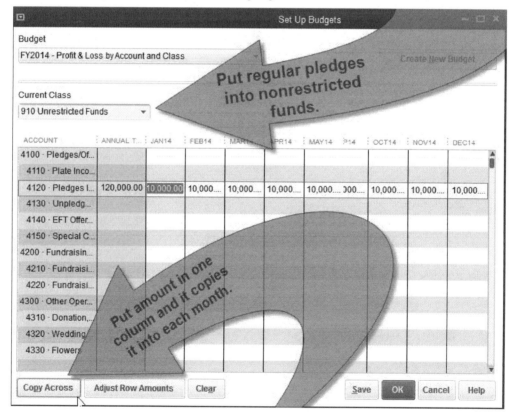

At the top, you will see the year and type of **Budget**. Below that is **Current Class**. You will need to change this box each time you enter a new program. But be sure to select *Save* first. Hitting *OK* will take you out of this screen.

Enter the budget information at the subaccount level if you have that much data. If you enter an amount in the **Jan** column and highlight it, you can then select *Copy Across,* and the system will put the same amount in all twelve months. You can then manually adjust the months.

Perhaps, after you had input $1000 per month in the plate collections account, the treasurer suggested increasing the budget by 10%.

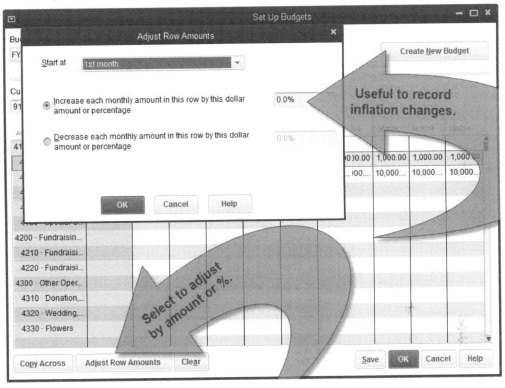

Highlight the first month's amount and select *Adjust Row Amounts.* Select *Increase each monthly amount* and type in the percentage. Once you click *OK*, plate collections will show $1100 monthly.

Input the budget data program by program, saving the work frequently. When you are finished, select *OK* or select *Create New Budget* if you would like to set up a grant or top-level budget. You do not need to set up a top-level budget separately if your classes all total the complete budget.

If you only want an annual budget, key the total amount by account into the month of January without spreading across the months. Throughout the year, the comparison to budget reports will then show dollars left in the budget.

I recommend taking the time to spread it monthly. You'll have much more useful information.

Let's see what kind of reports we can generate once a budget is input. Open the sample nonprofit company if you would like to follow along with the data. Go to the Report Center and select *Budgets & Forecasts* or *Budgets* if you are using the Pro version. Select *Budget Overview*.

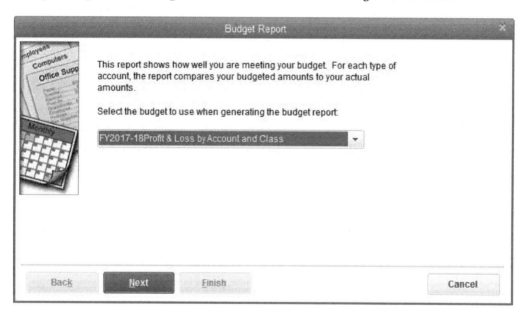

Select your budget report and hit *Next* to see options for the top of the report. We'll choose by month.

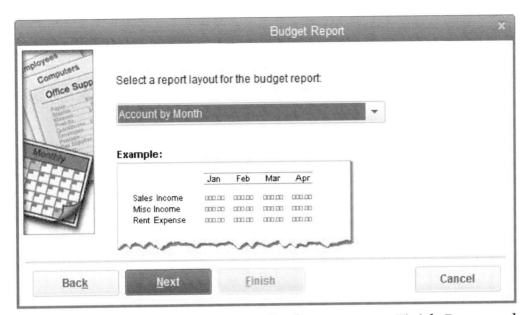

After you select *Next*, a dialog box will ask you to press *Finish*. Do so, and you will see a report displaying the budget by month.

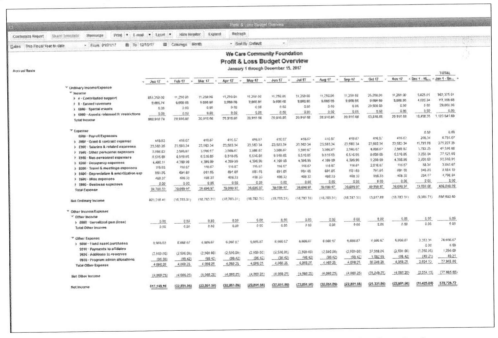

I realize this report is too small for you to read in the book, but you can scroll through it on your screen. As you compile your budgets, use this report to see the monthly trends in the budget and to check your data entry.

Comparing your actual revenues and expenses to budgets will help your church track their financial goals. Go back to the **Budgeting and Forecasting** reports and select *Budget vs Actual*. You'll see similar screens to the ones before. When it asks for the report layout, choose *Account by Class*.

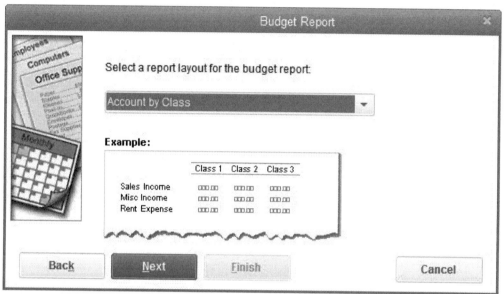

Click through the screens until the report is displayed.

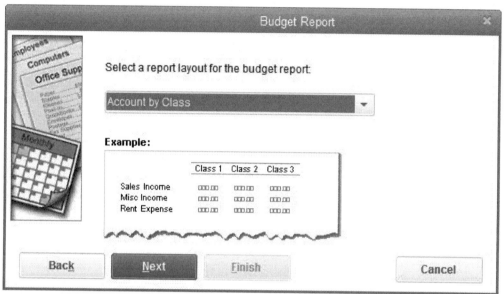

This report will show you how your programs expenses are comparing to their expectations. The **TOTAL** columns give you the variance for the entire church. Filter the report to each of the individual programs and give a copy to the program director each month.

Graphs are also available through the Report Center.

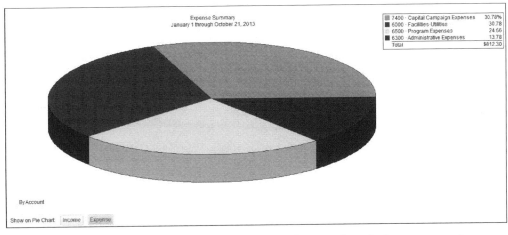

Near the bottom of the reports menus for each of the categories are standard graphs.

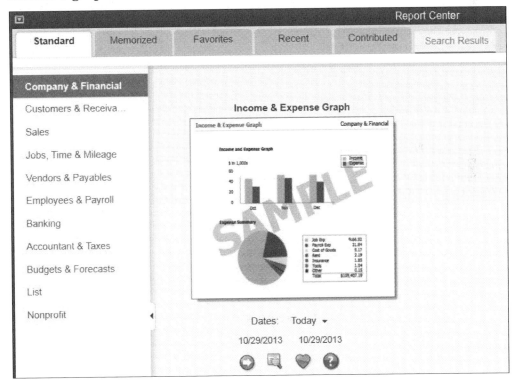

From the **Report Center**, select the area of interest and then scroll down to see the options. The graphs can be shown as bar graphs or pie charts displaying the breakdown of income or expenses. You decide the range of dates, programs, and/or customers.

Experiment with the various budget reports and graphs. Change the parameters and see what is most useful for your church. Export the reports to spreadsheets for further analysis or to make them more aesthetically pleasing.

C.   Forecasts

Budgets are typically created annually and stay stable throughout the year. **Forecasts** are used as a "what if" tool and are useful when change is anticipated. Perhaps you are considering hiring some new personnel to run an expanded children's program. You could create a forecast making assumptions on the additional costs of payroll and program expenses offset by any anticipated growth in your organization. The Premier and Nonprofit versions of QuickBooks offer this tool, but the Pro version does not.

The system can populate the data with the previous year's information by account and by month for you to change based on your new assumptions. This saves you from using the alternative: blank data fields for you to enter amounts from scratch for each account.

Go to *Company, Planning & Budgeting, Set up Forecasts.* The dialog boxes will look very similar to the **Budgets**.

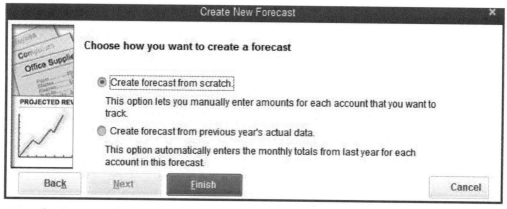

Specify the year for the forecast and select *Next*.

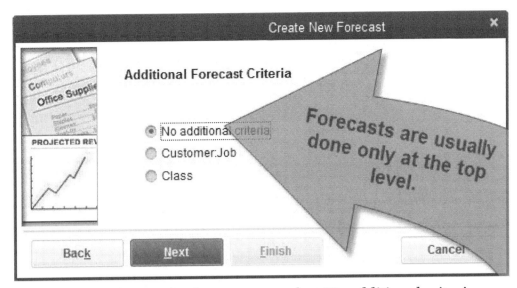

Unless you are forecasting by program, select *No additional criteria.*

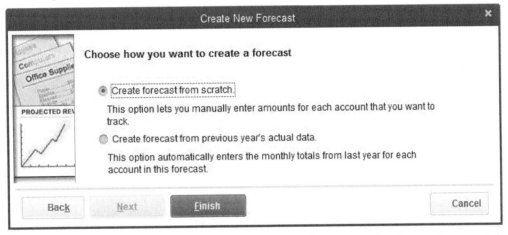

Create forecast from previous year's actual data is useful, especially if your collections have a normal variance throughout the year, i.e. high in spring around Easter, low in the summer, and high around the end of the year. You will see the differences in the months using the previous year's information. Otherwise, you can select *Create forecast from scratch* to enter all the data manually.

The forecast screen is in the same format as the screen to enter budgets. Enter the data by account and month, and the **ANNUAL TOTAL** column will sum up the data. Save frequently and select *OK* when finished.

D. Cash Flow Projector

The other tool QuickBooks offers is a cash-flow projector. It looks at the invoices not yet received in accounts receivables and those not yet paid in accounts payable. The system estimates the cash balance on a weekly basis for six weeks. It does not take into account any memorized bills or invoices, so you would need to input that data manually. Here is what the report looks like.

We Care Community Foundation
Weekly Cash Flow Projection
December 16, 2017 through January 27, 2018

	Current Week	12/17/17	12/24/17	12/31/17	1/7/18	1/14/18	1/21/18
Cash:							
Beginning Cash	417,647	417,647	437,266	456,885	476,504	496,123	515,742
Cash Receipts	0	19,619	19,619	19,619	19,619	19,619	19,619
Adjustments	0	0	0	0	0	0	0
Total Cash	417,647	437,266	456,885	476,504	496,123	515,742	535,361
Business Expenses:							
None	0	0	0	0	0	0	0
Adjustments	0	0	0	0	0	0	0
Total Business Expenses	0	0	0	0	0	0	0
Cash Available for Disbursement	417,647	437,266	456,885	476,504	496,123	515,742	535,361
Accounts Payable:							
Adjustments	0	0	0	0	0	0	0
Total Accounts Payable	0	0	0	0	0	0	0
Ending Cash Balance	417,647	437,266	456,885	476,504	496,123	515,742	535,361

Unless a significant amount of your donations and bills go through accounts receivable and accounts payable, most of the information will need to be entered manually. This is an area I'd recommend not worrying about until you are more familiar with the system.

> *We are coming close to the end! You have set up the system, learned to enter transactions, run reports, and understand how budgeting and forecasting work in QuickBooks. Let's move on to the next chapter to see what needs to be done at month end and at year end.*

XV. It's Month End and/or Year End—What do I do?

You have entered all your transaction and reconciled your bank account. Before you print out the financial statements for the treasurer or board, let's do a review of the data.

On the next page is a checklist of things to do each month and the additional requirements for year end. You may need to add a few other things for your particular organization, but this should get you started.

As you look down the list, you will see that we have covered almost everything except allocating the fund balances. In the first chapter, I explained how QuickBooks is designed for businesses which only have one equity account for net income to post to: Retained Earnings. Your church, however, has three different equity accounts: Unrestricted Net Assets, Temporarily Restricted Net Assets, and Permanently Restricted Net Assets. Additionally, you may have funds you need to track that carry forward year after year and are never closed out. In this chapter, I'll show you how to develop the funds report and how to record your net income (or loss) into the correct net assets account.

A sample Month-End Checklist is shown on the next page. There is a free pdf version on www.accountantbesideyou.com to print out and use.

A.   **Month & *Year-End Checklist**

Duties	Chapter	Completed
Enter all bills	X	
Enter any vendor credits	X	
Pay all bills	X	
Enter any manual checks	X	
Enter all online banking payments	X	
Enter all bank drafts	X	
Enter payroll	X	
Pay any payroll liabilities	X	
Enter any invoices required	IX	
Enter all donations	IX	
Enter any other receipts	IX	
Record postage expense	XI	
Enter credit card charges	X	
Reconcile credit card bill	XI	
Reconcile bank account to statement	XI	
Charge prepaid expenses	XIV	
Review *Receivable Aging* Report	XII	
Review *Payable Aging* Report	XII	
Review *Statement of Financial Position* (Balance Sheet)	XII	
Review *Statement of Activities by Class* (Income Statement)	XII	
Review *Income Statement Comparison to Budget*	XIII	
*Allocate fund balances	XIV	
*Set year-end closing date	XIV	
*Mail 1099s and 1096	XIV	
*Mail W-2s and W-3	XIV	

B. Reviewing your transactions

The first step is to be certain that everything has been accounted for correctly. I like to start with the Statement of Financial Position (or Balance Sheet as it is known in the for-profit world).

Go to *Reports, Company & Financial, Balance Sheet Standard*. Run the report with the month-end date you are closing. Be sure to select the *Accrual* option.

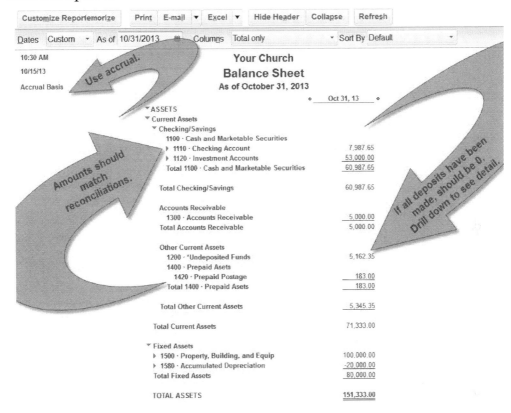

Make sure the report is expanded (you should see the **Collapse** button at the top). This report will list all the assets and liabilities for your church. I like to print out a copy to make notes on.

At the top are the cash accounts. Check your reconciliation summaries to see that each account ties to the reconciliation you performed. If you have a petty cash account, it should tie to the amount of cash in the drawer. Investments should tie to the brokerage reconciliations. If there are any differences, investigate and correct the errors or the reconciliations.

Undeposited funds should only have a balance if a deposit has not been taken to the bank. In this example, the undeposited funds account is showing a $5162.35 balance, but we know the church has made all the deposits. Let's drill down (double click) on the account and see what is left.

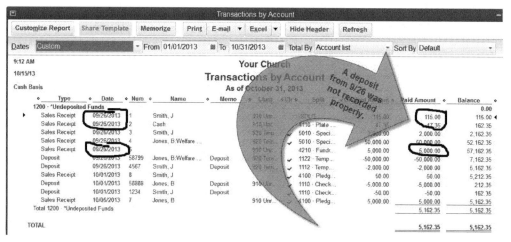

Looking through the detail, you can see the sales receipts go in and related deposit subtracted for all but three of the amounts. To correct this, go back to *Banking, Make Deposits,* and you will see all of the undeposited amounts.

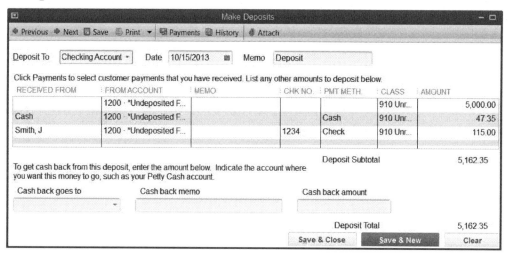

Select the receipts and change the transaction date to the date of the actual deposit. Select *Save & New.* Your balance sheet will no longer show undeposited funds as it has a $0 balance.

Next, print out the A/R Aging Report from the **Customers** report options. The date of the report should be the closing date. This report should tie to the receivable amounts.

For prepaid expenses, you can drill down on the balance to see what is included. On the balance sheet above, there is only a postage account; the balance of which should match the balance in the postage meter. Other expenses paid in advance can be recorded in the prepaid account. It is used to record property or liability insurance or items needed for a fundraising event that won't occur until next year.

A journal entry is required to move the expense out of the prepaid asset account and into an expense account. Here is an example entry.

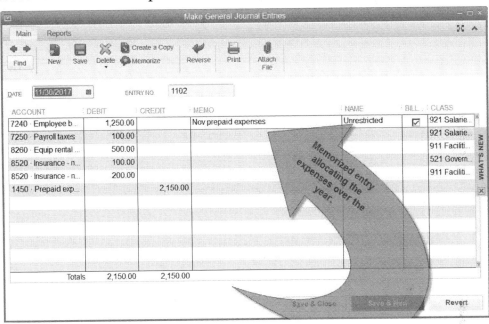

This organization is charging out various expenses paid in advance: copier rental, insurance, health benefits, etc. If the amount is the same each month, it should be memorized and automated.

To make certain the ending balance in the prepaid accounts are correct, you would need to go through the details and see what amount is leftover in each area. Set up a spreadsheet to summarize the balance by type and print it out.

	A	B	C	D
1		We Care Community		
2		Prepaid Balance		
3		11/30/2017		
4				
5				
6				
7		Property Insurance	1000	
8		D&O Insurance	4750	
9		HMO for Dec.	1250	
10		Total Acct 1450 Prepaid	$ 7,000	
11				

If you update it each month, this simple spreadsheet will save you lots of time at year end when the auditors want to know what is in the account. It will also keep you from overcharging the expense accounts.

> *I recommend setting up subaccounts for insurance, postage, and any other recurring prepaid expenses. You will still need to review them on a monthly basis, but it should go much quicker.*

Continue down the balance sheet this same way, documenting the balances.

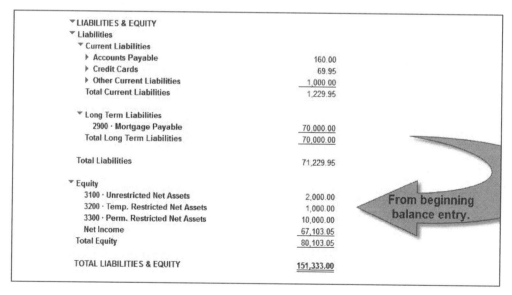

Print out the A/P Aging report from the **Vendors** reports for the accounts payable balance. The credit card balance will be any charges entered not yet paid.

You will really impress your treasurer (or your auditor) if you hand him a package each month of the balance sheet with supporting documentation for each area.

C.   **Allocate Fund Balances**

The bottom of the balance sheet has only one equity line called **Net Income**. But you need to know how much is in your restricted versus non-restricted net assets. To do this, run a **Profit & Loss by Class** report for the same time period.

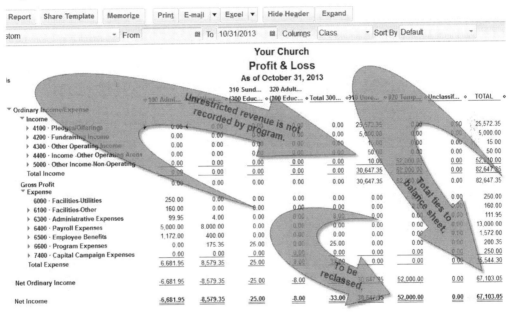

Monthly, you can review this report to see the breakout between restricted and unrestricted funds, but, at least annually, a journal entry will be necessary to reclassify the funds into their net asset accounts. The example below shows the entry necessary to reclass the restricted balance of $52,000 from the unrestricted equity account to the restricted account.

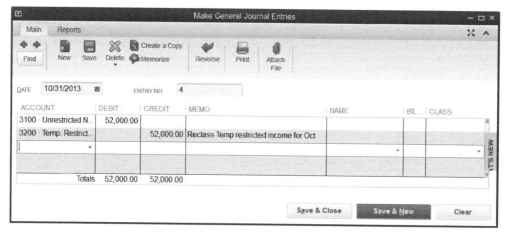

NOTE: Do Not Use Classes for this entry.

If you use an outside accountant, they may prefer to do the reclass for you. The system will warn you that this is out of the ordinary.

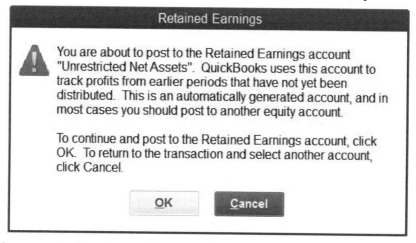

Once the year is closed out, the current net income will be rolled into the unrestricted net assets.

If you allocate the funds monthly, memorize the journal entry to save time next month.

D.   Restricted versus Unrestricted Cash

Another important item to review is the restricted versus unrestricted cash. If you have used the subaccount method, you will see your restricted cash on the detail balance sheet. Otherwise, you will need to design a report showing the cash basis of the various funds.

From the menu bar, select *Reports, Custom Reports, Summary.*

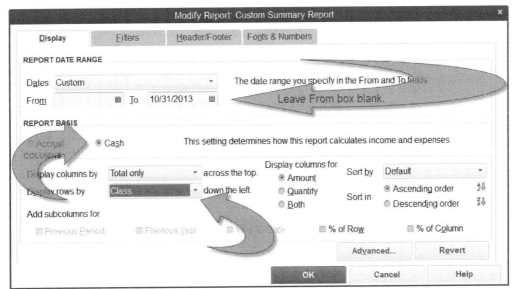

In the **Dates** box, select *Custom*. It will be at the bottom of the drop-down menu. Leave the first box blank after **From**, but type in the end of the last month (or period you are looking at) in the **To** box. Choose *Cash* under **Report Basis** and under **Columns**, choose **Display rows by** *Class*.

Select the *Filters* tab.

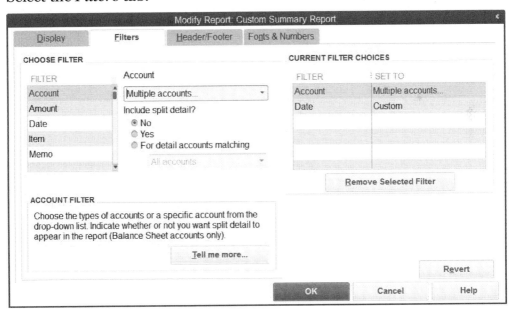

Under **Account**, select *Multiple accounts*. A drop-down menu will appear with your complete chart of accounts listed. I'm afraid the next part is a little tedious, but you can memorize the report and not have to do it again.

Click each account and subaccount **except** the cash and investment accounts, the accounts receivables, and the accounts payables (including payroll). All fixed and prepaid assets, mortgages, equity, revenue, and expense accounts should be selected. A check to the left will indicate the account was successfully selected. Select *OK*.

The **Header/Footer** tab can be selected to change the name of the report to *Funds Summary Report* or *Available Funds Report*. Select *OK*.

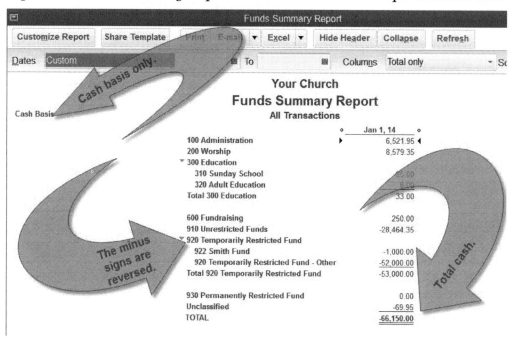

The **TOTAL** on this report will match the total cash and investments on your balance sheet. Of the $66,150 total cash, $53,000 is temporarily restricted.

This report is a little odd as the positive cash is shown as a negative. I'm afraid a report cannot be designed in QuickBooks to fix this, but you can export it to a spreadsheet, change the signs, summarize the data, and have something to hand out to the board.

E. Year-End Adjusting Entries

Any year-end journal entries outside of the normal monthly entries, including audit adjusting entries, should be recorded as of the last day of the accounting period (12/31/xx, if using a calendar year). If possible, record all regular donations and checks prior to that day (12/30/xx), so you know anything recorded on the last day of the year is an adjustment. This will allow you to run reports with and without the adjustments by changing the date.

F. Board Reports

Speaking of the governing board, I recommend you put together the following monthly reports for them and offer any more details as needed.

- Balance Sheet or Statement of Financial Position
- Budget versus Actual
- Profit & Loss by Class
- Funds Summary showing Restricted vs Non-restricted Cash

Additionally, you may wish to do some analysis and ratios showing:

percentage of pledges received to date and

percentage of donations received to budgeted amount.

G. Year-End Closing

After you have completed your year-end tasks, you will want to lock the data so no one can change it. This is what accountants call closing the books. In QuickBooks, there is not a true locking of the numbers. Instead, the data is password protected and warnings are issued if you try to post something to a closed period.

A closing date needs to be designated. Go to *Edit, Preferences, Accounting, Company Preferences* to see the following screen.

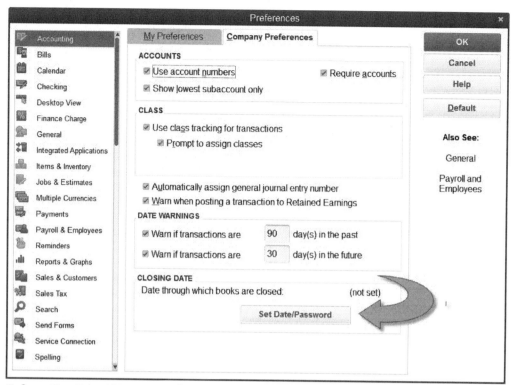

Select *Set Date/Password.*

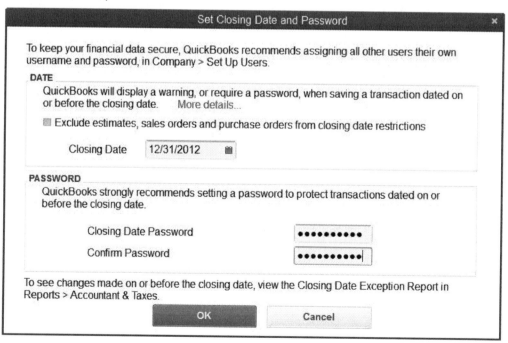

Choose the date of the fiscal year you just closed and designate a password. Anytime you post an entry that asks for this password, think to yourself, do I really want to do this?

> *If you forget the closing date password, the system will let the administrator delete it in the screen above and enter a new one. So protect the administrator's password!*

H.   Year-End Donor Acknowledgments

Another year-end task is acknowledging the donations made by your members and donors. IRS regulations do not require churches to provide acknowledgement for donations if the only benefit received by the donor is an *intangible religious benefit.* Per IRS Publication 1828 (www.irs.gov/pub/irs-pdf/p1828.pdf), intangible religious benefits include admission to a religious ceremony. Therefore, you are not required by law to send acknowledgements of pledges and donations received from your services. However, you are required to acknowledge any donation over $250 for **other** gifts. For additional information regarding donations, please read my *Church Accounting: The How-To Guide for Small & Growing Churches.*

Just because you are not required to do something does not mean you shouldn't do it. Thanking your members for their support is always a good idea. Additionally, you can use this communication as an internal accounting control tool and pledge reminder. At least annually, and preferably quarterly, send your members a list of contributions and remaining pledge balance. Besides including thanks, ask the member to contact a designated person not involved in the bookkeeping if there is a problem with their statement.

The designated person should then meet with the bookkeeper and investigate any discrepancies. If the member has made a donation that has not been recorded, the designated person will need to see if the check ever cleared the member's bank and, if so, who endorsed it.

> *The donation may have been lost in the mail, accidentally posted to the wrong member, or the bookkeeper may have stolen the money. Regardless, this would have been hard to catch without sending out the acknowledgment letters.*

Donor acknowledgment reports can be designed from the **Sales by Customer Detail** report in the **Sales** section of the reports menu.

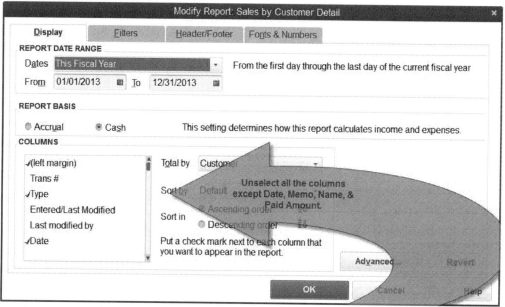

Under *Customize Report*, choose the period, (many churches like to send quarterly), and select *Cash* for the **Report Basis**. The **Columns** list determines which columns will display on the report. As you are sending this to your member, you only need the date, name, and amount. Include the memo if it is informative to the member. Now go to the **Header/Footer** tab.

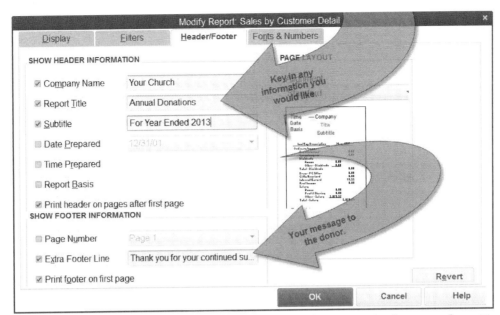

You can change the fonts or filter the report for a particular member. For now, select *OK*.

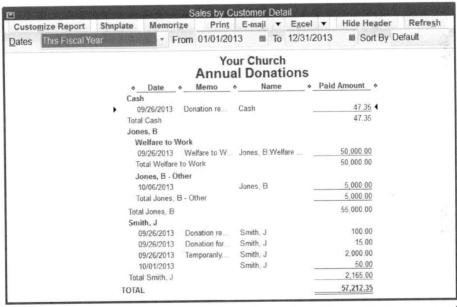

This report shows each member and their donations. But you need to separate this information in order to mail it out. Select *Print* to bring up some additional options.

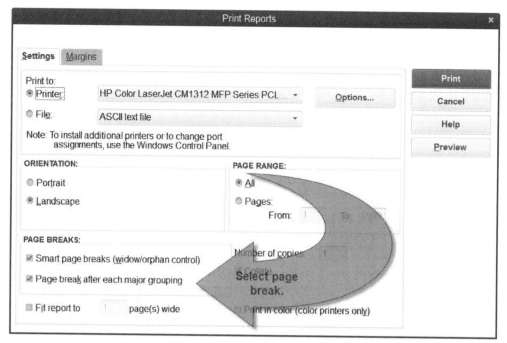

Select *Page break after each major grouping*. This will separate each member onto a new page. Select *Preview* to see the reports.

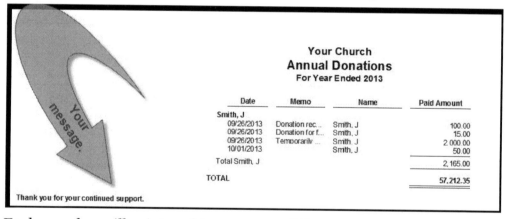

Each member will print on his own page. When you are ready, print and mail the reports to the members with a cover letter.

I.   Other Year-End Requirements

1.   1099 Filings

Annually, the IRS requires all organizations to send a Form 1099 to **Independent Contractors** paid over $600 (as of the time of this writing). 1099s are not sent to corporations or for payroll or reimbursements to employees. My book, *Church Accounting: The How-*

To Guide for Small & Growing Churches, explains in more detail who should be treated as an employee versus an independent contractor and how to filing requirements.

The good news is QuickBooks makes it easy to print these forms. Go to the menu bar and select *Vendors, Print/E-file 1099s, 1099 Wizard.*

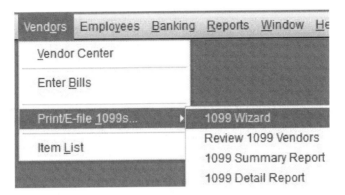

This will bring up QuickBooks' 1099 Wizard.

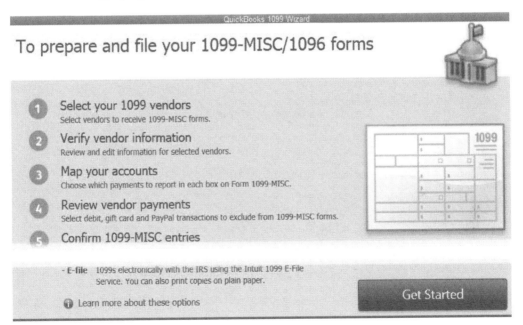

I'll walk you through the six steps. First, select *Get Started.*

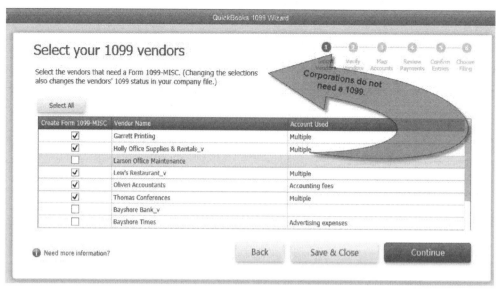

In this screen, you will select the vendors who are not a corporation. If you have a copy of the 1099s filed last year, take a look at them to make certain you are selecting the appropriate vendors.

Be aware, when you select or deselect a vendor, it changes the tax option in the vendor file. This is handy if you didn't set up a vendor as needing a 1099 when initially entering the vendor data. Once you have selected the vendors, select *Continue*.

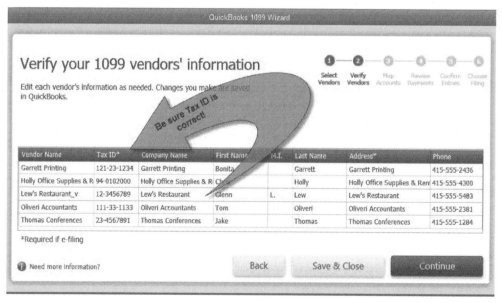

This screen will display the selected vendors, tax ID numbers, and addresses. Review this and make any corrections or changes. The **Tax ID** and the **Address** columns need to be complete and correct as they will be printed on the forms and mailed to the vendor and the IRS.

> *Even if you don't have the tax ID numbers of some vendors, go through the Wizard. It will show you which vendors were paid enough to need a 1099 and how many 1099 forms you will need to order. Select **Save & Close** and contact the vendors for any missing information. You can return to the Wizard when you have the data.*

Press *Continue* to see the next screen.

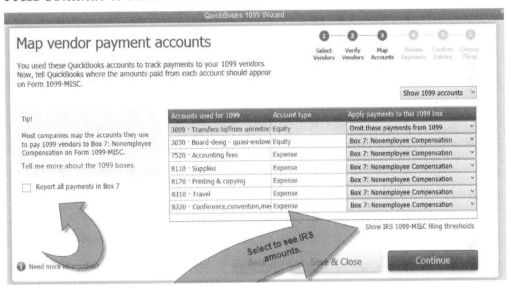

Notice the **Tip!** from QuickBooks. Unless your accountant tells you otherwise, you can select the box beside **Report all payments in Box 7.** Select *Show IRS 1099-MISC filing thresholds* near the bottom right corner.

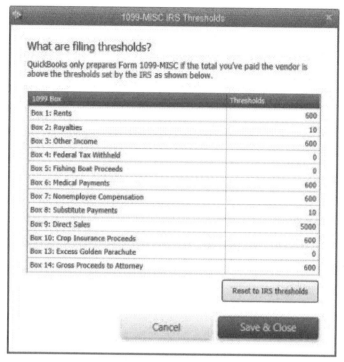

This lets you see what each box on the 1099 is for and the minimum amount paid which requires a 1099. Notice **Box 7: Nonemployee Compensation** has a minimum of $600.

If you see the message, **Your settings do not match the current IRS thresholds**, select *Reset to IRS thresholds*. Select *Save & Close* to go back to the previous screen. Then select *Continue*.

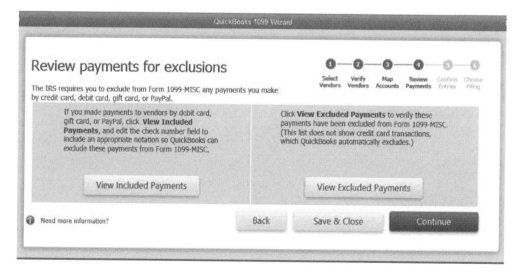

This screen allows you to see a report detailing payments made by credit card, debit card, or PayPal and whether they were excluded or not. Select *Continue* to confirm the vendor balances.

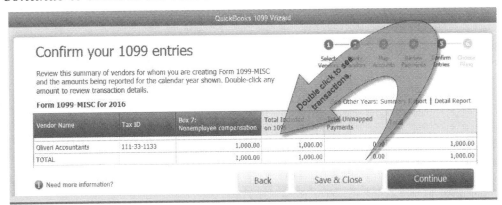

You can drill down on any entry to see the transactions included for any vendor slated to receive a 1099. Notice that even though we had selected five vendors for 1099s, only one is displayed here. Threshold payments were below the minimum required for the other four, so no 1099 is required. Select *Continue*.

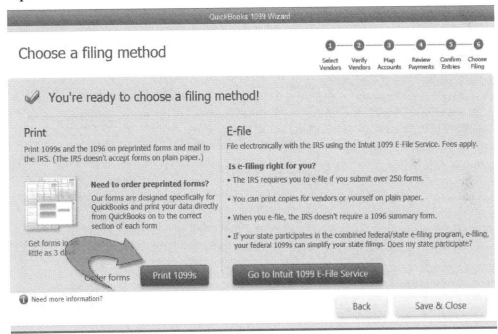

This screen allows you to E-file or print. Intuit will walk you through the necessary steps if you choose to E-file. For this example, select *Print 1099s*.

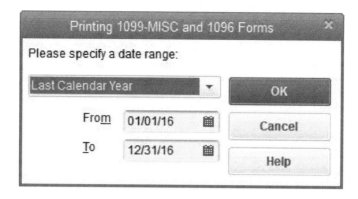

QuickBooks needs to know which year you want the 1099s to reflect. As 1099s must be mailed by the end of January in the year following the payments, this will usually be the *Last Calendar Year*. Select *OK*.

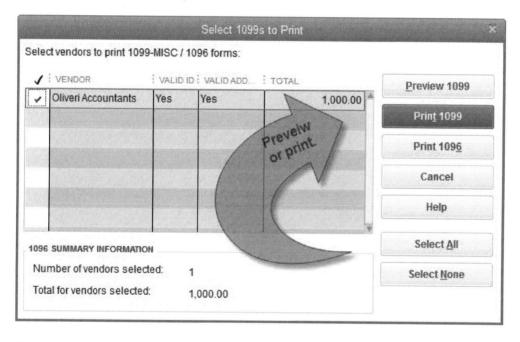

This screen lists the vendors who met the threshold amount and need a 1099. You can print just one or a range of the vendors by clicking the box next to their name.

Along the right side of the screen, you have options to preview the form or print it. There is also an option to print Form 1096, a summary transmittal form required by the IRS. Select *Print 1096*.

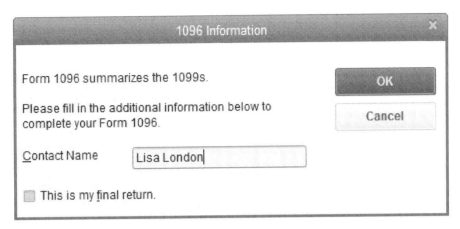

You will need to type in the name of the person the IRS should contact at your church if there are any problems and choose *OK*. The form will then be available to print or preview on the screen.

Back on the **Select 1099s to Print** screen, select *Preview 1099*.

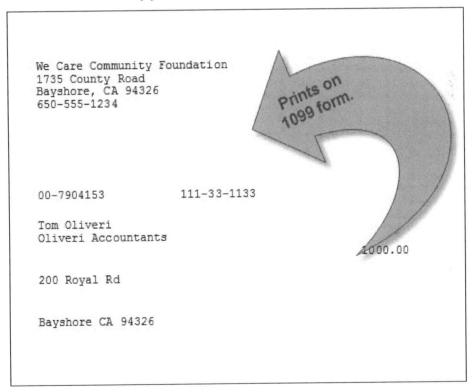

This is an example of the data that is printed. Hold up the print out to a blank IRS Form 1099 to see if the numbers fit the boxes correctly. Using the dialog box after selecting *Print, Align*, you can change the margins so the data prints on the form correctly.

2.   File W-2s for Employees

By the end of January, you will need to send W-2s to your employees.

From the IRS website http://www.irs.gov/uac/Form-W-2,-Wage-and-Tax-Statement:

> Every employer engaged in a trade or business who pays remuneration, including noncash payments of $600 or more for the year (all amounts if any income, social security, or Medicare tax was withheld) for services performed by an employee must file a Form W-2 for each employee (even if the employee is related to the employer) from whom:
>
> • Income, Social Security, or Medicare tax was withheld.
> • Income tax would have been withheld if the employee had claimed no more than one withholding allowance or had not claimed exemption from withholding on Form W-4, Employee's Withholding Allowance Certificate.

If you are using an outside payroll service, they should prepare and possibly mail the W-2s to employees and file Form W-3, the summary transmittal, to the IRS with copies of the W-2s. If you are preparing them in-house, refer to my *Church Accounting: The How-To Guide for Small & Growing Churches* for detailed instructions and requirements.

Great job! You've made it through all of the transactions for a year and know how to design and produce reports. In the next chapter, I'll go over some miscellaneous tasks that may come up.

XVI.   What About...???

We've covered the essentials of setting up your accounting system and running it efficiently. Until this point, the last thing I wanted to do was overwhelm you with lots of additional information about things that may not come up. In this last chapter, we'll address how to account for a few non-ordinary items, system features you may find useful, and reports you will probably need to run for your annual audit. You can also check my website www.accountantbesideyou.com for updated information and downloads to assist you.

A.   How Do I Account For ...?

1.   Mission Trips or Member-Specific Accounts

If your church offers mission trips or other events which the members raise money for their church-related expenses, there are a few extra steps to take. You will need to set up the system to track the fundraisers and revenue coming in by member and also track the expenses by member.

First let's add an item called Mission Fundraiser. Go to *Lists, Item List, Item, Add New*. Next add a new subclass under fundraisers called Mission Trip. To do this, go to *Lists, Class List, Class, Add New*. When the new class box appears, select *Subclass of* and chose Fundraisers.

Next, add each person going on the trip as a **Customer** with a **Job** called Mission Trip. See Chapter VI for how to set up Customer:Job.

With these accounts set up, you are ready to record the money coming in. If the donation does not need to be kept under the donor's name (i.e. cash received at a fundraiser), use the Customer:Job name of the person going in the sales receipt screen. Select the **Item** to be *Mission Fundraiser*, adjust the description as necessary, and use the new subclass you set up as the **Class.**

If the fundraiser is being shared by several members, you can allocate the receipts using the **Create Batch Invoices** option in the Premier & Nonprofit versions. See my video at accountantbesideyou.com/blog/mission-trips for details.

If a check or other donation was received, it needs to be under the actual donor's name. In this case, use the mission trip item and a mission trip class under the actual donor's name. Then under the attendees customer:job name, create an invoice for the donation under the mission job and class and enter the amount of the donation.

You now have the same donation in twice, so you'll need to enter a credit under the customer account of the attendee. Under *Customers, Create Credit Memos*, issue a credit for the amount of the donation. Select *Use credit to apply to invoice*. This time, use only the customer name, not the job. That way the job will show the donation, but the overall account for the person going does not show the additional amount. Be sure to use the same Mission Trip class.

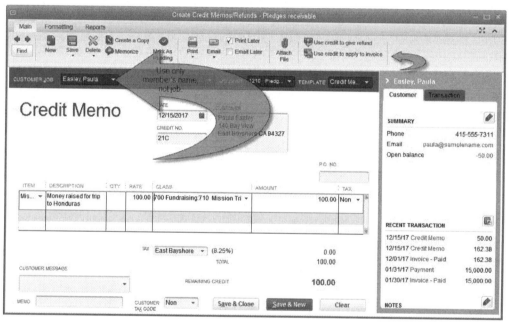

When the trip expenses need to be paid, you will go to the **Enter Bills** screen. In the following example, I'm assuming we bought tee shirts for the trip. The **Expense Account** is supplies. If this were the airline bill, it would be travel. Notice the expense is allocated to everyone going on the trip via the **Customer:Job** column. The **Class** goes to the subclass for the mission trip. **Save & Close**.

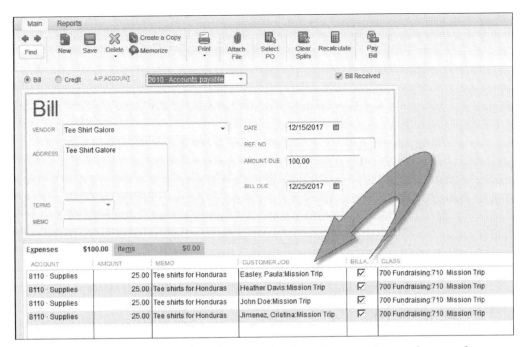

To see how much money has been raised and spent by each member, we need to go to the **Job Profitability Detail Report.**

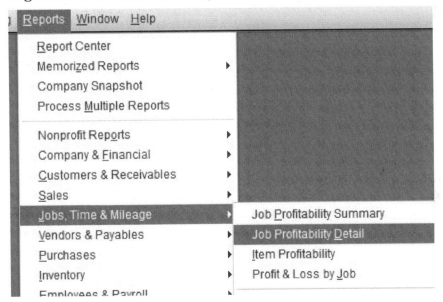

A screen will pop up with a drop-down box for you to select which member you are running the report for.

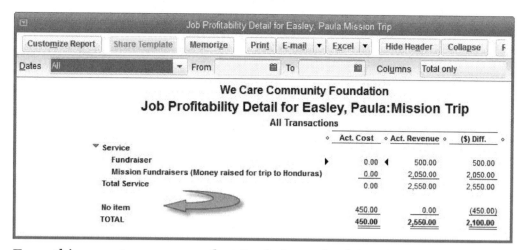

From this report, we can see that Paula has raised $2550 towards the trip and has spent $450. Since the bills were entered as Expense accounts instead of as Items, the system does not detail out the expenditures. You can, however, drill down to see the detail. If you would like the report to show the detail, set up items for each type of expenditures, i.e. air travel, food, etc.

Once you know what each member has raised and spent, you may wish to know how the total trip is looking. To do this, you will design a *Profit & Loss Statement by Class* customized for the mission trip.

Go to *Reports, Company & Financial, Profit & Loss by Class*. When the report comes up, select *Customize Report* in the upper left hand corner.

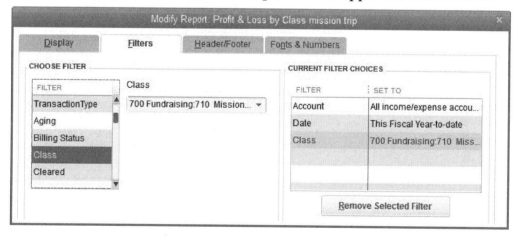

Under the **Filters** tab, select *Class* and then the Mission Trip sub class. Hit *OK*. You will now have a report showing the total Mission Trip revenue and expenses.

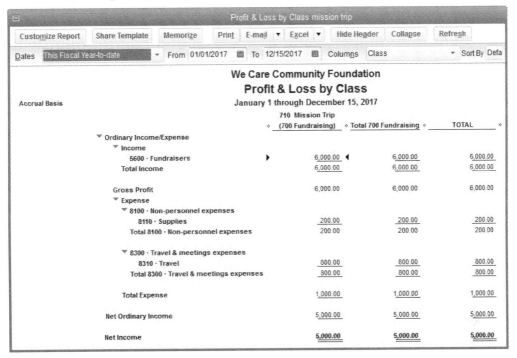

Memorize the report to save time next month.

2.   Fundraisers

What I recommend for tracking fundraisers will seem a bit odd. When you have a fundraiser, the governing board doesn't typically ask for the details of tickets sales versus sponsorship, etc. They want to know how much money the fundraiser netted (money in less the money paid out). So I suggest you set up a parent account with an income type for each fundraiser. There can be as few as two subaccounts or as many as your system will hold.

If you look at the chart of accounts in the appendix, you will see I have set up a parent account for **Fundraising Income**. Under it are two events, and each event has a revenue and an expense subaccount. The unusual thing is that the expenses have an income type. This allows the reports to show only the net profit from the fundraiser on the financial statements.

◦ 4200 · Fundraising Income	Income
◦4210 · Fundraising Event 1	Income
◦4211 · Event 1 Revenues	Income
◦4215 · Event 1 Expenses	Income
◦4220 · Fundraising Event 2	Income
◦4221 · Event 2 Revenues	Income
◦4225 · Event 2 Expense	Income

If you would like to track the types of revenues received or detail types of expenses from a fundraiser, set up items for each (sponsorship, ticket sales, printing, advertising, etc.). Reports can then be run on the items.

3. In-Kind Donations

There are times churches receive donations of items or professional services instead of cash. These are called in-kind donations. Typical examples of in-kind donations are computers, paintings, office supplies, legal services (this is only considered an in-kind donation if the church would have otherwise had to pay for the service), or use of space without being charged rent.

*Every church should have written guidelines for accepting **in-kind donations**. You do not have to accept everything that is offered. If the church cannot use it or sell it, do not accept it.*

When you receive an in-kind gift, it is appropriate to acknowledge it. However, do not value the gift in the acknowledgement; simply thank them for the item. For the donor's tax purposes, valuation is the donor's responsibility. An exception to that rule is the donation of a car, boat, or plane received for resell. Call your accountant or ask a member who is a CPA how to handle tax implications and reporting of vehicle donations or see my book, *Church Accounting: The How-To Guide for Small & Growing Churches.*

To record an in-kind donation in QuickBooks, set up an income account titled *In-Kind Contribution* and an expense account titled *Donated*

Goods & Services. In the proposed chart of accounts in the appendix, these are numbered 4380 and 6800, respectively.

If you plan to use the items donated, you can enter the transaction as a journal entry or as a sales receipt. If you enter it as a sales receipt, you will need to set up items related to the donation. This method is useful if you a have large number of in-kind donations and would like to run an item report to see what types of goods are being received. Otherwise, it is probably easier to record it as a journal entry.

From the menu bar, select Company, Make General Journal Entries.

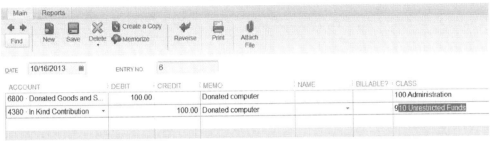

Use your best estimate to value the donation. Charge the donated goods expense line as a **DEBIT** and the in-kind contribution as a **CREDIT** for the same amount, assigning it to the appropriate program or fund. Select *Save & Close* and you are finished.

If you are using the donated goods or services, you don't need to do anything else in QuickBooks. However, if you sell the donated item, you will need to record the sale. Go back to the journal entry screen.

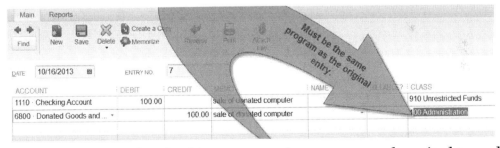

This time, **DEBIT** the checking account the money was deposited to and **CREDIT** the donated goods expense. You must be certain to assign the donated good to the same program as the original entry.

4. Volunteer Hours

Your church probably has a lot of people who generously give their time to assist in various programs. If you would like to quantify this time, use the **Timesheet** function in QuickBooks.

First you will need to set the preferences to allow time tracking. From the menu, choose *Edit, Preferences, Time & Expense, Company Preferences.*

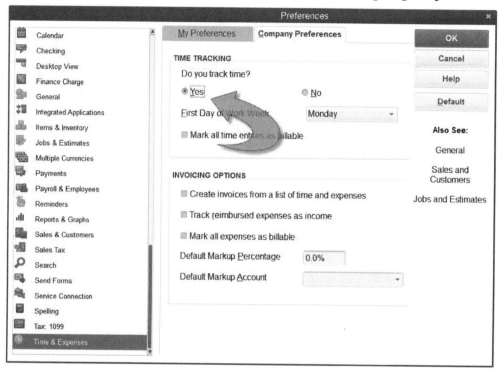

Select *Yes* under **Do you track time?** and leave the other boxes blank. Hit *OK* to close. QuickBooks will then close all of the open windows in order to save the change in the preference.

Next, you will set up items for the different types of volunteer duties. Go to the new item screen (*Lists, Item List, Item, New*). Select **Type** to be *Service* with a **Rate** of *$0*. Enter the name of the donated service under **Item Name/Number**. Select *Donated goods and services* for the **Account** box. Hit *OK*.

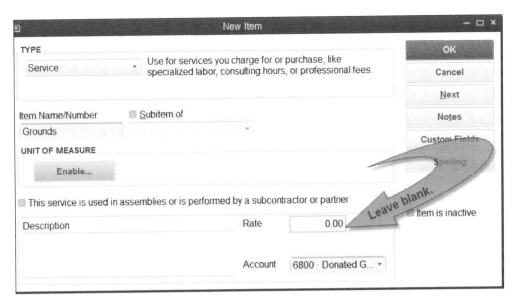

The names of your volunteers must be entered in the **Other Names List**. Go to *Lists, Other Names List, Other Names, New.*

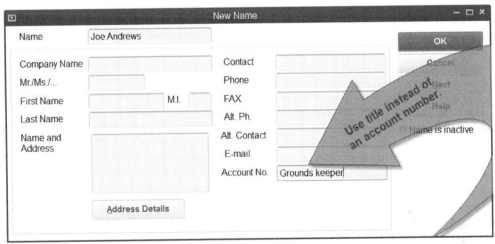

Enter the volunteer's name, email, and phone numbers. Use the **Account No.** box to input the title of his primary responsibility. You will then be able to run reports by the account number to pull up all volunteers who are plumbers, lawyers, teachers, administrative help, etc.

Run the other names report by going to Reports, List, Other Names Contact List, Customize Report.

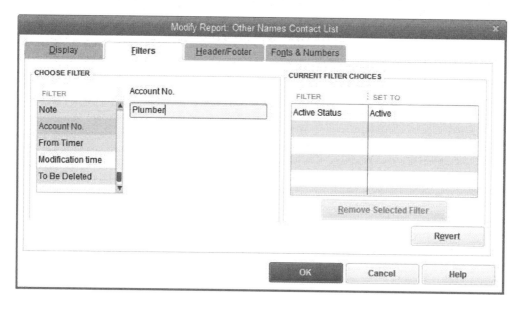

Choose the **Filters** tab in the **Modify Report** that appears. Scroll down the list under FILTER and highlight *Account No.* Type *Plumber* (or other title) in the box and select *OK* to see a report with names and contact information of everyone you've designated as a plumber.

To enter the time, go to the menu bar and select *Employees, Enter Time, Time/Enter Single Activity.*

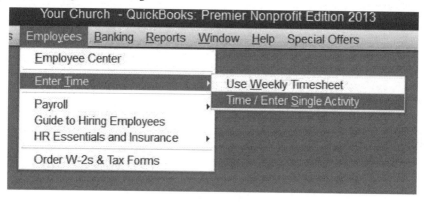

Notice the two choices above. You can enter one item of time or you can fill in a timesheet for the week. Let's enter a single activity first.

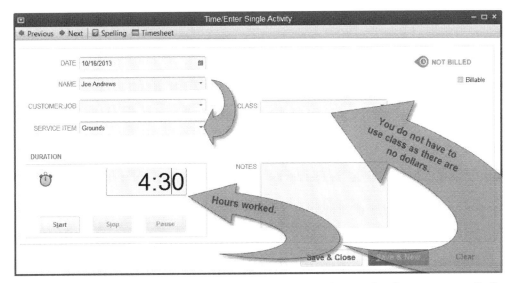

Enter the date the volunteer work was performed, the name of the volunteer, and the service item related to his work. Then key in the hours worked under **DURATION**. In this example, Joe worked 4 ½ hours on the grounds on October 16.

Do not select the icon labeled **Timesheet** along the top menu bar before you save your work. This will take you to the same screen as the **Use Weekly Timesheet** from the menu, but will clear the data from this screen if you haven't saved it. After selecting *Save & New*, you may select the *Timesheet* icon.

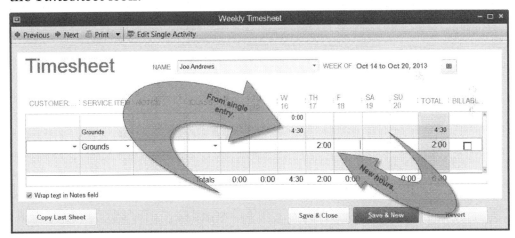

Once you input Joe's name and make sure the **WEEK OF** box is selected correctly, you will see the entry we just posted through the single activity screen. Now you can input hours under different service items and different days. Save this screen and let's look at the report options. From the Report Center, select *Jobs, Time & Mileage*.

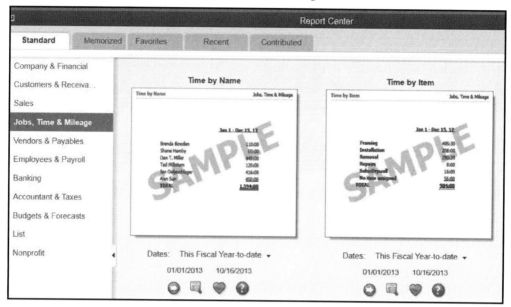

There are two standard reports, **Time by Name** and **Time by Item**. As you are by now familiar with how to filter and run reports, I'll skip a screen shot of the reports.

5.   Show a Reserve Account on the Income Statement

Many churches like to set up a reserve at a bank and designate an amount of money to be transferred to that account on a monthly or quarterly basis. Because the reserve account is a bank or investment account, the transfer of the funds does not show on the income statement.

If your governing board or treasurer would like to see the amount of money moved to the reserve account on the income statement, add two accounts to your chart of accounts list: **Reserve Transfer Deposit** and **Reserve Transfer Payment**. Add the accounts by selecting *Lists, Chart of Accounts, Account, New*. Under **Other Account Types,** select the *Other Income* account type and hit *Continue*.

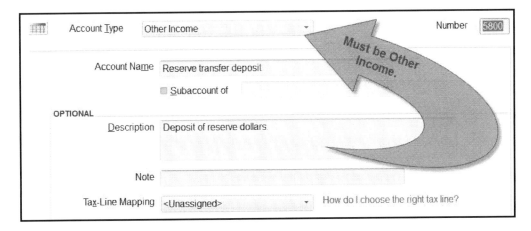

The deposit account must have an account type of *Other Income* in order to show below the operating expense line. Save this account and enter the payment account.

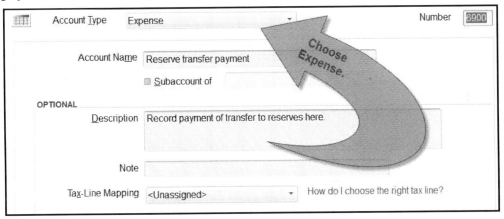

This time you will select an account type of *Expense* and save the entry.

When you write the check to make the transfer, instead of assigning it to the investment account, charge it to the reserve transfer payment account.

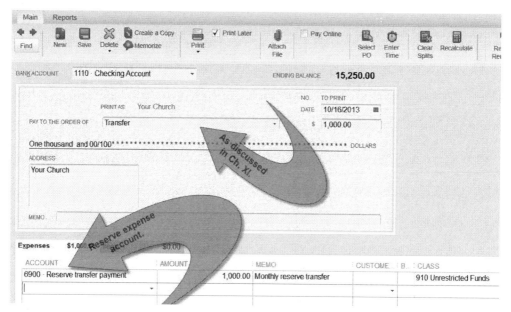

For the deposit, go to *Banking, Make Deposits.*

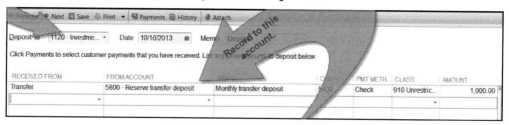

On the screen to input deposits, you will change the **Deposit to** account in the upper left corner to your investment account. The **FROM ACCOUNT** should be the *Reserve transfer deposit* account. Once saved, your income statement will show the expense in operations and the deposit as other income.

Your Church
Statement of Financial Income and Expense
January through October 2013

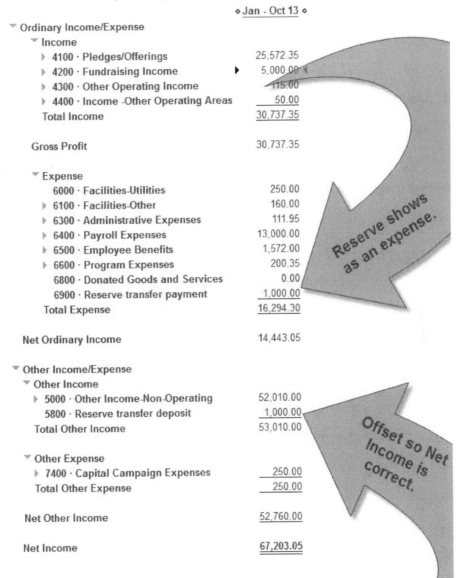

	◇ Jan - Oct 13 ◇
▼ Ordinary Income/Expense	
▼ Income	
▷ 4100 · Pledges/Offerings	25,572.35
▷ 4200 · Fundraising Income	5,000.00
▷ 4300 · Other Operating Income	115.00
▷ 4400 · Income -Other Operating Areas	50.00
Total Income	30,737.35
Gross Profit	30,737.35
▼ Expense	
6000 · Facilities-Utilities	250.00
▷ 6100 · Facilities-Other	160.00
▷ 6300 · Administrative Expenses	111.95
▷ 6400 · Payroll Expenses	13,000.00
▷ 6500 · Employee Benefits	1,572.00
▷ 6600 · Program Expenses	200.35
6800 · Donated Goods and Services	0.00
6900 · Reserve transfer payment	1,000.00
Total Expense	16,294.30
Net Ordinary Income	14,443.05
▼ Other Income/Expense	
▼ Other Income	
▷ 5000 · Other Income-Non-Operating	52,010.00
5800 · Reserve transfer deposit	1,000.00
Total Other Income	53,010.00
▼ Other Expense	
▷ 7400 · Capital Campaign Expenses	250.00
Total Other Expense	250.00
Net Other Income	52,760.00
Net Income	67,203.05

Reserve shows as an expense.

Offset so Net Income is correct.

6. Inter-fund Transfers

When a church receives a donation, it is recorded it in the fund or program it was designated for or into the general unrestricted fund. Sometimes, the governing board may decide to allocate some of the unrestricted funds into a specific program or fund. Assuming the funds are all being handled through the same cash account, you will need to record an inter-fund transfer.

To do this, set up a new **Other Expense** account called **Inter-Fund Transfers**. Go to *Company, Make General Journal Entries.*

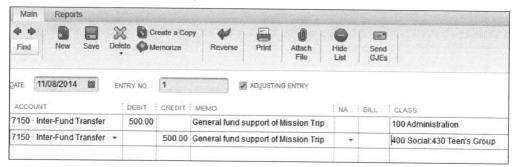

Record a debit to the Inter-Fund account for the amount that is being transferred. Assign the class of the fund **GIVING** the money. On the next line, use the same account, but change the class to the **RECEIVING** fund.

If you run a **Profit & Loss by Class**, the net impact will be correct for each fund. There is no net impact on the consolidated Profit & Loss, as the entry cancels itself out.

B. How Do I ...???

1. Set Up Multiple-Users and Passwords

QuickBooks allows you to set up multiple users and limit what they can do in the system. If you pay for additional licenses, these users can access the system from your computer network. If you have a single-user license, all of the users must work on only one machine.

If you would like to purchase additional licenses, follow the next screen.

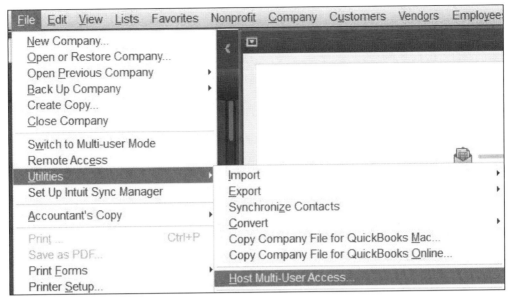

A dialog box will appear asking if you are hosting the company file on this computer for others to access. Select *Yes* and the system will take you to Intuit's website to purchase additional licenses.

However, if every user works on just one computer, go to *Company, Set Up Users & Passwords, Set Up Users.*

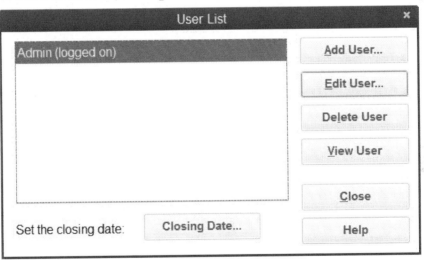

Currently, the administrator does not have a password. If you are going to allow other users on the system, you must first set up an administrator's password. To do this, highlight *Admin* and select *Edit User.*

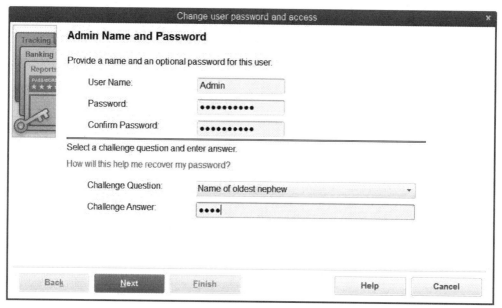

Enter a strong password (at least 6 characters with numbers or symbols as well as letters). Do not make it a variation of the church's name or something anyone who knows you could figure out. Type in the password a second time to make sure there is no mistake and choose a challenge question and answer. The challenge question is to allow you to reset the password if you forget it. Just make sure you don't forget the answer to the challenge question!

Select *Next* to see the following screen.

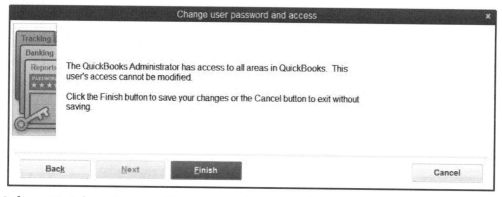

Select *Finish* and you will be taken back to the **User List** screen. Select *Add User*.

Here we will add a volunteer who enters the bills and volunteer time sheets. We need to give her a user name and password and hit *Next*.

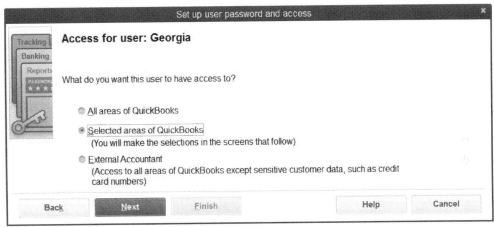

She only needs to use certain areas of QuickBooks, so choose *Selected areas of QuickBooks* and hit *Next*.

You will be taken through a series of screens pertaining to each area of QuickBooks where you will select whether the user has no access, full access, or selective access. Rather than printing each screen here, I'll show an example.

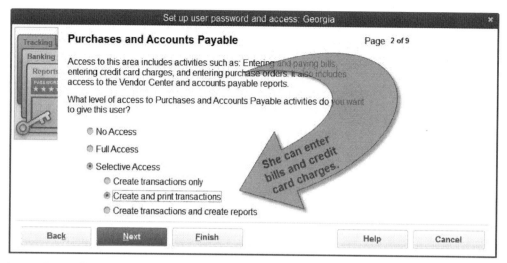

Georgia will now be able to enter the bills and credit card charges and print out any transactions she may want you to look at but cannot look at donor records or make journal entries.

After going through the nine screens, you will see a summary of your selections.

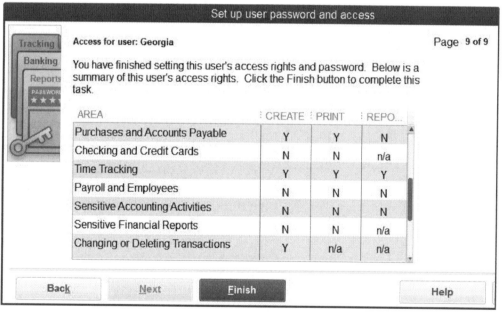

Georgia can now enter and print reports on volunteer time, and she can enter bills in accounts payable. In accounts payable, she can only change or delete transactions.

The treasurer and pastor would probably like to see financial reports in QuickBooks. When setting them up, choose *Selective Access* and only give permission in the **Sensitive Financial Reporting** screen.

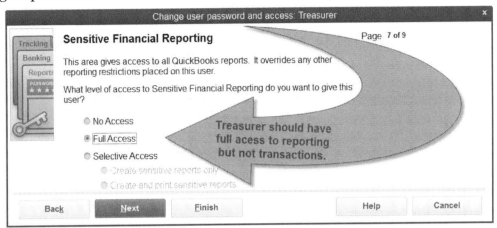

Now the treasurer can review the financials but not make any changes to the transactions.

2.   Send an Accountant Copy

If you have an accountant to review your books at the end of the month, quarter, or year, there is a handy tool in QuickBooks to facilitate this. **Accountant's Copy** is an option to send a working file to your CPA. Assuming he has an accountant version of QuickBooks, he can make changes in the file and send it back to you to upload. His changes will not affect any new transactions you have since put in the system.

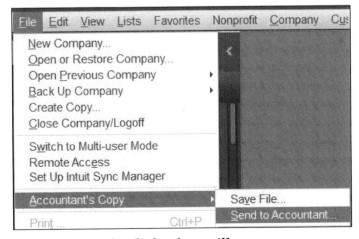

Follow the steps above and a dialog box will appear.

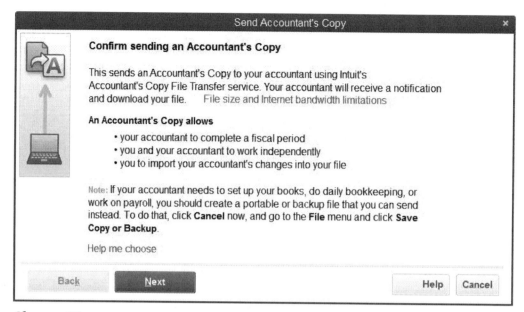

Choose *Next*.

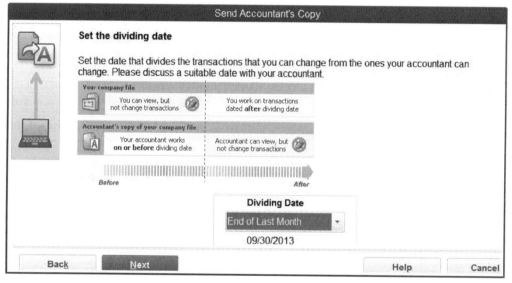

The **Dividing Date** delineates which periods the accountant can make changes to and which you can be working on. By selecting *End of Last Month*, you can post current transactions but no corrections to previous months. Select *Next* to input the email address it should be sent to and what address it should be sent from. From there, select *Next* again to see this step.

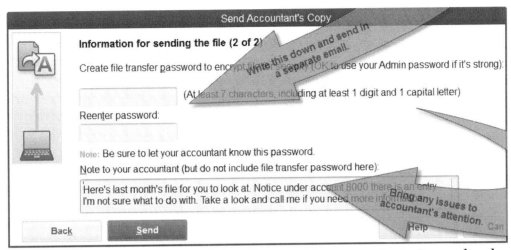

Here you will set a password for the outside accountant. It can be the same as your administrator password as he will also need that. As your outside accountant should not have access to the church's money, this should not be a control issue. It should be written down and emailed to him separately. The bottom part of the screen allows you to convey any information which might be helpful. Select *Send* and numerous informational dialog boxes will appear.

Once the accountant has reviewed the files, he can make changes and send the file back to you.

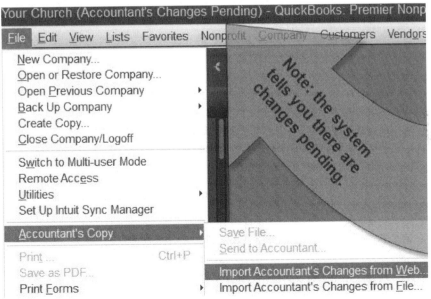

An email will be sent stating accountant changes are available. To upload these changes, select *File, Accountant's Copy, Import Accountant's Changes from Web*. A screen with a list of changes will appear. Select *Expand* to see the details in the account.

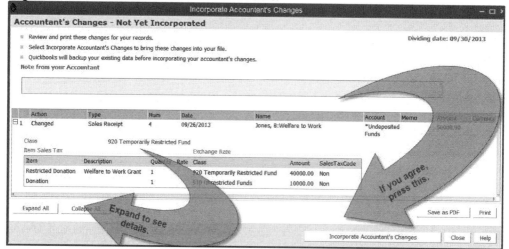

In this example, the accountant noticed the $50,000 receipt included $10,000 of unrestricted giving. He changed the sales receipt entry to move $10,000 into unrestricted funds. If you agree, select *Incorporate Accountant's Changes*.

Several dialog boxes will appear including a requirement to backup your system before the change will be recorded. Once you have backed up and accepted the changes, the system confirms they were incorporated and asks if you would like to change the closing date. If you change the closing date to the last month, this keeps anyone from accidentally recording any transactions after the accountant has looked at it.

3. Record a Mortgage

If your church has a mortgage, you will need to set up a few accounts before you get started. Under *Lists, Chart of Accounts*, you will need to add the following (if you haven't already):

- a **Fixed Asset** account to record the building or land. This may also be called Construction in Progress for a building under construction.
- a **Long-Term Liability** account to record the loan
- a **Prepaid Asset** account for any escrow payments
- **Expense** accounts for any loan expenses.

Additionally, you will need to set up your mortgage company as a vendor.

When you receive the money for the loan, you can go through **Make Deposit** screen. Be sure to show the receipt from the mortgage holder, and the account must be the liability account.

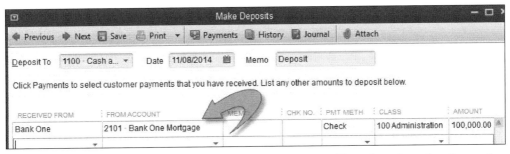

When you pay for the building or land, you will write the check to the seller charging the appropriate fixed asset account. This way, the accounting records show the cash being received and paid out and an asset with its related liability.

To make loan payments, go to *Enter Bills*. Select the mortgage holder as the **Vendor.**

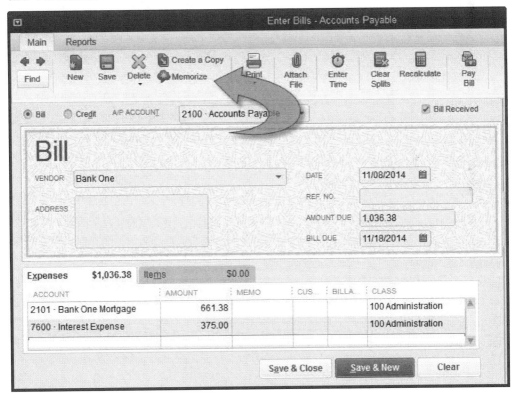

Using either the notice from the bank or an amortization schedule, split the payment between principal and interest payments. If you have an escrow, record it to the escrow account. *Memorize* the entry to remind you the following month. You will need to adjust the principal and interest numbers each time, but it will save you entering the rest of the data.

There is an option called **Loan Manger** option under **Banking,** but it is more informational than helpful. The What-If scenarios are useful, if you would like to see the impact of a change in interest rates or number of payments.

4.   Send a Thank You from the Receipts Screen

Here's a way to email a donor a thank-you note directly from the sales receipt screen. It takes a bit of time to design and layout the template, but once you do, it is easy to access for future donations. The steps may be a bit hard to follow, so go to **www.accountantbesideyou.com** where I have a complementary video to guide you through it.

Go to *Customers, Enter Sales Receipts.*

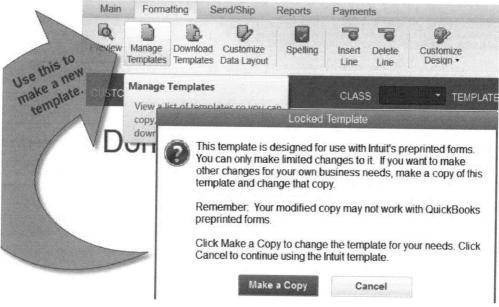

From the sales receipt screen, select *Formatting, Manage Templates.* A warning box may appear. Select *Make a Copy.* Otherwise you will see a screen listing all of the templates. Highlight the one you wish to copy and select *Copy* at the bottom left corner and *OK*. The screen below will appear.

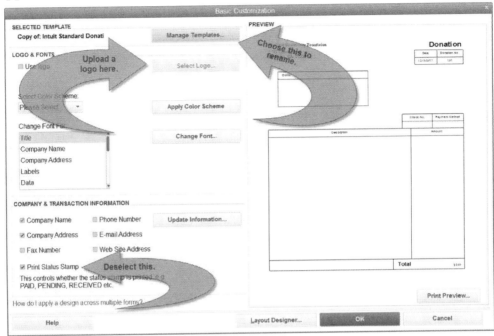

The screen will show the default sales or donation receipt. Under **LOGO & FONTS**, you can upload your church's logo to be shown on the receipt. **COMPANY & TRANSACTION INFORMATION** lets you select what information you would like the receipt to show. Deselect the **Print Status Stamp** as we are going to make this a thank-you note instead of a sales receipt.

The template needs a new, descriptive name. Select *Manage Templates* to see the following screen.

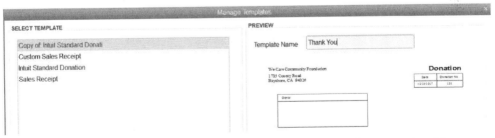

Highlight *Copy of Intuit Standard Donation* (or *Sales Receipt* if you are not using the Nonprofit edition). In the box next to **Template Name**, input a new name. I have used *Thank You*. Select *OK* to save.

You will be directed back to the **Basic Customization** screen. Choose *Additional Customization* at the bottom of the screen to alter the rows and columns.

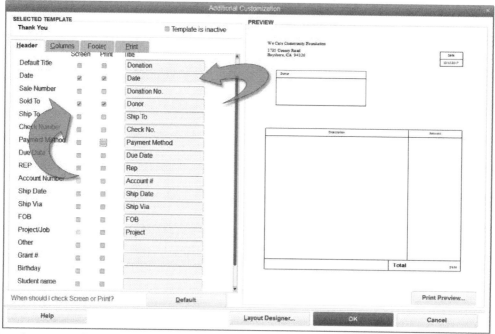

Under **Header**, you can choose what will display on the screen versus what will show up when you print. For a thank-you note, you need the date and the donor (select **Sold To**).

Now select the **Columns** tab.

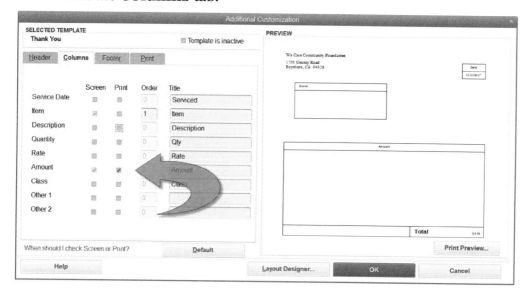

The only column we need is *Amount.* You can even erase the word **Amount** out of the box. Select the **Footer** screen and unselect all of the areas. Don't worry about the **Print** tab. Now it is time to change the way the receipt looks.

We'll do that by selecting *Layout Designer.* There is an irritating warning box that pops up every time you change an option, but don't worry about it.

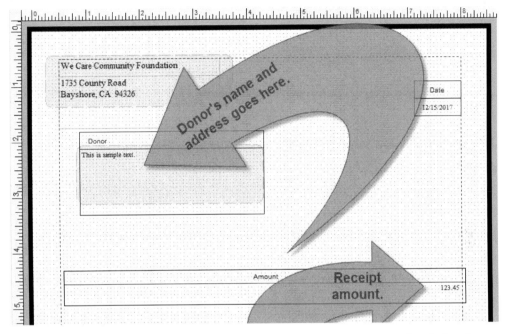

This is where it gets a little tedious. You need to get rid of the boxes around the information, add some text thanking the donor, and move things around a bit.

*Most importantly, the receipt **must** include a statement indicating:*

"The donor did not receive goods or services in exchange for their donation other than intangible religious benefits."

*Unless something WAS received. If so, it is considered a quid pro quo gift. Refer to **Church Accounting: The How-To Guide for Small & Growing Churches** for specifics on acknowledging donations.*

If you double click on a field, a **Properties** dialog box will appear.

Within this box, you can justify the print and change the font size, style, and color. Select *Font* and change it to *Times New Roman Size 14*. Now select *Border*.

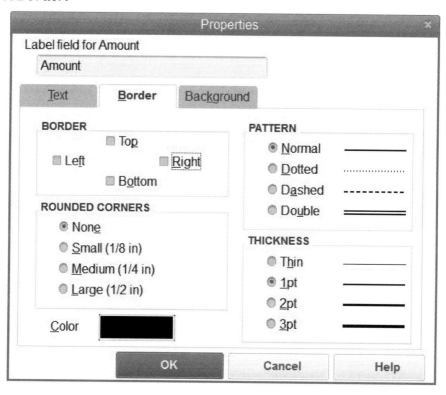

Here you will want to deselect the boxes next to **Top, Right, Left,** and **Bottom** to remove the border. Select *OK* to save. You will be back to the **Layout Designer screen.** Double click on every box on the screen and remove the borders using the process above.

At the top of the screen, you will see the layout designer menu options.

Select *Add, Text Box* to add a new text box to include your message. Input the text desired at the top of the inside box and change the fonts.

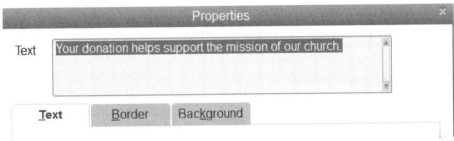

If you click on any of the boxes on the screen, you will notice the change in the borders. Like working in a spreadsheet, you can expand or contract the sizes of the boxes or move them around. It is rather difficult to show this statically, but you can experiment to suit your needs.

In this example, I made the amount box smaller and moved it closer to a text box.

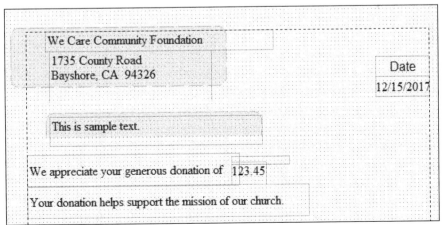

In the following example, Mr. Dunn sent in a $1000 donation. I entered it in the sales receipt screen with the **Thank You** template.

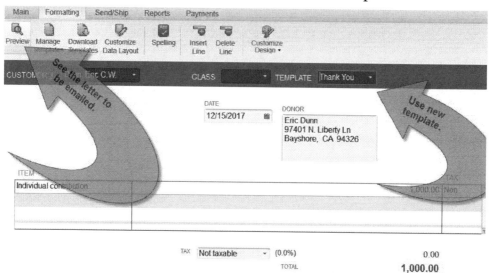

Select *Preview* under *Formatting* to see the following.

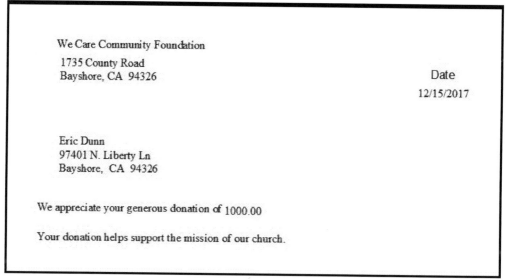

We Care Community Foundation

1735 County Road
Bayshore, CA 94326

Date

12/15/2017

Eric Dunn
97401 N. Liberty Ln
Bayshore, CA 94326

We appreciate your generous donation of 1000.00

Your donation helps support the mission of our church.

As you can see, it isn't perfect, but you can easily email it directly to the donor from the sales receipt main menu.

Just make sure the template is at **Thank You** before emailing it.

You can change the template back to sales receipt and print or email the data in the traditional format. The system allows you to toggle between all of the templates.

5. Merge duplicated donor or vendor accounts

While looking through the donor or vendor lists, you may find some duplicate donor or vendor names. This often occurs when the naming protocol isn't clear. Luckily, QuickBooks makes this easy to correct.

Go to ***Customers, Customer Center***. Write down the exact customer name of the account you wish to keep. Then double-click on the customer or job you don't want to use. This will bring up their **Edit Customer** window. Change the customer or job name to the same name as the entry you want to keep and click *OK*. The names are not case sensitive. A warning box will appear.

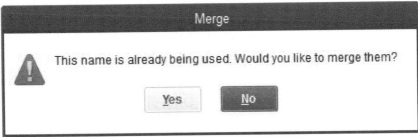

Click *Yes* to confirm that you want to merge the two names under the same name. All of the transactions from the deleted name will be merged into the name you input.

Please note that you cannot combine the names if they both have jobs. Delete or move the jobs from the customer name you will be removing before attempting the merge. Vendor names can be merged using the same process.

C. What About .....?

1. Reports I Need for an Audit

Though every audit is different, there are some basic reports your auditor will probably request. Some are financial and others are managerial. In planning for your audit, I'd recommend you gather, print, or have in an electronic file the following information as of the last day of the period being audited:

- Board minutes
- Contracts, including employment, rent, insurance, etc.
- Accounts receivable aging detail (list of amounts due from donors)
- Accounts payable aging detail (list of amounts due to vendors)
- Payroll reports from the outside service or detail files.

Additionally, your auditor will ask for a number of very detailed reports. This is where the **Accountant & Taxes** section of the Report Center comes in handy. These reports include the audit trail for changes to transactions, detail listings of all entries into accounts, and information needed for tax preparation.

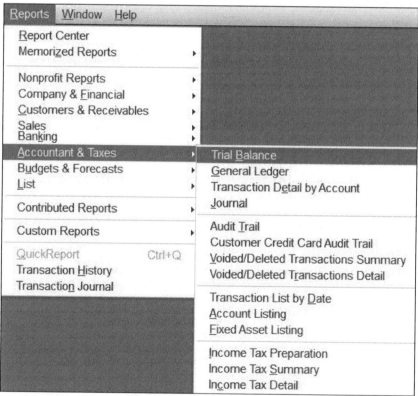

I won't explain what each of these reports include, but auditors love them. They can be filtered for a range or type of account and can be exported to a spreadsheet for the accountants to work with. So if you don't quite understand what information they need from a report, ask them to sit next to you as you bring up these reports and customize them.

> *Once you and the auditor have the reports needed, memorize them for next year and save yourself a lot of trouble.*

2. Tax Stuff

I am not offering any tax advice. Even though religious organizations are considered tax exempt, they may have activities that are taxable or, at least, have reporting requirements. Download IRS Publication 1828 (www.irs.gov/pub/irs-pdf/p1828.pdf) for a summary of IRS regulations as related to churches. It also gives you the length of time required for record retention and what reporting requirements there are for different activities. Additionally, ask your local accountant or tax attorney if your church has any taxable activities.

States may also have different taxing requirements, especially with sales tax. If you sell books or clothing, you may be required to collect and remit these taxes. Some states exempt churches and nonprofits from paying sales taxes on purchases or they reimburse them for the taxes paid. As every state is different, I'm afraid it is outside the scope of this book to cover them all, but I've included links to state departments of revenue and secretary of state websites at www.accountantbesideyou.com/state-weblinks.

> *You did it!*
>
> *Doesn't it feel great to realize you can set up QuickBooks for your church, enter transactions, run reports, prepare budgets, and all kinds of other useful tasks? The system has much more functionality than I could cover in this book, so experiment, explore, and have fun with it. I've enjoyed being the Accountant Beside You through the process. Keep an eye on my website www.accountantbesideyou.com for more books in the series, downloads, seminar locations, and future QuickBooks edition updates.*

XVII.   **Appendix**

- Before You Start Checklist
- Proposed Chart of Accounts
- How to Upload the Chart of Accounts
- Example Item List

A.   Before You Start Checklist

Here is a list of items you will need to set up QuickBooks for your church. It is also available as a free download on www.accountantbesideyou.com.

Setting up the Church File

- ☐ Legal name and address of the church
- ☐ Federal EIN
- ☐ First month of the accounting year (usually January)
- ☐ Name of your church's annual income tax form if applicable

Completing Lists and Entering Balances

Chart of Accounts:

- ☐ Names, numbers, and descriptions for the Chart of Accounts
- ☐ Financial statements as of the end of the prior year
- ☐ Trial balances as of the QuickBooks start date—balance by account and fund from
- ☐ List of programs and grants (for the Class List)
- ☐ Bank, credit card, loan, and lines of credit account numbers and data, including
- ☐ Value of assets (including original cost and accumulated depreciation for fixed

Member and Grants Information

- ☐ Members names, addresses, email, etc.
- ☐ Grant documents
- ☐ Outstanding invoices or pledges as of your church's transition to QuickBooks start

Vendor Information

- ☐ Vendor names, addresses, other contact information
- ☐ List of 1099 vendors and their tax ID numbers
- ☐ List of outstanding bills as of your QuickBooks' start date

Other Information

- ☐ Employee names and contact information
- ☐ Volunteer names and responsibilities

B. Proposed Chart of Accounts

Account	Type	Description
1100 · Cash and Marketable Securities	Bank	
1110 · Checking Account	Bank	Rename with your bank name
1120 · Investment Accounts	Bank	Rename with your investment account name
1190 · Petty Cash	Bank	For cash or gift cards held at the church
1300 · Accounts Receivable	Accounts Receivable	Unpaid or unapplied customer invoices and credits
1310 · Pledges Receivable	Accounts Receivable	Unpaid pledges by members
1320 · Accounts Receivable	Accounts Receivable	Monies due from others.
1330 · Sales Tax Receivable	Accounts Receivable	Only necessary if your state reimburses sales taxes paid
1200 · *Undeposited Funds	Other Current Asset	Funds received but not yet deposited to a bank account
1210 · Inventory Asset	Other Current Asset	Costs of inventory purchased for resale
1400 · Prepaid Assets	Other Current Asset	
1410 · Prepaid Insurance	Other Current Asset	Record the future periods portion of the insurance paid here
1420 · Prepaid Postage	Other Current Asset	Postage Meter Balance
1500 · Property, Building, and Equip	Fixed Asset	

1510 · Land	Fixed Asset	Land owned by the church (put address or plot number here)
1520 · Building	Fixed Asset	Put address here
1530 · Computers	Fixed Asset	
1540 · Furniture and Equipment	Fixed Asset	Furniture and equipment with useful life exceeding one year
1550 · Vehicle	Fixed Asset	
1580 · Accumulated Depreciation	Fixed Asset	Only needed if you record depreciation
1900 · Other Assets	Other Asset	
1910 · Other Assets-Suspense Account	Other Asset	Use this if you aren't sure which asset account to post to
2100 · Accounts Payable	Accounts Payable	Money owed to others
2150 · Credit Card	Credit Card	Add a subaccount for each credit card
2200 · Unearned Revenue/Prepaid Pledge	Other Current Liability	
2210 · Unearned Revenue/Prepaid Pledge	Other Current Liability	Record pledges received before the pledge period here
2300 · Accrued Liabilities	Other Current Liability	
2400 · Payroll Liabilities	Other Current Liability	Unpaid payroll liabilities. Amounts withheld or accrued, but not yet paid
2410 · Wages Payable	Other Current Liability	Only needed if not using an outside service
2900 · Mortgage Payable	Long Term Liability	

3000 Opening Balance Net Assets	Equity	System account. Should be $0
3100 Unrestricted Net Assets	Equity	General Fund
3200 · Temp. Restricted Net Assets	Equity	Fund balances of temporarily restricted funds
3300 · Perm. Restricted Net Assets	Equity	Endowments and other permanently restricted funds
4100 · Pledges/Offerings	Income	Normal donations
4110 · Plate Income	Income	Cash from the plate not designated to a member
4120 · Pledges Income	Income	Pledge commitments
4130 · Unpledged Support	Income	Money received from a member not pledged
4140 · EFT Offerings	Income	Electronic Funds Transfers of Donations
4150 · Special Collections-Operating	Income	Use for special collections for church operations
4200 · Fundraising Income	Income	Design a subaccount for each significant fundraiser
4210 Fundraising Event 1	Income	Income from annual fundraiser
4211 · Event 1 Revenues	Income	
4215 · Event 1 Expenses	Income	
4220 Fundraising Event 2	Income	
4221 · Event 2 Revenues	Income	
4225 ·Event 2 Expense	Income	
4300 Other Operating Income	Income	Money or goods received for services offered by the church

4310 · Donation, Gift, Bequest Income	Income	
4320 · Wedding, Funeral, & Memorials	Income	
4330 · Flowers	Income	
4380 · In-Kind Contribution	Income	Receipt of goods or services instead of money
4390 · Other Miscellaneous Income	Income	
4400 · Income -Other Operating Areas	Income	
4420 · Books/Pamphlets Sales	Income	
4430 · Cemetery Plots	Income	
4490 · Other Income-Other Operating	Income	
4500 · Investment Income	Income	Record interest, dividend and investment gains and losses in the subaccounts
4510 · Interest Income	Income	Interest from money market or bank accounts
4520 · Realized Gain/Loss - Investment	Income	Money made or lost from dividends or actual sales of stock. From your brokerage account statements
4530 · Unrealized Gain/Loss-Investment	Income	Change in the market prices. Data is on your brokerage statements
4800 Net Assets Released	Income	Used to reclassify dollars that are no longer restricted

5999 · Cost of Goods Sold	Cost of Goods Sold	Costs of items purchased and then sold to customers
6000 · Facilities-Utilities	Expense	Water, electricity, garbage, and other basic utilities expenses
6100 · Facilities-Other	Expense	
6105 · Rent Expense	Expense	Facility rental expense
6110 · Church Building Repairs & Main	Expense	
6120 · Grounds Maintenance	Expense	
6130 · Custodial Supplies	Expense	
6140 · Insurance	Expense	Includes all insurances except payroll related
6150 · Building and Property Security	Expense	Building and property security monitoring expenses
6160 · Pastor Housing Expense	Expense	
6161 · Pastor Housing Repairs & Main	Expense	
6190 · Miscellaneous Facilities	Expense	
6300 · Administrative Expenses	Expense	
6310 · Office Supplies	Expense	Office supplies expense
6320 · Postage and Delivery	Expense	Postage, and delivery services
6330 Telephone Expense	Expense	Telephone and long distance charges, faxing, and other fees
6340 Printing Expense	Expense	Printing and copying expenses

6350 · Software and Technology	Expense	Software, website, and computer support
6360 · Advertising and Promotions	Expense	
6370 · Conventions and Conferences	Expense	Costs for attending conferences and meetings
6372 · Dues and Subscriptions	Expense	Subscriptions and membership dues for civic, service, professional, trade organizations
6380 · Financial Fees	Expense	Any charges for financial services-payroll processing, credit card discounts, etc.
6381 · Bank Service Charges	Expense	Bank account service fees, bad check charges, and other bank fees
6382 · Professional Fees	Expense	Payments to accounting professionals and attorneys for accounting or legal services
6390 · Miscellaneous Administrative	Expense	
6400 · Payroll Expenses	Expense	Payroll expenses
6500 · Employee Benefits	Expense	
6560 · Other Payroll Tax Expense	Expense	
6600 · Program Expenses	Expense	Use for expenses that do not fall into other categories
6610 · Worship Program Expense	Expense	Use only if the expense doesn't fall in another account
6620 · Youth Program Expenses	Expense	Use only if the expense doesn't fall in another account

6630 · Adult Education Program Exp	Expense	Use only if the expense doesn't fall in another account
6690 · Other Program Expense	Expense	Use only if the expense doesn't fall in another account
6700 · National Church Allocation Exp.	Expense	For charges, dues, etc. owed to a supervising organization
6800 · Donated Goods and Services	Expense	Offset account for the receipt of goods or services instead of money
6900 · Reserve transfer payment	Expense	Record payment of transfer to reserves here
5000 · Other Income-Non-Operating	Other Income	Income received not from normal operations of the church
5020· Capital Campaign	Other Income	
5030 Endowment Donations	Other Income	
5040· Specific Bequests	Other Income	
5080 Sale of Fixed Assets	Other Income	
5090 · Misc. Other Inc.-Non-Operating	Other Income	
5010 · Specific Gifts Restr. -Non-Oper	Other Income	Specific gifts received for designated non-operating purposes
5100 · Special Collections Pass Thru	Other Income	Use this account to record donations received for other charitable organizations
5800 · Reserve Transfer Deposit	Other Income	Deposit of reserve dollars
7100 · Payments of Donations to Others	Other Expense	Use to pay pass-through donations to other organizations

7200 · Extraordinary Repairs	Other Expense	For large repairs outside the normal operations
7300 · Capital Expenditures	Other Expense	
7400 · Capital Campaign Expenses	Other Expense	
7500 · Grant Expense	Other Expense	Only for unusual expenses specifically required by a grant
7600 · Interest Expense	Other Expense	Interest payments on loans, credit card balances, or other debt
7700 · Depreciation Expense	Other Expense	Depreciation on fixed assets
8000 · Ask My Accountant	Other Expense	To be discussed with accountant

C.   How to Upload a Chart of Accounts File

If you have purchased the chart of account download from www.accountantbesideyou.com or need to upload a chart of accounts file from another source, I'll walk you through the steps.

> *The Chart of Account download is an IIF file. If you already have accounts in your Quickbooks file, it will try to match them up with the new accounts. You can then delete or hide any old ones you do not wish to use.*
>
> *The website also offers a Premium Download which is a QuickBooks Backup File (QBB) When you restore this file, it will erase anything already in the company file, but sets up the chart of accounts, items, classes and preferences used in this book. Use the QBB only for new setups.*

First, save the downloaded file where you can find it. I find the desktop a good place to put files temporarily. Just remember to move or delete them when you are done or your computer screen becomes rather cluttered.

Select *File, Utilities, Import, IIF Files.*

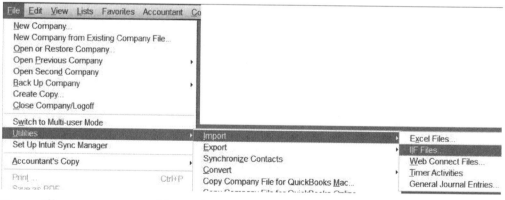

You will see a screen asking where to import the file from.

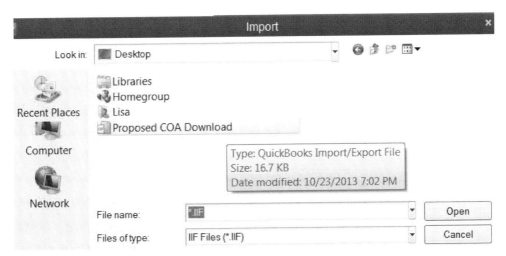

Select the chart of accounts download and press *Open*.

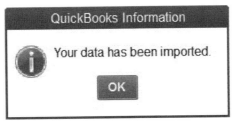

And you will be rewarded with the above information.

If you purchased a company file with basic start-up church data including the chart of accounts, preferences, and items already loaded, use the restore function. Go to *File, Open or Restore Company.*

Select *Restore a backup copy* in the screen below.

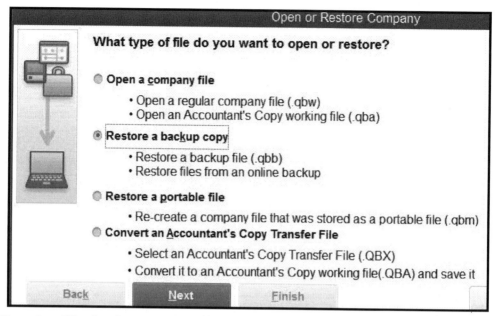

Next, it will ask where the file is stored.

After designating local or online, click *Next* to specify the area where the file is saved in the screen below:

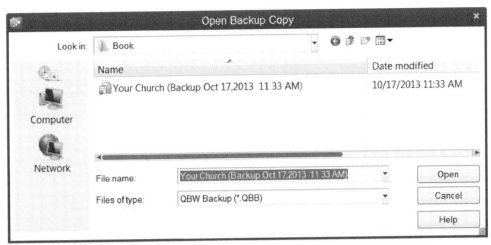

Choose *Open* and QuickBooks will reflect a basic startup church. Go to the top menu and select *Company, My Company.* By clicking on the pencil icon, you can edit the company file for your particular church.

D. Basic Item List: Donations, Expenses, & Volunteers

Item	Description	Type
Capital Campaign	Capital campaign contribution	Service
Donation	Donation to the church	Service
Electric	Electricity charges	Service
Employee Withholdings	Payroll withholdings	Service
Employer Taxes	Payroll taxes	Service
Fundraiser	Income from fundraisers—may have sub-items.	Service
Gross Payroll	Gross pay before deductions	Service
Grounds	Volunteer hours for grounds maintenance	Service
Memorials	Memorial donations	Service
Pass Thru Donation	Receipt of donations to other organizations	Service
Plate Donation	Donation received during service	Service
Pledge Offering	Pledge offering	Service
Plumbing	Donated plumbing services	Service
Restricted Donation	Temporarily restricted donation	Service
Sunday School	Volunteer time spent on Sunday School	Service
Altar Flowers	Donation for flowers for the altar	Non-inventory Part
Electric Allocations	Allocation of electric bill	Group
Payroll	Allocation of payroll	Group

Thank you for reading my book. I've enjoyed being

The Accountant Beside You.

If you enjoyed it, please go to your favorite retailer's website and give it a favorable rating.

If not, please contact me at questions@accountantbesideyou.com and let me know how to improve the series.

Look for more titles in

The Accountant Beside You

series:

Church Accounting: The How-To Guide for Small & Growing Churches

Using QuickBooks® for Nonprofit Organizations, Associations & Clubs

QuickBooks® para Iglesias y Otras Organizaciones Religiosas

Also see www.accountantbesideyou.com for videos, helpful links, and time-saving downloads.

Index